BARRON'S
STUDENTS' #1 CHOICE

PASS KEY

TO THE

PSAT/ NMSQT®

BARRON'S
STUDENTS' #1 CHOICE

PASS KEY

TO THE

PSAT/NMSQT®

Fifth Edition

Sharon Weiner Green, M.A.
Former Instructor in English
Merritt College, Oakland, California

Ira K. Wolf, Ph.D.
President, PowerPrep, Inc.
Former High School Teacher, College Professor,
and University Director of Teacher Preparation

BARRON'S EDUCATIONAL SERIES, INC.

Adapted from *PSAT/NMSQT,* 14th Edition © 2008 by Barron's Educational Series, Inc.
Math section also adapted from *Pass Key to the SAT I,* 4th Edition © 2001
by Barron's Educational Series, Inc.

All inquiries should be addressed to:
Barron's Educational Series, Inc.
250 Wireless Boulevard
Hauppauge, New York 11788
www.barronseduc.com

Library of Congress Control No. 2008929853

ISBN-13: 978-0-7641-3868-3
ISBN-10: 0-7641-3868-5

PRINTED IN THE UNITED STATES OF AMERICA
9 8 7 6 5 4 3 2 1

Contents

Preface

Welcome to the Fifth Edition of *Barron's Pass Key to the PSAT/NMSQT*. If you are preparing for today's PSAT, this is the book you need.

It features two full-length sample tests modeled on the PSAT in length and difficulty, two crucial "dress rehearsals" for the day you walk into the examination room.

It prepares you for the writing skills section, teaching you how to spot errors and polish rough drafts so that you can shine on the PSAT, and eventually on the SAT.

It briefs you on vocabulary-in-context and reading comprehension questions, giving you key tips on how to tackle these important critical reading question types.

It takes you step by step through the double reading passages, showing you how to work your way through a pair of reading passages without wasting effort or time.

It introduces you to the nonmultiple-choice questions in the mathematics section, teaching you shortcuts to solving problems and entering your own answers on a sample grid.

It offers you advice on how (and when) to use a calculator in dealing with both multiple-choice and "grid-in" questions.

It gives you the 300-word PSAT High Frequency Word List, 300 vital words that have been shown by computer analysis to occur and reoccur on actual published PSATs.

Getting ready for the PSAT is your first step in preparing for your most important college-entrance test—the SAT. Go for your personal best; take the time to learn how to prepare for the PSAT.

Acknowledgments

The authors gratefully acknowledge all those sources who granted permission to use materials from their publications:

Pages 14–15: From *Summer of '49* by David Halberstam © 1989 by David Halberstam. Reprinted by permission of HarperCollins Publishers Inc.

Page 15: From *Take Time for Paradise* © 1989 by the Estate of A. Bartlett Giamatti.

Pages 161–162: From *King Solomon's Ring* by Konrad Z. Lorenz, © 1952, Harper & Row, pp. 128–129.

Pages 163–164: Excerpts from *Renaissance to Modern Tapestries in The Metropolitan Museum of Art* (pp. 4–6) by Edith Appleton Standen. Copyright © 1987 The Metropolitan Museum of Art. Reprinted courtesy of the Metropolitan Museum of Art.

Pages 175–176: From "Yonder Peasant, Who Is He?" by Mary McCarthy in *Memories of a Catholic Girlhood,* copyright © 1948 and 1975, p. 57. Reprinted with permission of Harcourt Brace & Co.

Page 176: From *Reinventing Womanhood* by Caroline G. Heilbrun copyright © 1979. Reprinted with permission of W.W. Norton & Company, Inc., pp. 56–57.

Pages 222–223: From "Huge Conservation Effort Aims to Save Vanishing Architect of the Savannah" by William K. Stevens, © 2001 by the New York Times Co. Reprinted by permission.

Pages 234–235: From "Let's Say You Wrote Badly This Morning" by David Huddle in *The Writing Habit,* University Press of New England, Hanover, 1994.

Pages 235–236: From "My Two One-Eyed Coaches" by George Garrett. Virginia Quarterly Review, V. 63N. 2.

PSAT/NMSQT Test Time 2 Hours and 10 Minutes

Section 1:	**Critical Reading**	8 Sentence Completions
		16 Reading Comprehension Questions
Time—25 minutes		

Section 2:	**Mathematical Reasoning**	20 Multiple-Choice Questions
Time—25 minutes		

5-Minute Break

Section 3:	**Critical Reading**	5 Sentence Completions
		19 Reading Comprehension Questions
Time—25 minutes		

Section 4:	**Mathematical Reasoning**	8 Multiple-Choice Questions
		10 Student-Produced
		Response (Grid-In) Questions
Time—25 minutes		

1-Minute Break

Section 5:	**Writing Skills**	20 Improving Sentences
		14 Identifying Sentence Errors
		5 Improving Paragraphs
Time—30 minutes		

1 The PSAT/National Merit Scholarship Qualifying Test

Your plan to take the PSAT/NMSQT is perhaps your first concrete step toward planning a college career. The PSAT/NMSQT and the SAT—what do they mean to you? When do you take them? Where? What sort of hurdle do you face? How do these tests differ from the tests you ordinarily face in school? In this chapter we answer these basic questions so that you will be able to move on to the following chapters and concentrate on preparing yourself for this test.

SOME BASIC QUESTIONS ANSWERED

What Is the PSAT/NMSQT?

The PSAT/NMSQT is a standardized test designed to measure your ability to do college work. It is given once a year, in mid-October. Most schools administer the exam on a Saturday; some, however, give it on a weekday.

While many students take the test "for practice" as sophomores, most students take it only once, in their junior year.

The test consists of five sections: two test critical reading skills, two test mathematical reasoning skills, and one tests writing skills. The time allowed for each of the reading and math sections is twenty-five minutes; the time allowed for the writing skills section is thirty minutes.

Why Is the Test Called the PSAT/NMSQT?

This preliminary SAT also serves as the National Merit Scholarship Qualifying Test (NMSQT). Approximately 50,000 students nationally gain recognition in the NMSQT competition by their scores on the PSAT.

What Are Merit Scholarships?

Merit Scholarships are prestigious national awards that carry with them a chance for solid financial aid. Conducted by NMSC, an independent, nonprofit organization with offices at 1560 Sherman Avenue, Suite 200, Evanston, Illinois 60201-4897, the Merit Program today is supported by grants from more than 500 corporations, private foundations, colleges and universities, and other organizations.

The top-scoring PSAT/NMSQT participants in every state are named Semifinalists. Those who advance to Finalist standing by meeting additional requirements compete for one-time National Merit $2500 Scholarships and renewable, four-year Merit Scholarships, which may be worth as much as $10,000 a year for four years.

Check out Merit Scholarships at *www.nationalmerit.org.*

What Is the National Achievement Scholarship Program for Outstanding Black Students?

This is a program aimed at honoring and assisting promising African American high school students throughout the country. It is also administered by NMSC. Students who enter the Merit Program by taking the PSAT/NMSQT and who are also eligible to participate in the Achievement program mark a space on their test answer sheets asking to enter this competition as well. Top-scoring African American students in each of the regions established for the competition compete for nonrenewable National Achievement $2500 Scholarships and for four-year Achievement Scholarships supported by many colleges and corporate organizations.

Note: To be considered for this program, you *must* mark the appropriate space on your answer sheet.

Check out the National Achievement Scholarship Program at *www.nationalmerit.org.*

How Can the PSAT/NMSQT Help Me?

If you are a high school junior, it will help you gauge your potential scores on the SAT that you will take in the spring. It will give you some idea of which colleges you should apply to in your senior year. It will give you access to scholarship competitions. It will definitely give you practice in answering multiple-choice questions where timing is an important factor.

In addition, you may choose to take advantage of the College Board's Student Search Service. This service is free for students who fill out the biographical section of the PSAT/NMSQT. If you fill out this section, you will receive mail from colleges and search programs.

How Do I Apply for This Test?

You apply through your school. Fees, when required, are collected by your school. Fee waivers are available for students whose families cannot afford the test fee; if this applies to you, talk to your counselor.

The test is given in October. In December the results are sent to your school and to the scholarship program that you indicated on your answer sheet in the examination room. Your school will send you your score report.

What if I am a Home-Schooled Student?

If you are a home-schooler, you must make arrangements with the principal or counselor of a nearby high school (public or independent) to take the test. Do not wait until the school year starts to make your arrangements. If you want to take the test in October, start the process the previous June.

Because you are a home-schooler, your score report is supposed to be sent to your home address. When you fill out your answer sheet, you must enter the state's home school code in the school code section of the answer sheet. This will ensure that you will receive your score report. You should be able to get this number from the exam proctor or supervisor.

What Makes the PSAT Different from Other Tests?

The PSAT is trying to measure your ability to reason using facts that are part of your general knowledge or facts that are included in your test booklet. You are not required to recall any history or literature or science. You are not even required to recall most math formulas—they are printed right in the test booklet.

Your score depends upon how many correct answers you get within a definite period of time. You can't go too slowly; however, accuracy is even more important than speed. You have to pace yourself so that you don't sacrifice speed to gain accuracy (or sacrifice accuracy to gain speed).

The biggest mistake most students make is to answer too many questions. It is better to answer fewer questions correctly, even if you have to leave some out at the end of a section.

How Is the PSAT Different from the SAT?

The PSAT is a mini-version of the SAT. For most students, it serves as a practice test. The PSAT takes two hours and ten minutes; the SAT takes almost twice as long. You have to answer fewer reading, math, and writing skills questions on the PSAT than you do on the SAT; however, the questions are similar in level of difficulty.

The PSAT, unlike the SAT, has *no* essay-writing section. *You do not have to write an essay.* Your school may recommend that you participate in the College Board's practice essay-writing program, *Score Write*. However, your participation in *Score Write* will *not* affect your PSAT score.

How is the PSAT Scored?

The PSAT has three parts: critical reading, math, and writing skills. On each part you will receive a score between 20 and 80, and a combined Selection Index, which is the sum of your three scores. For example, if your score report listed scores of 53 in critical reading, 61 in math, and 48 in writing skills, your Selection Index would be 53 + 61 + 48 = 162.

Score Format

Critical Reading	Math	Writing Skills	Selection Index
53	61	48	162

For each individual score, as well as the Selection Index, you will receive a percentile ranking that shows how your scores compare with those of the other students who took the PSAT the same day you did.

Because SAT scores range from 200 to 800, many students multiply their PSAT scores by 10 to make them look like SAT scores. So, if you earned the scores given in the previous paragraph, you might say that your PSAT score was a 1620.

How are the results of your PSAT/NMSQT reported?

Sometime between December 5 and 10, you will receive from your school the following:
1. an official score report that includes:
   a) the answer you gave for each question
   b) the correct answer for each question
   c) the difficulty level of each question
   d) a Selection Index, which is used to determine eligibility for NMSC programs
2. a copy of the original test booklet that you used in the examination room

Can I do anything if I miss the test but still want to participate in scholarship competitions?

If you fail to take the PSAT/NMSQT because you were ill or involved in an emergency, you still may be able to qualify for a National Merit or National Achievement Scholarship. You need to contact the NMSC to find out about alternative testing arrangements that would enable you to take part in the National Merit competitions.

If you are of Hispanic descent, you need to contact the National Hispanic Scholar Recognition Program run by the College Board. You can arrange to be considered for this program by communicating with The College Board, Suite 600, 1233 20th Street NW, Washington, DC 20036.

HOW TO APPROACH THE PSAT

Test-Taking Tactics

What Tactics Can Help Me When I Take the PSAT?

1. Memorize the directions given in this book for each type of question. These are only slightly different from the exact words you'll find on the PSAT you'll take. During the test, do not waste even a few seconds reading any directions or sample questions.
2. Know the format of the test. The number and kinds of questions break down as follows:

   48 Critical Reading Questions (2 Sections, 25 minutes each)
   13 sentence completion questions
   8   short paragraph critical reading questions
   27 long paragraph critical reading questions

   38 Math Questions (2 Sections, 25 minutes each)
   28 standard multiple-choice questions
   10 student-produced response (grid-in) questions

   39 Writing Skills Questions (1 Section, 30 minutes)
   14 identifying sentence errors questions
   20 improving sentence questions
   5   improving paragraph questions

3. Expect easy questions at the beginning of many sets of the same question type. Within these sets (except for the reading comprehension and improving paragraph questions), the questions progress from easy to difficult. In other words, the first sentence completion question in a set will be easier than the last sentence completion in that set; the first grid-in question will be easier than the last grid-in question.

4. Take advantage of the easy questions to boost your score. Remember, each question is worth the same number of points. Whether it is easy or difficult, whether it takes you ten seconds or two minutes to answer, you get the same number of points for each question you answer correctly. Your job is to answer as many questions as you possibly can without rushing ahead so fast that you make careless errors or lose points for failing to give some questions enough thought. So take enough time to get those easy questions right!

5. *First* answer all the easy questions; *then* tackle the hard ones if you have time. You know that the questions in each segment of the test get harder as you go along (except for the reading comprehension question and the improving paragraph questions). But there's no rule that says you have to answer the questions in order. You're allowed to skip. So, if the last three sentence completion questions are driving you crazy, move on to the short reading passages right away. Test-wise students know when it's time to move on.

6. Eliminate as many wrong answers as you can and then make an educated guess. Deciding between two choices is easier than deciding among five. Whenever you guess, every answer you eliminate improves your chances of guessing correctly.

7. Change answers *only* if you have a reason for doing so. Don't give in to last-minute panic. It's usually better for you not to change your answers on a sudden hunch or whim.

8. Calculators are permitted in the test room, so bring along a calculator that you are comfortable using. No question on the test will *require* the use of a calculator, but it may be helpful for some questions. Bring whatever calculator you use in your math class at school.

9. Remember that you are allowed to write anything you want in your test booklet. Make good use of it. Circle questions you skip, and put big question marks next to questions you answer but are unsure about. In sentence completion questions, circle or underline key words such as *although*, *therefore*, *not*, and so on. In reading passages, circle key words and underline or put a mark in the margin next to any major point. On math questions, mark up diagrams, adding

lines when necessary. And, of course, use all the space provided to solve the problem. In short, write anything that will help you, using whatever symbols you like. But remember, the only thing that counts is what you enter on your answer sheet. No one will ever see anything that you write in your test booklet.

10. Be careful not to make any stray marks on your answer sheet. This test is graded by a machine, and a machine cannot tell the difference between an accidental mark and a filled-in answer. When the machine sees two marks instead of one, the answer is marked wrong.

11. Check frequently to make sure you are answering the questions in the right spots. No machine is going to notice that you made a mistake early in the test, answered question 4 in the space for question 5, and all your following answers are in the wrong place. One way to avoid this problem is to mark your answers in your test booklet and transfer them to your answer sheet by blocks.

12. Line up your test book with your answer sheet to avoid making careless errors. Whether you choose to fill in the answers question by question or in blocks, you will do so most efficiently if you keep your test book and your answer sheet aligned.

13. Be particularly careful in marking the student-produced responses on the math grid. Before you fill in the appropriate blanks in the grid, write your answer at the top of the columns. Then go down each column, making sure you're filling in the right spaces.

14. Don't get bogged down on any one question. By the time you get to the actual PSAT, you should have a fair idea of how much time to spend on each question. If a question is taking too long, leave it and go on to the next question. This is no time to try to show the world that you can stick to a job no matter how long it takes. All the machine that grades the test will notice is that after a certain point you didn't have any correct answers.

Reducing Anxiety

How Can I Prevent PSAT Anxiety from Setting In?

1. The best way to prepare for any test you ever take is to get a good night's sleep before the test so that you are well rested and alert.
2. Eat breakfast for once in your life. You have a full morning ahead of you; you should have a full stomach as well.

3. Allow plenty of time for getting to the test site. Taking a test is pressure enough. You don't need the extra tension that comes from worrying about whether you will get there on time.

4. Be aware of the amount of time the test is going to take. There are five sections. They will take two hours and ten minutes total. Add to that a five-minute break after the third section, a one-minute break between the others, plus thirty minutes for paper pushing. If the test starts at 8:00 A.M., don't make a dentist appointment for 11:00. You can't possibly get there on time, and you'll just spend the last half-hour of the test worrying about it.

5. The College Board tells you to bring two sharpened No. 2 pencils to the test. Bring four. They don't weigh much, and this might be the one day in the decade when two pencil points decide to break. Bring full-size pencils, not little stubs. They are easier to write with, and you might as well be comfortable.

6. Speaking of being comfortable, wear comfortable clothes. This is a test, not a fashion show. Aim for the layered look. Wear something light, but bring a sweater. The test room may be hot, or it may be cold. You can't change the room, but you can put on the sweater.

7. Bring a watch or small travel clock that can fit on your desk. You need one. The room in which you take the test may not have a clock, and some proctors are not very good about posting the time on the blackboard. Don't depend on them. Each time you begin a test section, write down in your booklet the time according to your watch. That way you will always know how much time you have left.

8. Smuggle in some quick energy in your pocket—trail mix, raisins, a candy bar. Even if the proctors don't let you eat in the test room, you can still grab a bite en route to the rest rooms during the five-minute break. Taking the test can leave you feeling drained and in need of a quick pickup—bring along your favorite comfort food.

9. There will be a break after the third section. Use this period to clear your thoughts. Take a few deep breaths. Stretch. Close your eyes and imagine yourself floating or sunbathing. In addition to being under mental pressure, you're under physical pressure from sitting so long in an uncomfortable seat with a No. 2 pencil clutched in your hand. Anything you can do to loosen up and get the kinks out will ease your body and help the oxygen get to your brain.

10. Most important of all, remember: very little, if anything, is riding on the result of this test. If you do poorly, no one will know; your PSAT scores are not reported to the colleges to which you plan to apply. So relax!

Guessing

If you don't know the answer to a question on the PSAT, should you guess? The answer to the above question is very simple: in general, *it pays to guess.* To understand why this is so and why so many people are confused about it, you must understand how the PSAT is scored.

On the PSAT, every question is worth exactly the same amount: 1 point. A correct answer to a critical reading question for which you may have to read a whole paragraph is worth no more than a correct response to a sentence completion question that you can answer in a few seconds. You get no more credit for a correct answer to the hardest math question than you do for the easiest. For each question that you answer correctly, you receive 1 raw score point. For each multiple-choice question that you answer incorrectly, you lose ¼ point. Questions that you leave out have no effect on your score. Here's how it works:

$$\# \text{ Right} - \frac{\# \text{ Wrong}}{4} = \text{Raw Score}$$

There are 48 critical reading questions on the PSAT. If you answer 34 correctly, get 9 wrong, and leave out 5, what will your reading raw score be?

$$34 - \frac{9}{4} = 31\frac{3}{4}, \text{ or a rounded raw score of 32}$$

If you answer 34 correctly, get 0 wrong, and leave out 14, what will your raw score be? 34!

Does this mean you should skip every question that puzzles you and answer only questions that you are *sure* of getting right? No. It means you need to slow down to avoid making careless errors and to give yourself the best chance to answer questions correctly. You also need to learn *how* and *when* to guess.

The rule is, if you have worked on a problem and are sure you can eliminate even one of the choices, you *must* guess. This is what is called an *educated guess.* You are not guessing wildly, marking answers at random. You are working on the problem, ruling out answers that make no sense. The more choices you can rule out, the better your chance is of picking the right answer and earning one more point.

You can almost always rule out some answer choices. Most math questions contain at least one or two answer choices that are absurd (for example, negative choices when you know the answer must be positive). In the critical reading section, once you have read the passage, you'll see that some of the answer choices just don't make sense. Cross out those answer choices that you *know* are incorrect. Once you've narrowed down your choices, go for that educated guess.

SAMPLE PSAT QUESTIONS

The purpose of this section is to familiarize you with the kinds of questions that appear on the PSAT by presenting questions like those on recent PSATs. Knowing what to expect when you take the examination is an important step in preparing for the test and succeeding in it.

The directions that precede the various types of questions are similar to those on the PSAT. For all except the student-produced response questions, you are to choose the best answer and fill in the corresponding blank on the answer sheet.

CRITICAL READING

The critical reading sections consist of forty-eight questions to be answered in fifty minutes. A typical test is made up of thirteen sentence completion questions, eight short-paragraph critical reading questions, and twenty-seven long-paragraph critical reading questions.

Sentence Completions

Select the best answer to the following questions, then fill in the appropriate space on your Answer Sheet.

Each of the following sentences contains one or two blanks; these blanks indicate that a word or set of words has been left out. Below the sentence are five words or phrases, lettered A through E. Select the word or set of words that best completes the sentence.

EXAMPLE:

Fame is ----; today's rising star is all too soon tomorrow's washed-up has-been.

(A) rewarding   (B) gradual   (C) essential
    (D) spontaneous   (E) transitory

---

1. Folk dancing is ---- senior citizens, and it is also economical; they need neither great physical agility nor special equipment to enjoy participating in the dance.

   (A) bewildering to   (B) costly for   (C) foreign to   (D) appropriate for

   (E) impracticable for

2. Holding her infant son, the new mother felt an ---- greater than any other joy she had known.

   (A) affluence   (B) incentive   (C) assurance   (D) incredulity   (E) elation

3. The author maintained that his insights were not ----, but had been made independently of others.

   (A) derivative   (B) esoteric   (C) fallacious   (D) hypothetical   (E) concise

4. Suspicious of the ---- actions of others, the critic Edmund Wilson was in many ways a ---- man, unused to trusting anyone.

   (A) altruistic . . cynical
   (B) questionable . . contrite
   (C) generous . . candid
   (D) hypocritical . . cordial
   (E) benevolent . . dauntless

5. Although Roman original contributions to government, jurisprudence, and engineering are commonly acknowledged, the artistic legacy of the Roman world continues to be judged widely as ---- the magnificent Greek traditions that preceded it.

   (A) an improvement on   (B) an echo of
   (C) a resolution of   (D) a precursor of
   (E) a consummation of

6. ---- though she appeared, her journals reveal that her outward maidenly reserve concealed a passionate nature unsuspected by her family and friends.

   (A) Effusive   (B) Suspicious   (C) Tempestuous   (D) Domineering
   (E) Reticent

7. Crabeater seal, the common name of *Lobodon carcinophagus*, is ----, since the animal's staple diet is not crabs, but krill.

   (A) a pseudonym   (B) a misnomer   (C) an allusion   (D) a digression
   (E) a compromise

Answer Explanations

Sentence Completion Questions

1. **(D)** *Because* senior citizens don't need great physical agility to enjoy folk dancing, it is an *appropriate* activity for them.

2. **(E)** If the missing word is an emotion greater than *any other joy*, then it too must be a form of joy. *Elation* is a feeling of great joy.

3. **(A)** If the author got his insights independently, then he did not get or derive them from the insights of other people. In other words, his insights were not *derivative*.

4. **(A)** Someone given to distrusting the motives and actions of others is by definition *cynical*. Such a person would question even the *altruistic*, unselfish deeds of others, suspecting there to be ulterior motives for these charitable acts.

5. **(B)** The view of Rome's contributions to government, law, and engineering is wholly positive: these original additions to human knowledge are generally acknowledged or recognized. *In contrast*, Rome's original contributions to art are *not* recognized; they are seen as just an *echo* or imitation of the art of ancient Greece.

   Note that *Although* sets up the contrast here.

6. **(E)** Her outward appearance was one of "maidenly reserve" (self-restraint; avoidance of intimacy). Thus, she seemed to be *reticent* (reserved; disinclined to speak or act freely), even though she actually felt things passionately.

7. **(B)** Because these seals eat far more krill than crabs, it *misnames* them to call them crabeater seals. The term is thus a *misnomer*, a name that's wrongly applied to someone or something.

   Beware of eye-catchers. Choice A is incorrect. A *pseudonym* isn't a mistaken name; it's a false name that an author adopts.

Critical Reading

Your ability to read and understand the kind of material found in college texts and the more serious magazines is tested in the critical reading section of the PSAT/NMSQT. There are two types of passages on the test, short passages and long passages. Short passages are approximately 100 words in length; long passages generally range from 400–850 words. Some passages are paired: you will also be asked to answer two or three questions that compare the viewpoints of two passages on the same subject. You can expect to spend most of your verbal testing time reading the passages and answering the critical reading questions.

> The passage below is followed by questions based on its content. The correct answer may be stated outright or merely suggested in the passage and in any introductory or footnoted material included.

Questions 8–9 are based on the following passage.

"Ladybug, ladybug, fly away home. Your house is on fire; your children do roam." Few farmers would seek to chase away ladybugs, or ladybird beetles, with this familiar children's rhyme, for ladybugs are known as
Line the farmer's friend. Clusters of ladybugs are often gathered and sold to
(5) farmers, who employ them to control the spread of insect pests. In 1888, for example, when California's orange orchards were threatened by an outbreak of cottony-cushion scale, farmers imported the Australian ladybird beetle to devour the scale. In less than two years, the ladybugs had saved the orchards.

8. The quotation in the opening lines of the passage primarily serves to
    (A) alert the ladybugs to an actual danger
    (B) introduce the passage's subject informally
    (C) demonstrate a common misapprehension
    (D) provide a critical literary allusion
    (E) diminish the importance of ladybird beetles

9. As used in line 8, the word "scale" most likely refers to

(A) a form of cotton
(B) a variety of insect
(C) a type of orange
(D) a plant nutrient
(E) a measure of weight

The questions that follow the two passages in this section relate to the content of both, and to their relationship. The correct response may be stated outright or merely suggested in the passages and in any introductory or footnoted material included.

Questions 10–16 are based on the following passages.

The following passages are excerpted from books on America's national pastime, baseball.

Passage 1

DiMaggio had size, power, and speed. McCarthy, his longtime manager, liked to say that DiMaggio might have stolen 60 bases a season if he had given him the green light. Stengel, his new manager, was equally
Line impressed, and when DiMaggio was on base he would point to him as
(5) an example of the perfect base runner. "Look at him," Stengel would say as DiMaggio ran out a base hit, "he's always watching the ball. He isn't watching second base. He isn't watching third base. He knows they haven't been moved. He isn't watching the ground, because he knows they haven't built a canal or a swimming pool since he was last there.
(10) He's watching the ball and the outfielder, which is the one thing that is different on every play."

DiMaggio complemented his natural athletic ability with astonishing physical grace. He played the outfield, he ran the bases, and he batted not just effectively but with rare style. He would glide rather than run, it
(15) seemed, always smooth, always ending up where he wanted to be just when he wanted to be there. If he appeared to play effortlessly, his team-mates knew otherwise. In his first season as a Yankee, Gene Woodling, who played left field, was struck by the sound of DiMaggio chasing a fly ball. He sounded like a giant truck horse on the loose, Woodling thought,
(20) his feet thudding down hard on the grass. The great, clear noises in the open space enabled Woodling to measure the distances between them without looking.

He was the perfect Hemingway hero, for Hemingway in his novels romanticized the man who exhibited grace under pressure, who withheld
(25) any emotion lest it soil the purer statement of his deeds. DiMaggio was

that kind of hero; his grace and skill were always on display, his emotions always concealed. This stoic grace was not achieved without a terrible price: DiMaggio was a man wound tight. He suffered from insomnia and ulcers. When he sat and watched the game he chain-smoked and drank
(30) endless cups of coffee. He was ever conscious of his obligation to play well. Late in his career, when his legs were bothering him and the Yankees had a comfortable lead in a pennant race, columnist Jimmy Cannon asked him why he played so hard—the games, after all, no longer meant so much. "Because there might be somebody out there
(35) who's never seen me play before," he answered.

Passage 2

Athletes and actors—let actors stand for the set of performing artists—share much. They share the need to make gestures as fluid and economical as possible, to make out of a welter of choices the single, precisely right one. They share the need for thousands of hours of
(40) practice in order to train the body to become the perfect, instinctive instrument to express. Both athlete and actor, out of that abundance of emotion, choice, strategy, knowledge of the terrain, mood of spectators, condition of others in the ensemble, secret awareness of injury or weakness, and as nearly an absolute concentration as possible so that
(45) all externalities are integrated, all distraction absorbed to the self, must be able to change the self so successfully that it changes us.

When either athlete or actor can bring all these skills to bear and focus them, then he or she will achieve that state of complete intensity and complete relaxation—complete coherence or integrity between what
(50) the performer wants to do and what the performer has to do. Then, the performer is free; for then, all that has been learned, by thousands of hours of practice and discipline and by repetition of pattern, becomes natural. Then, intellect is upgraded to the level of an instinct. The body follows commands that precede thinking.

(55) When athlete and artist achieve such self-knowledge that they trans-
form the self so that we are re-created, it is finally an exercise in power. The individual's power to dominate, on stage or field, invests the whole arena around the locus of performance with his or her power. We draw from the performer's energy, just as we scrutinize the performer's
(60) vulnerabilities, and we criticize as if we were equals (we are not) what is displayed. This is why all performers dislike or resent the audience as much as they need and enjoy it. Power flows in a mysterious circuit from performer to spectator (I assume a "live" performance) and back, and while cheers or applause are the hoped-for outcome of performing,
(65) silence or gasps are the most desired, for then the moment has occurred—then domination is complete, and as the performer triumphs, a unity rare and inspiring results.

10. In Passage 1, Stengel is most impressed by DiMaggio's

    (A) indifference to potential dangers

    (B) tendency to overlook the bases in his haste

    (C) ability to focus on the variables

    (D) proficiency at fielding fly balls

    (E) overall swiftness and stamina

11. It can be inferred from the content and tone of Stengel's comment (lines 5–11) that he would regard a base runner who kept his eye on second base with

    (A) trepidation   (B) approbation

    (C) resignation   (D) exasperation

    (E) tolerance

12. The phrase "a man wound tight" (line 28) means a man

    (A) wrapped in confining bandages

    (B) living in constricted quarters

    (C) under intense emotional pressure

    (D) who drank alcohol to excess

    (E) who could throw with great force

13. Which best describes what the author is doing in the parenthetical comment "let actors stand for the set of performing artists" (lines 36 and 37)?

    (A) Indicating that actors should rise out of respect for the arts

    (B) Defining the way in which he is using a particular term

    (C) Encouraging actors to show tolerance for their fellow artists

    (D) Emphasizing that actors are superior to other performing artists

    (E) Correcting a misinterpretation of the role of actors

14. To the author of Passage 2, freedom for performers depends on

    (A) their subjection of the audience

    (B) their willingness to depart from tradition

    (C) the internalization of all they have learned

    (D) their ability to interpret material independently

    (E) the absence of injuries or other weaknesses

15. The author's attitude toward the concept of the equality of spectators and performers (lines 57–61) is one of

    (A) relative indifference

    (B) mild skepticism

    (C) explicit rejection

    (D) strong embarrassment

    (E) marked perplexity

16. The author of Passage 2 would most likely react to the characterization of DiMaggio presented in lines 30–35 by pointing out that DiMaggio probably

    (A) felt some resentment of the spectator whose good opinion he supposedly sought
    (B) never achieved the degree of self-knowledge that would have transformed him
    (C) was unaware that his audience was surveying his weak points
    (D) was a purely instinctive natural athlete
    (E) was seldom criticized by his peers

Answer Explanations

Critical Reading Questions

8. **(B)** Rather than launch immediately into a formal discussion of the beneficial qualities of ladybugs or ladybird beetles, the author chooses to *introduce the subject informally* by quoting a familiar nursery rhyme.

9. **(B)** Cottony-cushion scale is just one of the insect pests combatted by ladybird beetles. The correct answer is Choice B, *a variety of insect*.

10. **(C)** Stengel's concluding sentence indicates that DiMaggio watches "the one thing that is different on every play." In other words, DiMaggio *focuses on the variables*, the factors that change from play to play.

11. **(D)** The sarcastic tone of Stengel's comment suggests that he would be *exasperated* or irritated by a base runner who had his eye on second base when he should have been watching the ball and the outfielder.

12. **(C)** Look at the sentences following this phrase. They indicate that DiMaggio was a man *under intense emotional pressure*, one who felt so much stress that he developed ulcers and had problems getting to sleep.

13. **(B)** The author is taking a moment away from his argument to make sure the reader knows exactly who the subjects of his comparison are. He is not simply comparing athletes and actors. He is comparing athletes and *all* performing artists, "the set of performing artists," to use his words. Thus, in his side comment, he is *defining* how he intends to use the word *actors* throughout the discussion.

14. **(C)** Performers are free when all they have learned becomes so natural, so internalized, that it seems instinctive. In other words, freedom depends on the *internalization* of what they have learned.

15. **(C)** The author bluntly states that we spectators are not the performers' equals. Thus, his attitude toward the concept is one of *explicit rejection*.

16. (A)   Passage 1 indicates DiMaggio always played hard to live up to his reputation and to perform well for anyone in the stands who had never seem him play before. Clearly, he wanted the spectators to have a good opinion of him. Passage 2, however, presents a more complex picture of the relationship between the performer and his audience. On the one hand, the performer needs the audience, needs its good opinion and its applause. On the other hand, the performer also resents the audience, resents the way spectators freely point out his weaknesses and criticize his art. Thus, the author of Passage 2 might well point out that DiMaggio *felt some resentment* of the audience, whom he hoped to impress with his skill.

MATHEMATICAL REASONING

There are two types of questions on the Mathematics portion of the PSAT:

1. multiple-choice questions
2. grid-in questions

The math questions are in Sections 2 and 4 of the PSAT. You are allowed twenty-five minutes to complete each section.

- Section 2 will have twenty multiple-choice questions (Questions 1–20)
- Section 4 will have eight multiple-choice questions (Questions 21–28) followed by ten grid-in questions (Questions 29–38).

Within each group, the questions are presented approximately in order of increasing difficulty. In fact, on the score report, which you will receive about seven weeks after taking the PSAT, each question will be rated E (Easy), M (Medium), or H (Hard), depending on how many students answered that question correctly. A typical ranking of the math questions would be as follows:

	Easy	Medium	Hard
Section 2: Multiple-choice	1–6	7–14	15–20
Section 4: Multiple-choice	21–22	23–25	26–28
Section 4: Grid-in	29–31	32–35	36–38

As a result, the amount of time you spend on any one question will vary greatly.

Multiple-Choice Questions

Twenty-eight of the thirty-eight mathematics questions on the PSAT are multiple-choice questions. Although you have certainly taken multiple-choice tests before, the PSAT uses a few different types of questions in these sections, and you must become familiar with all of them. By far, the most common type of question is one in which you are asked to solve a problem. The straightforward way to answer such a question is to do the necessary work, get the solution, then look at the five choices and choose the one that corresponds to your answer. In Chapter 5 we will discuss other techniques for answering these questions, but for now let's look at a couple of examples.

EXAMPLE 1

What is the average (arithmetic mean) of $-2, -1, 0, 1, 2, 3$, and 4?

(A) 0 (B) $\dfrac{3}{7}$ (C) 1 (D) $\dfrac{7}{6}$ (E) $\dfrac{7}{2}$

To solve this problem requires only that you know how to find the average of a set of numbers. Ignore the fact that this is a multiple-choice question. *Don't even look at the choices.*

- Calculate the average by adding the 7 numbers and dividing by 7.

- $\dfrac{-2+-1+0+1+2+3+4}{7} = \dfrac{7}{7} = 1$

- Now look at the five choices. Find 1 listed as Choice C, and blacken in C on your answer sheet.

EXAMPLE 2

Emily was born on Wednesday, April 15, 1987. Her sister Erin was born exactly 1200 days later. On what day of the week was Erin born?

(A) Tuesday   (B) Thursday   (C) Friday   (D) Saturday   (E) Sunday

Again, you are not helped by the fact that this question is a multiple-choice question. You need to determine the day of the week on which Erin was born and then select the choice that matches your answer.

- The 7 days keep repeating in exactly the same order: 1 day after Emily was born was a Thursday, 2 days after Emily was born was a Friday, and so on. Make a table.

	Thurs.	Fri.	Sat.	Sun.	Mon.	Tues.	Wed.
Days after Emily	1	2	3	4	5	6	7
was born	8	9	10	11	12	13	14
	and so on.						

- Note that whenever the number of days is a multiple of 7 (7, 14, 21, . . . , 70, . . .) a whole number of weeks has gone by, and it is again a Wednesday.
- If 1200 were a multiple of 7, the 1200th day would be a Wednesday.
- Is it? To find out, use your calculator: $1200 \div 7 = 171.4285 \ldots$
- 1200 days is <u>not</u> a whole number of weeks; it is a little more than 171 weeks.
- Since $171 \times 7 = 1197$, the 1197th day completes the 171st week, and hence is a Wednesday.
- The 1198th day starts the next week. It is a Thursday; the 1199th day is a Friday; and the 1200th day is a Saturday.
- The answer is D.

NOTE: Did you notice that the solution didn't use the fact that Emily was born on April 15, 1987? This is unusual. Occasionally, but not often, a PSAT problem contains extraneous information.

In contrast to Examples 1 and 2, some questions *require* you to look at all five choices in order to find the answers. Consider Example 3.

EXAMPLE 3

For any numbers *a* and *b*: $a \odot b = a^2 + b^2$? Which of the following is *not* equal to 6 ☺ 8?
(A) −10 ☺ 0   (B) −8 ☺ −6   (C) 9 ☺ $\sqrt{19}$ (D) (6 ☺ 9) − (4 ☺ 1)
(E) 2(3 ☺ 4)

The words *which of the following* alert you to the fact that you are going to have to examine each of the five choices and determine which of them satisfies the stated condition—in this case, that it is *not* equal to 6 ☺ 8.

Do not be concerned that you have never seen the symbol "☺" used this way before. No one has. On the PSAT there is always at least one question that uses a symbol that the test makers have made up. All you have to do is read the question very carefully and follow the directions exactly. In this case we have: $6 ☺ 8 = 6^2 + 8^2 = 36 + 64 = 100$.

Now check each of the five choices, and find the one that is *not* equal to 100.

(A) $-10 ☺ 0 = (-10)^2 + 0^2 = 100 + 0 = 100$

(B) $-8 ☺ -6 = (-8)^2 + (-6)^2 = 64 + 36 = 100$

(C) $9 ☺ \sqrt{19} = 9^2 + (\sqrt{19})^2 = 81 + 19 = 100$

(D) $(6 ☺ 9) - (4 ☺ 1) = (6^2 + 9^2) - (4^2 + 1^2) = (36 + 81) - (16 + 1) = 117 - 17 = 100$

(E) $2(3 ☺ 4) = 2(3^2 1 4^2) = 2(9 + 16) = 2(25) = 50$, which is *not* equal to 100.

So, the correct answer is E.

Another kind of multiple-choice question that appears on the PSAT is the Roman numeral-type question. These questions actually consist of three statements labeled I, II, and III. The five answer choices give various possibilities for which statement or statements are true. Here is a typical example.

EXAMPLE 4

In $\triangle ABC$, $AB = 3$ and $BC = 4$. Which of the following could be the perimeter of $\triangle ABC$?

I. 8
II. 12
III. 16

(A) I only   (B) II only   (C) I and II only   (D) II and III only
(E) I, II, and III

• To solve this problem, examine each statement independently.

    I. Could the perimeter be 8? If it were, then the third side would be 1. But in any triangle, the smallest side must be greater than the difference of the other two sides. So, the third side must be *greater* than $4 - 3 = 1$. It cannot equal 1. I is false.

    II. Could the perimeter be 12? That is, could the third side be 5? Yes. The three sides could be 3, 4, and 5. In fact, the most common right triangle to appear on the PSAT is a 3-4-5 right triangle. II is true.

    III. Could the perimeter be 16? If it were, then the third side would be 9. But in any triangle, the largest side must be less than the sum of the other two sides. So, the third side must be less than $4 + 3 = 7$. It cannot equal 9. III is false.

• Only statement II is true. The answer is B.

Grid-in Questions

Ten of the forty mathematics questions on the PSAT are what the College Board calls Student-Produced Response Questions. These are the only questions on the PSAT that are not multiple-choice. Since the answers to these questions are entered on a special grid, they are usually referred to as *grid-in* questions. Except for the method of entering your answer, this type of question is probably the one with which you are most familiar. In your math class, most of your homework problems and test questions require you to determine an answer and write it down, and this is what you will do on the grid-in problems. The only difference is that once you have figured out an answer, you must record it on a special grid such as the one shown, so that it can be read by a computer. Here is a typical grid-in question.

EXAMPLE 5

John has a rectangular garden in his backyard. He decides to enlarge it by increasing its length by 20% and its width by 30%. If the area of the new garden is a times the area of the original garden, what is the value of a?

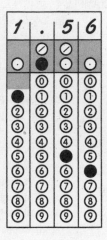

Solution. From the wording of the question, it is clear that the answer does not depend on the actual original dimensions. Therefore, pick an easy value. For example, assume that the original garden is a square whose sides are 10. Since 20% of 10 is 2 and 30% of 10 is 3, then the new garden is a 12 by 13 rectangle. Therefore, the area of the original garden is 100, and the area of the new garden is 156. So $156 = a(100)$, and $a = 1.56$.

To enter this answer, you write 1.56 in the four spaces at the top of the grid and blacken in the appropriate circle under each space. In the first column, under the 1, blacken the circle marked 1; in the second column, under the decimal point, blacken the circle with the decimal point; in the third column, under the 5, blacken the circle marked 5; and finally, in the fourth column, under the 6, blacken in the circle marked 6.

Note that the only symbols that appear in the grid are the digits from 0 to 9, a decimal point, and a fraction bar (/). The grid does not have a minus sign, so *answers to grid-in problems can never be negative.* In Chapter 6, you will read suggestions for the best way to fill in grids. You will also learn the special rules concerning the proper way to grid in fractions, mixed numbers, and decimals that won't fit in the grid's four columns.

WRITING SKILLS

The writing skills section consists of thirty-nine questions to be answered in thirty minutes. A typical test is made up of fourteen identifying sentence errors questions, twenty improving sentence questions, and five improving paragraph questions.

Identifying Sentence Error

The identifying sentence error questions test your ability to spot faults in usage and sentence structure.

The sentences in this section may contain errors in grammar, usage, choice of words, or idioms. There is either just one error per sentence or the sentence is correct. Some words or phrases are underlined and lettered; everything else in the sentence is correct.

If an underlined word or phrase is incorrect, choose that letter; if the sentence is correct, select No error. Then blacken the appropriate space on your Answer Sheet.

EXAMPLE:

The region has a climate so severe that plants   Ⓐ Ⓑ ● Ⓓ Ⓔ
                A
growing there rarely had been more than twelve
   B   C
inches high. No error
    D   E

---

1. Despite the fact that some states have resisted, the Congress have passed
         A   B   C
    legislation permitting highway speed limits to 65 miles per hour on rural
            D
    interstates. No error
          E

2. Mohandas Gandhi, to who the title "Father of Passive Resistance"
                      A
    may be given, bravely led the nationalist movement in India against
     B   C   D
    British rule. No error
         E

3. Joe DiMaggio, whose style was one of quiet excellence, was consistently the
_____A_____B
New York Yankees' outstanding player during his thirteen years on the team.
_____C_____D
No error
___
E

4. When Ms. Rivera was truly happy, she does not constantly complain that she
_____A___B_____C_____D
has no purpose in life. No error
_____E

Answer Explanations

1. **(C)** Error in subject-verb agreement. The antecedent, *Congress*, is singular. Change *have passed* to *has passed*.
2. **(A)** Error in case. Change *who* to *whom*. It is the object of the preposition *to*.
3. **(E)** Sentence is correct.
4. **(A)** Error in sequence of tenses. The sentence should read: *When Ms. Rivera is truly happy, she does not constantly complain.*

Improving Sentence Questions

The improving sentence questions test your ability to select the wording that makes the strongest sentence—the clearest, the smoothest, the most compact.

Some or all parts of the following sentences are underlined. The first answer choice, (A), simply repeats the underlined part of the sentence. The other four choices present four alternate ways to phrase the underlined part. Select the answer that produces the most effective sentence, one that is clear and exact, and blacken the appropriate space on your answer sheet. In selecting your choice, be sure that it is standard written English and that it expresses the meaning of the original sentence.

EXAMPLE:

The first biography of author Eudora Welty came out in 1998
and she was eighty-nine years old at the time.

(A)   and she was eighty-nine years old at the time
(B)   at the time when she was eighty-nine
(C)   upon becoming an eighty-nine year old
(D)   when she was eighty-nine
(E)   at the age of eighty-nine years old

Ⓐ Ⓑ Ⓒ ● Ⓔ

5. More than any animal, the wolverine exemplifies the unbridled ferocity of "nature red in tooth and claw."

(A) More than any animal
(B) More than any other animal
(C) More than another animal
(D) Unlike any animal
(E) Compared to other animals

6. The reviewer knew that Barbara Cartland had written several Gothic novels, she didn't remember any of their titles.

(A) novels, she didn't remember any of their titles
(B) novels, however she didn't remember any of their titles
(C) novels, their titles, however, she didn't remember
(D) novels without remembering any of their titles
(E) novels, but she remembered none of their titles

7. I think the United States will veto the resolution imposing sanctions against Israel regardless of the desires of the Arab nations for strong action.

(A) regardless of the desires of the Arab nations
(B) irregardless of the Arab nations' desires
(C) regardless of the Arab nations desires
(D) irregardless of the Arab nation's desires
(E) mindful of the desires of the Arab nations

Answer Explanations

5. (B) Choice B includes the necessary word *other*, which makes the comparison correct. Choice D changes the meaning of the sentence by its implication that the wolverine is *not* an animal.

6. (E) Choices A, B, and C are run-on sentences. Choice D changes the meaning of the sentence by implying that it was Barbara Cartland who could not remember the titles.

7. (A) *Irregardless* in Choices B and D is incorrect. Also, in Choices C and D, the case of *nations* is incorrect. The correct form of the plural possessive case of *nation* is *nations'*. Choice E changes the meaning of the sentence; in fact, it reverses it.

Improving Paragraph Questions

The improving paragraph questions test your ability to polish an essay by combining sentences or manipulating sentence parts. You may need to arrange sentences to improve the essay's logical organization, or to pick evidence to strengthen the writer's argument.

The passage below is the unedited draft of a student's essay. Some of the essay needs to be rewritten to make the meaning clearer and more precise. Read the essay carefully.

The essay is followed by three questions about changes that might improve all or part of its organization, development, sentence structure, use of language, appropriateness to the audience, or use of standard written English. Choose the answer that most clearly and effectively expresses the student's intended meaning. Indicate your choice by filling in the corresponding space on the answer sheet.

---

[1] As people grow older, quite obviously, the earth does too. [2] And with the process of the earth aging, we must learn to recycle. [3] The idea of using things over and over again to conserve our supply of natural resources is a beautiful one. [4] Those who don't see how easy it is to recycle should be criticized greatly.

[5] As we become more aware of the earth's problems, we all say "Oh, I'd like to help." [6] However, so few really do get involved. [7] Recycling is a simple, yet effective place to start. [8] Taking aluminum cans to the supermarket to be recycled is an ingenious idea. [9] It attracts those who want the money (5 cents a can), and it is also a convenient place to go to. [10] In addition, in almost every town, there is a Recycling Center. [11] I know that there are separate bins for paper, bottles, cans, etc. [12] This is a convenient service to those who recycle. [13] It is so easy to drive a few blocks to a center to drop off what needs to be recycled. [14] This is just another simple example of how easy it really is to recycle and to get involved. [15] Those who don't see its simplicity should be criticized for not doing their part to help make the world a better place.

[16] When I go to other people's houses and see aluminum cans in the garbage, I can honestly say I get enraged. [17] Often I say, "Why don't you just recycle those cans instead of throwing them out?" [18] What makes me even more angry is when they say "We have no time to recycle them." [19] Those people, I feel, should be criticized for not recycling in the past and should be taught a lesson about our earth and how recycling can conserve it.

8. Which of the following most effectively expresses the underlined portion of sentence 2 below?

And with the process of the earth aging, we must learn to recycle.

(A) with the aging process of the earth
(B) the process of the earth's aging
(C) as the earth ages
(D) with the aging earth's process
(E) as the process of the earth's aging continues

9. Considering the essay as a whole, which of the following best explains the main purpose of the second paragraph?

(A) to explain the historical background of the topic
(B) to provide a smooth transition between the first and third paragraphs
(C) to define terms introduced in the first paragraph
(D) to give an example of an idea presented in the first paragraph
(E) to present a different point of view on the issue being discussed

10. Which of the sentences below most effectively combines sentences 10, 11, and 12?

(A) Recycling centers offer recyclers convenience by providing separate bins for paper, bottles, and cans and by being located in almost every town.
(B) Recycling centers, located in almost every town, serve recyclers by providing convenient bins to separate paper, bottles, and cans.
(C) Almost every town has a recycling center with separate bins for paper, bottles, and cans, and this is a convenient service for people who want to recycle.
(D) People who want to recycle will find recycling centers in almost every town, providing a convenient separation of paper, bottles, and cans into bins.
(E) For the convenience of recyclers, separate bins for paper, bottles, and cans are provided by almost every town's recycling center.

Answer Explanations

8. (C) This question asks you to find an alternative to a rather awkward group of words, composed of two phrases, *with the process* and *of the earth aging*. The second is graceless and ungrammatical. It should have read *of the earth's aging*, because in standard usage, nouns and pronouns modifying gerunds are usually written as possessives. Knowing what it should have been, however, is not much help in answering the question. You still must select from the five alternatives the one best way to express the essay writer's idea. In the context of the whole sentence, two of the choices, B and D, make no sense at all. A also borders on incomprehensibility. Of choices C and E, the better choice is C because it is more concise and it expresses exactly what the writer intended.

9. **(D)** To answer this question you need to have read the whole essay. You also need to know the way individual paragraphs function in an essay—any essay. Here, all five choices describe legitimate uses of a paragraph, but they don't all apply to this particular essay. Choices A, C, and E can be quickly discarded. Choice B is a possibility because in a unified essay every paragraph (except the first and last) in some sense serves as a bridge between paragraphs. Because the second paragraph is the longest in the essay, however, its main function is probably more than transitional. In fact, it develops by example an idea originating in the first paragraph—how easy it is to recycle. Therefore, D is the best choice.

10. **(B)** In a series of short sentences, every idea carries equal weight. By combining short sentences, writers may emphasize the important ideas and subordinate the others. To answer this question, then, you have to decide which idea expressed by the three sentences ought to be emphasized. Since two of the sentences (11 and 12) refer to the convenient arrangement of recycling centers, that's the point to stress. In the context of the whole essay, the other sentence (10), which pertains to the location of recycling centers, contains less vital information. Usually, the main point of a sentence is contained in the main, or independent, clause, and secondary ideas are found in subordinate, or dependent, clauses.

   With that principle in mind, read each of the choices. A and C give equal weight to the location and convenience of recycling centers. D stresses the location rather than the convenience. E subordinates properly but changes the meaning. Therefore, B is the correct answer. In B, information about the location of recycling centers is contained in a subordinate clause included parenthetically inside the main clause.

2 The Sentence Completion Question

The sentence completion questions ask you to choose the best way to complete a sentence from which one or two words have been omitted. You must be able to recognize the logic, style, and tone of the sentence so that you can choose the answer that makes sense in this context. You must also be able to recognize the way words are normally used.

The sentences cover a wide variety of topics. However, this is not a test of your general knowledge. You may feel more comfortable if you are familiar with the topic the sentence is discussing, but you should be able to handle any of the sentences using your understanding of the English language.

Tips for Handling Sentence Completion Questions

1. Before you look at the answer choices, read the sentence, substituting the word *blank* for the missing word. Think of words you know that might make sense in the context. You may not come up with the exact word, but you may come up with a synonym. You will definitely have a feel for what word belongs in the frame.

EXAMPLE 1

See how the first tip works in dealing with the following sentence:

The psychologist set up the experiment to test the rat's _____: he wished to see how well the rat adjusted to the changing conditions it had to face.

Even before you look at the answer choices, you can figure out what the answer *should* be.

Look at the sentence. The psychologist is trying to test the rat's *blank*. In other words, the psychologist is trying to test some particular quality or characteristic of the rat. What quality? How do you get the answer?

Look at the second part of the sentence, the part following the colon (the second clause, in technical terms). This clause defines or clarifies what the psychologist is trying to test. He is trying to see how well the rat adjusts. What words does this suggest to you? *Flexibility*, possibly, or *adjustment* comes to mind. Either of these words could logically complete the sentence's thought.

Here are the five answer choices given:

(A) reflexes   (B) communicability   (C) stamina
   (D) sociability   (E) adaptability

Which one is the best synonym for *flexibility* or *adjustment*? Clearly, the closest synonym is *adaptability*, Choice E.

To make sure you are correct, reread the sentence, substituting the word *adaptability* in the blank.

The psychologist set up the experiment to test the rat's adaptability: he wished to see how well the rat adjusted to the changing conditions it had to face.

The correct answer is Choice E.

2. Look for words or phrases that indicate a contrast between one idea and another—words like *although, however, despite,* or *but*. In such cases, an antonym or near-antonym for another word in the sentence may be the correct answer.

EXAMPLE 2

See how the second tip works in dealing with the following sentence:

We expected the winner of the race to be jubilant about his victory, but he was _____ instead.

How do you expect someone to feel who has won a victory? Even if you do not know the word *jubilant*, you can guess that it means overjoyed and triumphant.

But signals a contrast. The winner is *not* jubilant. Instead, he is the opposite of jubilant: he is sad.

Here are the five answer choices given:

(A) triumphant   (B) mature   (C) morose
   (D) talkative   (E) culpable

You are looking for an antonym of *jubilant*. *Triumphant* is a synonym of *jubilant*, not an antonym; its antonym is *sad* or *disappointed*. You can cross out Choice A. *Mature* means grown-up; its antonym is *immature*. You can cross out Choice B. The next choice, *morose*, may be an unfamiliar word to you. For the moment, skip Choice C. The antonym of *talkative* is *silent* or *uncommunicative*. You can cross out Choice D. *Culpable* means guilty; its antonym is *innocent*. You can cross out Choice E. Only Choice C is left. *Morose* means gloomy and ill-humored; it is the opposite of *jubilant*.

   3. **Look for words or phrases that indicate support for a concept—words such as *likewise, similarly, in the same way, and, in addition, additionally,* and *also.*** What follows logically develops the writer's idea. In such cases, a synonym or near-synonym for another word in the sentence may provide the correct answer.

EXAMPLE 3

   See how the third tip works in dealing with the following sentence:

   The simplest animals are those whose bodies are least complex in structure, and that do the same things done by all animals, such as eating, breathing, moving, and feeling, in the most _____ way.

   The transition word *and* signals you that the writer intends to develop the idea of simplicity introduced in the sentence. Which of the answer choices is closest in meaning to *simplest* and to *least complex*?

   Here are the five answer choices given:

   (A) haphazard   (B) bizarre   (C) advantageous
       (D) primitive   (E) unique

   You are looking for a word that develops the idea of simplicity, possibly a synonym for the word *simplest*. In biology class, you most likely learned that primitive life forms were simple in structure, and that the more complex forms of life evolved later. Clearly, Choice D, *primitive*, is best. It is the only answer choice that develops the idea of simplicity.

   4. **Look for words or phrases that indicate that one thing causes another—words like *because, since, therefore,* or *thus.***

EXAMPLE 4

   See how the fourth tip works in dealing with the following sentence:

   Because her delivery was _____ , the effect of her speech on the voters was nonexistent.

Because signals a relationship of cause and effect. One thing causes another. Which of the answer choices expresses such a logical relationship?

Here are the five answer choices given:

(A) halting   (B) plausible   (C) moving
    (D) respectable   (E) audible

What sort of delivery would cause a speech to have no effect? Obviously you would not expect a *moving* (eloquent) delivery to have such a poor result. A *halting* or stumbling speech, however, might logically have little or no effect on its audience. Thus, Choice A is best.

5. Look for signals that indicate a word is being defined—phrases such as *in other words, that is,* or *which means*, and special punctuation clues. Commas, hyphens, and parentheses all are used to set off definitions.

EXAMPLE 5

See how the fifth tip works in dealing with the following sentence:

As a child, Menuhin was considered a _____ , gifted with extraordinary musical ability.

This sentence is a straightforward definition. The missing word is defined in the section set off by the comma. Ask yourself what word in the dictionary is defined as a person *gifted with extraordinary musical ability*?

Here are the five answer choices given:

(A) heretic   (B) prodigy   (C) mendicant
    (D) renegade   (E) precursor

Menuhin was a child *prodigy*. The correct answer is Choice B.

6. If you're having vocabulary trouble, look for familiar word parts— prefixes, suffixes, and roots—in unfamiliar words.

EXAMPLE 6

See how the sixth tip works in dealing with the following sentence:

After a tragedy, many people claim to have had a _____ of disaster.

Some of the following answer choices are unfamiliar words that you can figure out if you know the meaning of the prefixes, suffixes, and roots involved. Here are the five answer choices given:

(A) deviation   (B) proclamation   (C) presentiment
(D) brink   (E) verdict

Go through the answer choices, trying to figure out the meaning of any unfamiliar words by breaking them down into parts.

Deviation   The prefix *de-* means down or away.
The root *via* means way or road.
A *deviation* is a departure from the way, that is, a divergence or difference.

Does this word work in the context? If it does not, you can eliminate Choice A.

Proclamation   The prefix *pro-* means forward or in favor of.
The root *clam* means cry out.
A *proclamation* is a public statement or announcement, something cried out to the people.

Does this word work in the context? If it does not, you can eliminate Choice B.

Presentiment   The prefix *pre-* means before.
The root *sens* means feel. A *sentiment* is a feeling.
A *presentiment* is something you feel before it happens, a premonition or foreboding.

Presentiment works in the context. Your best answer is Choice C.

7. Work out whether the missing word is positive (+) or negative (−). Then test the answer choices for their positive or negative sense, eliminating those that don't work.

EXAMPLE 7

See how the seventh tip works in the following sentence.

No matter how hard Ichabod tried to appear smooth and debonair, he still struck those who met him as a particularly _____ young man.

The sentence contrasts Ichabod's desired image—smooth and debonair (both positive terms)—with the actual negative impression he makes. You are looking for a negative term. Ask yourself what negative words would describe a young man who is *not* smooth and debonair (suave; sophisticated; elegant).

Here are the five answer choices given:

(A) heroic   (B) promising   (C) mendacious
   (D) ungainly   (E) precocious

Heroic (gallant; brave), *promising* (likely to turn out well), and *precocious* (unusually advanced, especially mentally) are all positive terms. Since you are looking for a negative term, you can eliminate Choices A, B, and E.

Both *mendacious* and *ungainly* are negative terms. *Mendacious* means untruthful. Ichabod isn't being untruthful; he's just unsuccessful at looking cool and suave. No matter how hard he tries, he still looks *ungainly*: ungraceful and clumsy, the opposite of smooth. The correct answer is Choice D.

8. In a sentence completion question with two blanks, eliminate answer choices by testing one blank at a time. First read through the entire sentence and decide which blank you want to work on. Then insert the appropriate word of each answer pair in that blank. Ask yourself whether this particular word makes sense in this blank. If a word makes *no* sense in the sentence, you can eliminate that answer pair.

EXAMPLE 8

See how the eighth tip works in the following sentence.

The author portrays research psychologists not as disruptive _____ in the field of psychotherapy, but as effective _____ working ultimately toward the same ends as the psychotherapists.

Two additional tips can help you answer this question. **Tip 2:** Look for words that signal a contrast. The *not as…but as* structure signals a contrast; the missing words may be antonyms or near-antonyms. **Tip 7:** Test the answer choices for their positive or negative sense, eliminating those that don't work.

Here are the five answer choices given:

(A) proponents..opponents
(B) antagonists..pundits
(C) interlocutors..surrogates
(D) meddlers..usurpers
(E) intruders..collaborators

Turn to the second part of the sentence. The research psychologists are portrayed as effective "blanks" working ultimately toward the same ends as the psychotherapists. The key phrase here is "working ultimately toward the same ends." Thus, the research psychologists are in effect working together with the psychotherapists to achieve a common goal. This immediately suggests that the correct answer is *collaborators*, Choice E. Test the first word of that answer pair in the first blank. The adjective "disruptive" suggests that the first missing word is negative in tone. *Intruders* (people who rudely or inappropriately barge in) definitely have negative connotations. Choice E continues to look good.

Reread the sentence with both words in place, making sure both words make sense. "The author portrays research psychologists not as disruptive intruders in the field of psychotherapy, but as effective collaborators working ultimately toward the same ends as the psychotherapists." Both words make perfect sense. The correct answer is Choice E.

DID YOU KNOW?

Some sentences are actually two statements linked by a semi-colon (;) or a colon (:). The punctuation mark is your clue that the two statements support each other.

A semi-colon signals you that the second statement develops the idea expressed in the first statement.

EXAMPLE

It is foolish to boast about your wealth or accomplishments; no one likes a braggart.

Statement 1: It is foolish to boast about your wealth or accomplishments.
Why?
Statement 2: No one likes a braggart.

A colon signals you that the second statement serves to explain or clarify the first. It gives examples, or it defines terms.

EXAMPLE

Justice Brandeis was noted for his legal acumen: his biographers often comment about the keenness of his insights into the workings of the law.

Statement 1: Justice Brandeis was noted for his legal acumen.
What is legal acumen?
Statement 2: His biographers often comment about *the keenness of his insights into the workings of the law*.
Legal acumen is keenness of insight into the workings of the law.

Practice Exercises   Answers given on page 45.

The following exercises are set up to give even National Merit Scholars a challenge. If you don't get every answer right, it's No Big Deal. Just do your best, and check the answer explanations for tips on how to do even better next time round.

> Each of the following sentences contains one or two blanks; these blanks indicate that a word or set of words has been left out. Below the sentence are five words or phrases, lettered A through E. Select the word or set of words that best completes the sentence.

Exercise A

1. Although the play was not praised by the critics, it did not _____ thanks to favorable word-of-mouth comments.

   (A) succeed   (B) translate   (C) function
   (D) close   (E) continue

2. Because the hawk is _____ bird, farmers try to keep it away from their chickens.

   (A) a migratory   (B) an ugly   (C) a predatory
   (D) a reclusive   (E) a huge

3. If you are trying to make a strong impression on your audience, you cannot do so by being understated, tentative, or _____.

   (A) hyperbolic   (B) restrained   (C) argumentative
   (D) authoritative   (E) expressive

4. Despite the mixture's _____ nature, we found that by lowering its temperature in the laboratory we could dramatically reduce its tendency to vaporize.

   (A) resilient   (B) homogeneous   (C) insipid
   (D) volatile   (E) acerbic

5. Milton's poem *Lycidas* is renowned as an example of _____ verse, for it laments the death of the young clergyman Edward King.

   (A) satiric   (B) moribund   (C) elegiac
   (D) free   (E) didactic

6. Despite his _____ appearance, he was chosen by his employer for a job that required neatness and polish.

   (A) disheveled   (B) impressive   (C) prepossessing
   (D) aloof   (E) tardy

7. The earthquake caused some damage, but the tidal wave that followed was more _____ because it _____ many villages.

   (A) culpable..bypassed
   (B) surreptitious..absorbed
   (C) deleterious..renovated
   (D) beneficial..congested
   (E) devastating..inundated

8. Several manufacturers now make biodegradable forms of plastic: some plastic six-pack rings, for example, gradually _____ when exposed to sunlight.

   (A) harden   (B) stagnate   (C) inflate
   (D) propagate   (E) decompose

9. Although Barbara Tuchman never earned a graduate degree, she nevertheless _____ a scholarly career as a historian noted for her vivid style and _____ erudition.

   (A) interrupted..flawed
   (B) relinquished..immense
   (C) abandoned..capricious
   (D) pursued..prodigious
   (E) followed..scanty

10. Since the chief executive officer had promised to give us a definite answer to our proposal, we were _____ by his _____ reply.

    (A) pleased..equivocal
    (B) vexed..negative
    (C) annoyed..noncommittal
    (D) delighted..perfunctory
    (E) baffled..decisive

Exercise B

1. The insurance company rejected his application for accident insurance, because his _____ occupation made him a poor risk.

   (A) desultory   (B) haphazard   (C) esoteric
   (D) hazardous   (E) sedentary

2. No other artist rewards the viewer with more sheer pleasure than Miró: he is one of those blessed artists who combine profundity and _____.

   (A) education   (B) wisdom   (C) faith
   (D) depth   (E) fun

3. The tapeworm is an example of _____ organism, one that lives within or on another creature, deriving some or all of its nutriment from its host.

   (A) a hospitable   (B) an exemplary   (C) a parasitic
   (D) an autonomous   (E) a protozoan

4. The young woman was quickly promoted when her employers saw how _____ she was.

   (A) indigent   (B) indifferent   (C) assiduous
   (D) irresolute   (E) cursory

5. Though she was theoretically a friend of labor, her voting record in Congress _____ that impression.

   (A) implied   (B) created   (C) confirmed
   (D) belied   (E) maintained

6. The reasoning in this editorial is so _____ that I cannot see how anyone can be _____ by it.

   (A) coherent..convinced
   (B) astute..persuaded
   (C) cogent..moved
   (D) specious..deceived
   (E) dispassionate..incriminated

7. To _____ the problem of contaminated chicken, the panel recommends shifting inspections from cursory visual checks to a more scientifically _____ random sampling for bacterial and chemical contamination.

(A) alleviate..rigorous
(B) eliminate..perfunctory
(C) analyze..symbolic
(D) document..unreliable
(E) obviate..dubious

8. Unable to hide his _____ for the police commissioner, the inspector imprudently made _____ remarks about his superior officer.

(A) disdain..detached
(B) respect..ambiguous
(C) liking..unfathomable
(D) contempt..interminable
(E) scorn..scathing

9. We were amazed that a woman who had been up to now the most _____ of public speakers could, in a single speech, electrify an audience and bring them cheering to their feet.

(A) enthralling   (B) accomplished   (C) pedestrian
(D) auspicious   (E) masterful

10. Shy and hypochondriacal, Madison was _____ at public gatherings; his character made him a most _____ lawmaker and practicing politician.

(A) ambivalent..conscientious
(B) uncomfortable..unlikely
(C) inaudible..fervent
(D) aloof..gregarious
(E) awkward..effective

Exercise C

1. In place of the more general debate about abstract principles of government that many delegates expected, the Constitutional Convention put _____ proposals on the table.

   (A) theoretical   (B) vague   (C) concrete
   (D) tentative   (E) redundant

2. He was so _____ in meeting the payments on his car that the finance company threatened to seize the automobile.

   (A) dilatory   (B) mercenary   (C) solvent
   (D) diligent   (E) compulsive

3. The child was so spoiled by her indulgent parents that she pouted and became _____ when she did not receive all of their attention.

   (A) discreet   (B) suspicious   (C) elated
   (D) sullen   (E) tranquil

4. Modern architecture has abandoned the use of _____ trimming on buildings and has concentrated on an almost Greek simplicity of line.

   (A) flamboyant   (B) austere   (C) inconspicuous
   (D) hypothetical   (E) derivative

5. We lost confidence in him because he never _____ the grandiose promises he had made.

   (A) forgot about   (B) reneged on   (C) tired of
   (D) delivered on   (E) retreated from

6. Perhaps because something in us instinctively distrusts such displays of natural fluency, some readers approach John Updike's fiction with _____.

   (A) indifference   (B) suspicion   (C) veneration
   (D) enthusiasm   (E) eloquence

7. Because she had a reputation for _____ , we were surprised and pleased when she greeted us so _____ .

   (A) insolence..informally
   (B) insouciance..cordially
   (C) graciousness..amiably
   (D) arrogance..disdainfully
   (E) aloofness..affably

8. Just as disloyalty is the mark of the traitor, _____ is the mark of the
   _____.

   (A) timorousness..hero
   (B) temerity..renegade
   (C) avarice..philanthropist
   (D) cowardice..craven
   (E) vanity..flatterer

9. We now know that what constitutes practically all of matter is empty space:
   relatively enormous _____ in which revolve infinitesimal particles so
   _____ that they have never been seen or photographed.

   (A) crescendos..minute
   (B) enigmas..statio
   (C) conglomerates..vague
   (D) abstractions..colorful
   (E) voids..small

10. Brilliant yet disturbing, James Baldwin's *The Fire Next Time* is both so
    eloquent in its passion and so _____ in its candor that it is bound to
    _____ any reader.

    (A) bitter..soothe
    (B) romantic..appall
    (C) searing..unsettle
    (D) indifferent..disappoint
    (E) frank..bore

Exercise D

1. The scientist maintains that any hypothesis must explain what has already
   been discovered and must be constantly _____ by future findings.

   (A) confirmed   (B) invalidated   (C) disregarded
   (D) equaled   (E) reversed

2. Traffic speed limits are set at a level that achieves some balance between the
   danger of _____ speed and the desire of most people to travel as quickly
   as possible.

   (A) minimal   (B) normal   (C) prudent
   (D) inadvertent   (E) excessive

3. Written in an engaging style, the book provides a comprehensive overview of European wines that should prove inviting to everyone from the virtual _____ to the experienced connoisseur.

   (A) prodigal   (B) novice   (C) zealot
   (D) miser   (E) glutton

4. In view of the interrelationships among the African-American leaders treated in this anthology, a certain amount of _____ among some of the essays presented is inevitable.

   (A) overlapping   (B) inaccuracy   (C) pomposity
   (D) exaggeration   (E) objectivity

5. Most Antarctic animals _____ depend on the tiny shrimplike krill, either feeding on them directly, like the humpback whale, or consuming species that feed on them.

   (A) seldom   (B) ultimately   (C) needlessly
   (D) immediately   (E) marginally

6. Andy Warhol was an inspired _____ of his own art: he had a true gift for publicity.

   (A) assessor   (B) promoter   (C) curator
   (D) benefactor   (E) luminary

7. Japan's industrial success is _____ in part to its tradition of group effort and _____ , as opposed to the tradition of individual personal achievement common in many other industrial nations.

   (A) responsive..independence
   (B) related..misdirection
   (C) equivalent..solidarity
   (D) subordinate..individuality
   (E) attributable..cooperation

8. Aimed at _____ European attempts to seize territory in the Americas, the Monroe Doctrine was a strong warning to _____ foreign powers.

   (A) abetting..impertinent
   (B) eliminating..credulous
   (C) assisting..remote
   (D) preventing..overt
   (E) curbing..predatory

9. Because he was cynical, he was reluctant to _____ the _____ of any kind act until he had ruled out all possible hidden uncharitable motives.

    (A) question..benevolence
    (B) acknowledge..wisdom
    (C) credit..unselfishness
    (D) endure..loss
    (E) witness..outcome

10. The concept of individual freedom grew from political and moral convictions that _____ the closed and _____ world of feudalism into a more open and dynamic society.

    (A) galvanized..vibrant
    (B) converted..irreverent
    (C) transformed..hierarchical
    (D) recast..vital
    (E) merged..unregulated

Exercise E

1. Some students are _____ in choosing their classes; that is, they want to take only the courses for which they see immediate value.

    (A) theoretical   (B) impartial   (C) pragmatic
    (D) idealistic   (E) opinionated

2. Chaotic in conception but not in _____, Kelly's canvases are as neat as the proverbial pin.

    (A) conceit   (B) theory   (C) execution
    (D) origin   (E) intent

3. Although Josephine Tey was arguably as good a mystery writer as Agatha Christie, she was clearly far less _____ than Christie, having written only six books in comparison to Christie's sixty.

    (A) coherent   (B) prolific   (C) equivocal
    (D) pretentious   (E) gripping

4. In the North American tribes, men were the representational artists, creating drawings of hunters and animals; women, on the other hand, traditionally _____ abstract, geometrical compositions.

 (A) devised   (B) shunned   (C) decried
 (D) impersonated   (E) prefigured

5. The counselor viewed divorce not as a single circumscribed event but as _____ of changing family relationships—as a process that begins during the failing marriage and extends over many years.

 (A) a continuum   (B) an episode   (C) a parody
 (D) a denial   (E) an elimination

6. The systems analyst hesitated to talk to strangers about her highly specialized work, because she feared it was too _____ for people uninitiated in the field to understand.

 (A) intriguing   (B) derivative   (C) frivolous
 (D) esoteric   (E) rudimentary

7. Lavish in visual beauty, the film *Lawrence of Arabia* nevertheless boasts _____ of style: it knows how much can be shown in a single shot, how much can be said in a few words.

 (A) nonchalance   (B) economy   (C) autonomy
 (D) frivolity   (E) arrogance

8. The verbose and _____ style of the late Victorian novel is totally unlike the _____ of a minimalist like Hemingway.

 (A) chatty..prolixity
 (B) awkward..consistency
 (C) redundant..terseness
 (D) eloquent..logistics
 (E) concise..floridity

9. Both the popular shows *China Beach* and *Tour of Duty* reflect the way dissent has become _____ in America; what were radical antiwar attitudes in the 1960s are now _____ TV attitudes.

 (A) domesticated..mainstream
 (B) obsolete..militant
 (C) meaningful..unfashionable
 (D) sensationalized..trite
 (E) troublesome..conventional

10. He was a _____ employee, but the _____ and exhaustive research that he performed made it worthwhile for his employers to put up with his difficult moods.

(A) domineering..biased
(B) congenial..exemplary
(C) popular..pretentious
(D) fastidious..garbled
(E) cantankerous..meticulous

Answer Key

Exercise A

1. D	3. B	5. C	7. E	9. D
2. C	4. D	6. A	8. E	10. C

Exercise B

1. D	3. C	5. D	7. A	9. C
2. E	4. C	6. D	8. E	10. B

Exercise C

1. C	3. D	5. D	7. E	9. E
2. A	4. A	6. B	8. D	10. C

Exercise D

1. A	3. B	5. B	7. E	9. C
2. E	4. A	6. B	8. E	10. C

Exercise E

1. C	3. B	5. A	7. B	9. A
2. C	4. A	6. D	8. C	10. E

3 Improving Critical Reading Comprehension

Now more than ever, doing well on the critical reading questions can make the difference between success and failure on the PSAT. The most numerous questions in each verbal section, they are also the most time-consuming and the ones most likely to bog you down. However, you can handle them, and this chapter will show you how.

Frequently Asked Questions

1. **How can I become a better reader?**
   Read, Read, Read!
   Just do it.

   There is no substitute for extensive reading to prepare you for the PSAT and for college work. The only way to build up your proficiency in reading is by reading books of all kinds. As you read, you will develop speed, stamina, and the ability to comprehend the printed page. But if you want to turn yourself into the kind of reader the colleges are looking for, you must develop the habit of reading—closely and critically—every day.

2. **What sort of material should I read?**
   Challenge yourself. Don't limit your reading to light fiction, graphic novels, and Xbox reviews. Branch out a bit. Try to develop an interest in as many fields as you can.

   Check out some of these magazines:

   - *The New Yorker*
   - *Smithsonian*
   - *The New York Review of Books*
   - *National Geographic*
   - *Natural History*
   - *Harper's Magazine*

   Explore popular encyclopedias on the Web. You'll find articles on literature, music, science, philosophy, history, the arts—the whole range of fields touched on by the PSAT. If you take time to sample these fields, you won't find the subject matter of the reading passages on the PSAT strange.

3. **On the PSAT, is it better to read the passage first or the questions first?**

   The answer is, it depends on the passage, and *it depends on you*. If you are a super fast reader faced with one of the 100-word short reading passages, you may want to head for the questions first. It all depends on how good your visual memory is and on how good at scanning you are. If you're not a speed demon at reading, your best move may be to skim the whole passage before you read the questions. Only you can decide which method suits you best.

Tips for Handling Critical Reading Questions

1. **Tackle the short passages before the long ones.** Use them as a warm-up for the longer passages that follow.

2. **Tackle passages with familiar subjects before passages with unfamiliar ones.** It's hard to concentrate when you read about something wholly unfamiliar to you. Give yourself a break. In each section, first tackle the reading passage that interests you or deals with the topic about which you have a clue. Then move on to the other passage. You'll do better that way.

3. **If you are stumped by a tough reading question, move on, but do *not* skip the other questions on that passage.** Remember, the critical reading questions following each passage are not arranged in order of difficulty. They tend to be arranged sequentially: questions on paragraph 1 come before questions on paragraph 2. So try *all* the questions on the passage. That tough question may be just one question away from one that's easy for you.

4. **Do not zip back and forth between passages.** Stick with one passage until you feel sure you've answered all the questions you can on that passage. (If you don't, you'll probably have to waste time rereading the passage when you come back to it.) Before moving on to the next passage, be sure to go back over any questions you marked to come back to. In answering other questions on the passage, you may have acquired some information that will help you answer the questions you skipped.

5. **Read as fast as you can with understanding, but don't force yourself to rush.** Do not worry about the time. If you worry about not finishing the test, you will start taking shortcuts and miss the correct answer in your rush.

6. **Try to anticipate what the passage will be about.** As you read the italicized introductory material and tackle the passage's opening sentences, ask yourself who or what the author is talking about.

7. **Read with a purpose.** Try to spot what kind of writing this is, what techniques are used, who its intended audience is, and how the author feels about the subject. Be on the lookout for names, dates, and places. In particular, try to remember where in the passage the author makes major points. Then, when you start looking for the phrase or sentence that will justify your answer choice, you may be able to save time by zipping back to that section of the passage without having to reread the whole thing.

8. **Read the footnotes.** Duh!

9. **When you tackle the questions, go back to the passage to check each answer choice.** Do not rely on your memory, and above all, do not ignore the passage and just answer questions based on other things you've read. Remember, the questions are asking you about what this author has to say about the subject, not about what some other author you once read said about it in another book.

10. **Use the line references in the questions to get quickly to the correct spot in the passage.** It takes less time to locate a line number than to spot a word or phrase. Use the line numbers to orient yourself in the text.

11. **When dealing with the double passages, tackle them one at a time.** The questions are organized sequentially: questions about Passage 1 come before questions about Passage 2. So, do things in order. First read Passage 1; then jump straight to the questions and answer all the questions on Passage 1. Next read Passage 2; then answer all the questions on Passage 2. Finally, tackle the two or three questions that refer to both passages. Go back to both passages as needed.

    Occasionally a couple of questions referring to both passages will come before the questions on Passage 1. Do not let this throw you. Use your common sense. You've just read the first passage. Skip the one or two questions on both passages, and head straight for the questions about Passage 1. Answer them. Then read Passage 2. Answer the questions on Passage 2. Finally, go back to the questions you skipped and answer them (plus any other questions at the end of the set that refer to both passages). This is not rocket science. One thing, though: whenever you skip from question to question or from passage to passage, *be sure you are filling in the right spaces on your answer sheet.*

12. **Watch out for words or phrases in the questions that can clue you in to the kind of question being asked.** If you can recognize just what a given question is asking for, you'll be better able to tell which particular reading tactic to apply.

13. **Tackle vocabulary-in-context questions the same way you do sentence completion questions.** First, read the sentence, substituting "blank" for the word in quotes. Think of words you know that might make sense in the context. Then test each answer choice, substituting it in the sentence for the word in quotes. Ask yourself whether this particular answer choice makes sense in the specific context. Vocabulary-in-context questions take hardly any time to answer. If you're running out of time, answer them first.

14. **When asked to find a passage's main idea, be sure to check the opening and summary sentences of each paragraph.** Authors often orient readers with a sentence that expresses a paragraph's main idea concisely. Although such *topic sentences* may appear anywhere in the paragraph, you can usually find them in the opening or closing sentences.

    In PCAT reading passages, topic sentences are sometimes implied rather than stated directly. If you cannot find a topic sentence, ask yourself these questions:

    - Who or what is this passage about?
    - What feature of this subject is the author talking about?
    - What is the author trying to get across about this feature of the subject?

    You'll be on your way to locating the passage's main idea.

15. **When you answer specific detail questions, point to the precise words in the passage that support your answer choice.** You must be *sure* that the answer you select is in the passage. That means you must find a word or sentence or group of sentences that justifies your choice. Do *not* pick an answer just because it agrees with your personal opinions or with information on the subject that you've gotten from other sources.

16. **When you answer inference questions, look for what the passage logically suggests, but does *not* directly state.** Inference questions require you to use your judgment. You are drawing a conclusion based on what you have read in the text. Think about what the passage suggests. You must not take anything directly stated in the passage as an inference. Instead, you must look for clues in the passage that you can use in coming up with your own conclusion. Then you should choose as your answer a statement that logically follows from the information the author has given you.

17. **When asked to figure out an author's attitude, mood, or tone, look for words that convey emotion, express values, or paint pictures.** These images and descriptive phrases get the author's feelings across.

SHORT PASSAGES

Passage 1

Too many parents force their children into group activities. They are concerned about the child who loves to do things alone, who prefers a solitary walk with a camera to a game of ball. They want their sons to be *Line* "team players" and their daughters "good mixers." In such foolish fears
(5) lie the beginnings of the blighting of individuality, the thwarting of personality, the stealing of the wealth of one's capital for living joyously and well in a confused world. What America needs is a new army of defense, manned by young men and women who, through guidance and confidence, encouragement and wisdom, have built up values for themselves
(10) and away from crowds and companies.

1. According to the passage, too many parents push their children to be

   (A) unnecessarily gregarious
   (B) foolishly timorous
   (C) pointlessly extravagant
   (D) acutely individualistic
   (E) financially dependent

2. The primary point the author wishes to make is that

   (A) young people need time to themselves
   (B) group activities are harmful to children
   (C) parents knowingly thwart their children's personalities
   (D) independent thinking is of questionable value
   (E) America needs universal military training

3. The author puts quotation marks around the words "team players" and "good mixers" to indicate that he

   (A) is using vocabulary that is unfamiliar to the reader
   (B) intends to define these terms later in course of the passage
   (C) can readily distinguish these terms from one another
   (D) prefers not to differentiate roles by secondary factors such as gender
   (E) refuses to accept the assumption that these are entirely positive values

4. By "the wealth of one's capital for living joyously and well in a confused world" (lines 6–7), the author most likely means the

(A) financial security that one attains from one's individual professional achievements and overanalyzing it

(B) riches that parents thrust upon children who would far prefer to be left alone to follow their own inclinations

(C) hours spent in solitary pursuits that enable one to develop into an independent, confident adult

(D) happy memories of childhood days spent in the company of true friends

(E) profitable financial and personal contacts young people make when they engage in group activities

Passage 2

"Sticks and stones can break my bones,
But names will never harm me."

No doubt you are familiar with this childhood rhyme; perhaps, when
Line you were younger, you frequently invoked whatever protection it could
(5) offer against unpleasant epithets. But like many popular slogans and
verses, this one will not bear too close scrutiny. For names will hurt you.
Sometimes you may be the victim, and find yourself an object of scorn,
humiliation, and hatred just because other people have called you certain
names. At other times you may not be the victim, but clever speakers
(10) and writers may, through name calling, blind your judgment so that you
will follow them in a course of action wholly opposed to your own interests or principles. Name calling can make you gullible to propaganda
which you might otherwise readily see through and reject.

5. The author's primary purpose in quoting the rhyme in lines 1 and 2 is to

(A) remind readers of their childhood vulnerabilities

(B) emphasize the importance of maintaining one's good name

(C) demonstrate his conviction that only physical attacks can harm us

(D) affirm his faith in the rhyme's ability to shield one from unpleasant epithets

(E) introduce the topic of speaking abusively about others

6. By "this one will not bear too close scrutiny" (line 6), the author means that

(A) the statement will no longer seem valid if you examine it closely

(B) the literary quality of the verse does not improve on closer inspection

(C) people who indulge in name-calling are embarrassed when they are in the spotlight

(D) the author cannot stand having his comments looked at critically

(E) a narrow line exists between analyzing a slogan and over-analyzing it

7. According to the passage, name calling may make you more susceptible to

   (A) poetic language
   (B) biased arguments
   (C) physical abuse
   (D) risky confrontations
   (E) offensive epithets

8. The author evidently believes that slogans and verses frequently

   (A) appeal to our better nature
   (B) are disregarded by children
   (C) are scorned by unprincipled speakers
   (D) represent the popular mood
   (E) oversimplify a problem

Passage 3

The following passage was written by Phillips Brooks, a nineteenth-century Anglican bishop.

> To keep clear of concealment, to keep clear of the need of concealment, to do nothing which you might not do out on the middle of Boston Common at noonday—I cannot say how more and more it seems to
> *Line* me the glory of a young person's life. It is an awful hour when the first
> *(5)* necessity of hiding anything comes. The whole life is different thenceforth. When there are questions to be feared and eyes to be avoided and subjects which must not be touched, then the bloom of life is gone. Put off that day as long as possible. Put it off forever if you can.

9. The author regards the occasion when one first must conceal something as

   (A) anticlimactic
   (B) insignificant
   (C) fleeting
   (D) momentous
   (E) enviable

10. The author's tone throughout the passage can best be described as

    (A) hostile
    (B) condescending
    (C) playful
    (D) earnest
    (E) impersonal

11. The passage as a whole can best be described as

(A) an apology
(B) a rebuttal
(C) an exhortation
(D) an understatement
(E) a paradox

Passage 4

The following passage was written by a twentieth-century naturalist.

We were about a quarter mile away when quiet swept over the colony,
A thousand or more heado periscoped. Two thousand eyes glared. Save
for our wading, the world's business had stopped. A thousand avian per-
Line   sonalities were concentrated on us, and the psychological force of this
(5)   was terrific. Contingents of home-coming feeders, suddenly aware of four
strange specks moving across the lake, would bank violently and speed
away. Then the chain reaction began. Every throat in that rookery let go
with a concatenation of wild, raspy, terrorized trumpet bursts. With all
wings now fully spread and churning, and quadrupling the color mass,
(10)   the birds began to move as one, and the sky was filled with the sound
of Judgment Day.

12. The author's primary purpose in this passage is to

(A) explain a natural catastrophe
(B) issue a challenge
(C) criticize an expedition
(D) evoke an experience
(E) document an experiment

13. The "four strange specks" (lines 5–6) are

(A) wild birds
(B) animal predators
(C) intruding humans
(D) unusual clouds
(E) members of the colony

14. The word "bank" in line 6 means

    (A) cover
    (B) heap up
    (C) count on
    (D) tilt laterally
    (E) reserve carefully

15. The visitors' response to the episode described in this passage was most likely one of

    (A) impatience
    (B) trepidation
    (C) outrage
    (D) grief
    (E) awe

Passage 5

How is a newborn star formed? For the answer to this question, we must look to the familiar physical concept of gravitational instability. It is a simple concept, long-known to scientists, having been first recog-
Line nized by Isaac Newton in the late 1600's.
(5)   Let us envision a cloud of interstellar atoms and molecules, slightly admixed with dust. This cloud of interstellar gas is static and uniform. Suddenly, something occurs to disturb the gas, causing one small area within it to condense. As this small area increases in density, becoming slightly denser than the gas around it, its gravitational field likewise
(10) increases somewhat in strength. More matter now is attracted to the area, and its gravity becomes even stronger; as a result, it starts to con-tract, in process increasing in density even more. This in turn further increases its gravity, so that it accumulates still more matter and con-tracts further still. And so the process continues, until finally the small
(15) area of gas gives birth to a gravitationally bound object, a newborn star.

16. The primary purpose of the passage is to

    (A) demonstrate the evolution of the meaning of a term
    (B) support a theory considered outmoded
    (C) depict the successive stages of a phenomenon
    (D) establish the pervasiveness of a process
    (E) describe a static condition

17. The word "disturb" in line 7 means

    (A) hinder
    (B) perplex
    (C) unsettle
    (D) pester
    (E) inconvenience

18. It can be inferred from the passage that the author views the information contained within it as

    (A) controversial but irrefutable
    (B) commonly accepted and factual
    (C) speculative and unprofitable
    (D) original but obscure
    (E) sadly lacking in elaboration

19. The author provides information that answers which of the following questions?

    I.   How does the small region's increasing density affect its gravitational field?
    II. What causes the disturbance that changes the cloud from its original static state?
    III. What is the end result of the gradually increasing concentration of the small region of gas?

    (A) I only
    (B) II only
    (C) I and II only
    (D) I and III only
    (E) I, II, and III

20. Throughout the passage, the author's manner of presentation is

    (A) argumentative
    (B) convoluted
    (C) anecdotal
    (D) expository
    (E) hyperbolic

LONG PASSAGES

Passage 1

Although patience is the most important quality a treasure hunter can have, the trade demands a certain amount of courage, too. I have my share of guts, but make no boast about ignoring the hazards of diving.

Line As all good divers know, the business of plunging into an alien world
(5) with an artificial air supply as your only link to the world above can be as dangerous as stepping into a den of lions. Most of the danger rests within the diver himself.

The devil-may-care diver who shows great bravado underwater is the worst risk of all. He may lose his bearings in the glimmering dim light
(10) which penetrates the sea and become separated from his diving companions. He may dive too deep, too long and suffer painful, sometimes fatal, bends.

He may surface too quickly and force his lungs to squeeze their supply of high pressure air into his blood stream, causing an embolism—a
(15) bubble of air in the blood—which often kills. He may become trapped in a submarine rockslide, get lost in an underwater cave, or be chopped to bits by a marauding shark. These are not occasional dangers such as crossing a street in busy traffic. They are always with you underwater. At one time or another I have faced all of them except bends and
(20) embolism, which can be avoided by common sense and understanding of human physical limits beneath the surface.

Once, while salvaging brass from the sunken hulk of an old steel ship, I brushed lightly against a huge engine cylinder, which looked as if it were as solid as it was on the day the ship was launched. Although
(25) the pressure of my touch was hardly enough to topple a toy soldier, the heavy mass of cast iron collapsed, causing a chain reaction in which the rest of the old engine crumbled. Tons of iron dropped all around me. Sheer luck saved me from being crushed. I have been wary of swimming around steel shipwrecks ever since.

1. The title that best expresses the central point of this passage is

(A) Alien Adventures
(B) The Wrong Kind of Courage
(C) The Successful Skindiver
(D) Underwater Perils
(E) Hunting Treasure the Hard Way

2. The passage most probably appeared in

(A) a short story
(B) an autobiographical article
(C) a diver's logbook
(D) an article in an encyclopedia
(E) a manual of skin diving instructions

3. Which of the following does the author NOT do?

(A) define a term
(B) give an example
(C) make a comparison
(D) pose a question
(E) list a possibility

4. According to the passage, the solidity of the steel engine cylinder was

(A) flawless
(B) massive
(C) flexible
(D) illusory
(E) fortunate

5. The word "sheer" (line 28) most nearly means

(A) steep
(B) pure
(C) sharp
(D) filmy
(E) abrupt

Passage 2

The following passage is taken from a basic geology text.

Rocks which have solidified directly from molten materials are called igneous rocks. Igneous rocks are commonly referred to as primary rocks because they are the original source of material found in sedimentaries
Line and metamorphics. Igneous rocks compose the greater part of the
(5) earth's crust, but they are generally covered at the surface by a relatively thin layer of sedimentary or metamorphic rocks. Igneous rocks are distinguished by the following characteristics: (1) they contain no fossils; (2) they have no regular arrangement of layers; and (3) they are nearly always made up of crystals.

(10)   Sedimentary rocks are composed largely of minute fragments derived from the disintegration of existing rocks and in some instances from the remains of animals. As sediments are transported, individual fragments are sorted according to size. Distinct layers of such sediments as gravel, sand, and clay build up, as they are deposited by water and
(15)   occasionally wind. These sediments vary in size with the material and the power of the eroding agent. Sedimentary materials are laid down in layers called strata.

When sediments harden into sedimentary rocks, the names applied to them change to indicate the change in physical state. Thus, small
(20)   stones and gravel cemented together are known as conglomerates; cemented sand becomes sandstone; and hardened clay becomes shale. In addition to these, other sedimentary rocks such as limestone frequently result from the deposition of dissolved material. The ingredient parts are normally precipitated by organic substances, such as the shells
(25)   of clams or hard skeletons of other marine life.

Both igneous and sedimentary rocks may be changed by pressure, heat, solution, or cementing action. When individual grains from existing rocks tend to deform and interlock, they are called metamorphic rocks. For example, granite, an igneous rock, may be metamorphosed into a
(30)   gneiss or a schist. Limestone, a sedimentary rock, when subjected to heat and pressure may become marble, a metamorphic rock. Shale under pressure becomes slate.

6. The primary purpose of the passage is to

(A) explain the factors that may cause rocks to change in form
(B) show how the scientific names of rocks reflect the rocks' composition
(C) present a new hypothesis about the nature of rock formation
(D) define and describe several diverse kinds of rocks
(E) explain why rocks are basic parts of the earth's structure

7. The word "state" in line 19 means

(A) mood
(B) pomp
(C) territory
(D) predicament
(E) condition

8. According to the passage, igneous rocks are characterized by

   (A) their inability to be changed by heat or pressure
   (B) the wealth of fossils they incorporate
   (C) their granular composition
   (D) their relative rarity
   (E) their lack of regular strata

9. The passage contains information that would answer which of the following questions?

   I. Which elements form igneous rocks?
   II. What produces sufficient pressure to alter a rock?
   III. Why is marble called a metamorphic rock?

   (A) I only
   (B) III only
   (C) I and II only
   (D) II and III only
   (E) I, II, and III

10. The author does all of the following EXCEPT

    (A) provide an example
    (B) define a term
    (C) describe a process
    (D) cite an authority
    (E) enumerate specific attributes

THE DOUBLE PASSAGE

The following set of paired passages are excerpted from books on America's national pastime, baseball.

Passage 1

DiMaggio had size, power, and speed. McCarthy, his longtime manager, liked to say that DiMaggio might have stolen 60 bases a season if he had given him the green light. Stengel, his new manager, was equally
Line   impressed, and when DiMaggio was on base he would point to him as an
(5)   example of the perfect base runner. "Look at him," Stengel would say as DiMaggio ran out a base hit, "he's always watching the ball. He isn't watching second base. He isn't watching third base. He knows they haven't been moved. He isn't watching the ground, because he knows they haven't built a canal or a swimming pool since he was last there. He's
(10)   watching the ball and the outfielder, which is the one thing that is different on every play."

DiMaggio complemented his natural athletic ability with astonishing physical grace. He played the outfield, he ran the bases, and he batted not just effectively but with rare style. He would glide rather than run, it

(15) seemed, always smooth, always ending up where he wanted to be just when he wanted to be there. If he appeared to play effortlessly, his team-mates knew otherwise. In his first season as a Yankee, Gene Woodling, who played left field, was struck by the sound of DiMaggio chasing a fly ball. He sounded like a giant truck horse on the loose, Woodling thought,

(20) his feet thudding down hard on the grass. The great, clear noises in the open space enabled Woodling to measure the distances between them without looking.

He was the perfect Hemingway hero, for Hemingway in his novels romanticized the man who exhibited grace under pressure, who withheld

(25) any emotion lest it soil the purer statement of his deeds. DiMaggio was that kind of hero; his grace and skill were always on display, his emo-tions always concealed. This stoic grace was not achieved without a ter-rible price: DiMaggio was a man wound tight. He suffered from insomnia and ulcers. When he sat and watched the game he chain smoked and

(30) drank endless cups of coffee. He was ever conscious of his obligation to play well. Late in his career, when his legs were bothering him and the Yankees had a comfortable lead in a pennant race, columnist Jimmy Cannon asked him why he played so hard—the games, after all, no longer meant so much. "Because there might be somebody out there

(35) who's never seen me play before," he answered.

Passage 2

Athletes and actors—let actors stand for the set of performing artists—share much. They share the need to make gestures as fluid and economical as possible, to make out of a welter of choices the single, precisely right one. They share the need for thousands of hours of prac-

(40) tice in order to train the body to become the perfect, instinctive instru-ment to express. Both athlete and actor, out of that abundance of emotion, choice, strategy, knowledge of the terrain, mood of spectators, condition of others in the ensemble, secret awareness of injury or weak-ness, and as merely an absolute concentration as possible so that all

(45) externalities are integrated, all distraction absorbed to the self, must be able to change the self so successfully that it changes us.

When either athlete or actor can bring all these skills to bear and focus them, then he or she will achieve that state of complete intensity and complete relaxation—complete coherence or integrity between what

(50) the performer wants to do and what the performer has to do. Then, the performer is free; for then, all that has been learned, by thousands of hours of practice and discipline and by repetition of pattern, becomes natural. Then, intellect is upgraded to the level of an instinct. The body follows commands that precede thinking.

(55) When athlete and artist achieve such self-knowledge that they transform the self so that we are recreated, it is finally an exercise in power. The individual's power to dominate, on stage or field, invests the whole arena around the locus of performance with his or her power. We draw from the performer's energy, just as we scrutinize the performer's vul-

(60) nerabilities, and we criticize as if we were equals (we are not) what is displayed. This is why all performers dislike or resent the audience as much as they need and enjoy it. Power flows in a mysterious circuit from performer to spectator (I assume a "live" performance) and back, and while cheers or applause are the hoped-for outcome of performing,

(65) silence or gasps are the most desired, for then the moment has occurred—then domination is complete, and as the performer triumphs, a unity rare and inspiring results.

11. Stengel's comments in lines 5–11 serve chiefly to

(A) point out the stupidity of the sort of error he condemns
(B) suggest the inevitability of mistakes in running bases
(C) show it is easier to spot problems than to come up with answers
(D) answer the criticisms of DiMaggio's baserunning
(E) modify his earlier position on DiMaggio's ability

12. In line 18, the word "struck" most nearly means

(A) halted
(B) slapped
(C) afflicted
(D) enamored
(E) impressed

13. By quoting Woodling's comment on DiMaggio's running (lines 19–20), the author most likely intends to emphasize

(A) his teammates' envy of DiMaggio's natural gifts
(B) how much exertion went into DiMaggio's moves
(C) how important speed is to a baseball player
(D) Woodling's awareness of his own slowness
(E) how easily DiMaggio was able to cover territory

14. In the last paragraph of Passage 1, the author acknowledges which negative aspect of DiMaggio's heroic image?

(A) His overemphasis on physical grace
(B) His emotional romanticism
(C) The uniformity of his performance
(D) The obligation to answer the questions of reporters
(E) The burden of living up to his reputation

15. The author makes his point about DiMaggio's prowess through all the following except

(A) literary allusion
(B) quotations
(C) personal anecdotes
(D) generalization
(E) understatement

16. The phrase "stand for" in line 36 means

(A) tolerate
(B) represent
(C) advocate
(D) withstand
(E) surpass

17. The phrase "bring all these skills to bear" in lines 47 means

(A) come to endure
(B) carry toward
(C) apply directly
(D) cause to behave
(E) induce birth

18. Why, in line 63, does the author of Passage 2 assume a "live" performance?

(A) His argument assumes a mutual involvement between performer and spectator that can occur only when both are physically present.

(B) He believes that televised and filmed images give a false impression of the performer's ability to the spectators.

(C) He fears the use of "instant replay" and other broadcasting techniques will cause performers to resent spectators even more strongly.

(D) His argument dismisses the possibility of combining live performances with filmed segments.

(E) He prefers audiences not to have time to reflect about the performance they have just seen.

19. Which of the following characteristics of the ideal athlete mentioned in Passage 2 is NOT illustrated by the anecdotes about DiMaggio in Passage 1?

(A) Knowledge of the terrain

(B) Secret awareness of injury or weakness

(C) Consciousness of the condition of other teammates

(D) Ability to make gestures fluid and economical

(E) Absolute powers of concentration

20. Which of the following statements is best supported by a comparison of the two passages?

(A) Both passages focus on the development of a specific professional athlete.

(B) The purpose of both passages is to compare athletes with performing artists.

(C) The development of ideas in both passages is similar.

(D) Both passages examine the nature of superior athletic performance.

(E) Both passages discuss athletic performance primarily in abstract terms.

Answer Key

Short Passages

1. **A**	8. **E**	15. **E**
2. **A**	9. **D**	16. **C**
3. **E**	10. **D**	17. **C**
4. **C**	11. **C**	18. **B**
5. **E**	12. **D**	19. **D**
6. **A**	13. **C**	20. **D**
7. **B**	14. **D**	

Long Passages

1. **D**	6. **D**
2. **B**	7. **E**
3. **D**	8. **E**
4. **D**	9. **B**
5. **B**	10. **D**

The Double Passage

11. **A**	16. **B**
12. **E**	17. **C**
13. **B**	18. **A**
14. **E**	19. **C**
15. **E**	20. **D**

4 Building Your Vocabulary

Recognizing the meaning of words is essential to comprehending what you read. The more you stumble over unfamiliar words in a text, the more you have to take time out to look up words in your dictionary, the more likely you are to wind up losing track of what the author has to say.

To succeed in college, you must develop a college-level vocabulary. You must learn to use these words, and re-use them until they become second nature to you. The time you put in now learning vocabulary-building techniques for the PSAT will pay off later on, and not just on the PSAT.

In this chapter you will find a fundamental tool that will help you build your vocabulary: Barron's PSAT High-Frequency Word List. No matter how little time you have before the test, you still can familiarize yourself with the sort of vocabulary you will face on the PSAT. First, look over the words you will find on our list: each of these 300 words, ranging from everyday words such as *ample* and *meek* to less commonly known ones such as *esoteric* and *pervasive* has appeared (as answer choices or as question words) at least four times in PSATs in the past two decades.

Not only will looking over the high-frequency word list reassure you that you *do* know some PSAT-type words; but also it may well help you on the actual day of the test. These words have turned up on recent tests; some of them may appear on the test you take.

PSAT HIGH-FREQUENCY WORD LIST

absolve V. pardon (an offense); free from blame. The father confessor *absolved* him of his sins. absolution, N.

abstract ADJ. theoretical; not concrete; nonrepresentational. To him, hunger was an *abstract* concept; he had never missed a meal.

accessible ADJ. easy to approach; obtainable. We asked our guide whether the ruins were *accessible* on foot.

acclaim V. applaud; announce with great approval. The NBC sportscasters *acclaimed* every American victory in the Olympics and lamented every American defeat. acclamation, acclaim, N.

accommodate V. provide lodgings. Mary asked the room clerk whether the hotel would be able to *accommodate* the tour group on such short notice. accommodations, N.

accommodate V. oblige or help someone; adjust or bring into harmony; adapt. Mitch always did everything possible to *accommodate* his elderly relatives, from driving them to medical appointments to helping them with paperwork. accommodating, ADJ. (secondary meaning)

acknowledge V. recognize; admit. Although Ira *acknowledged* that the Beatles' tunes sounded pretty dated nowadays, he still preferred them to the punk rock songs his nephews played.

acrimony N. bitterness of words or manner. The candidate attacked his opponent with great *acrimony*. acrimonious, ADJ.

adversary N. opponent. "Aha!" cried Holmes. "Watson, I suspect this delay is the work of my old *adversary* Professor Moriarty." adversarial, ADJ.

adverse ADJ. unfavorable; hostile. The recession had a highly *adverse* effect on Father's investment portfolio: he lost so much money that he could no longer afford the butler and the upstairs maid. adversity, N.

aesthetic ADJ. artistic; dealing with or capable of appreciation of the beautiful. The beauty of Tiffany's stained glass appealed to Alice's *aesthetic* sense. aesthete, N.

affable ADJ. easily approachable; warmly friendly. Accustomed to cold, aloof supervisors, Nicholas was amazed by how *affable* his new employer was.

affinity N. kinship; attraction to. She felt an *affinity* with all who suffered; their pains were her pains. Her brother, in contrast, had an *affinity* for political wheeling-and-dealing; he manipulated people shamelessly, not caring who got hurt.

alleviate V. relieve; lessen. This should *alleviate* the pain; if it does not, we will use stronger drugs.

altruistic ADJ. unselfishly generous; concerned for others. The star received no fee for appearing at the benefit; it was a purely *altruistic* act. altruism, N.

ambiguous ADJ. unclear or doubtful in meaning. The proctor's *ambiguous* instructions thoroughly confused us; we didn't know which columns we should mark and which we should leave blank. ambiguity, N.

ambivalence N. having contradictory or conflicting emotional attitudes. Torn between loving her parents one minute and hating them the next, she was confused by the *ambivalence* of her feelings. ambivalent, ADJ.

amenable ADJ. readily managed; willing to give in; agreeable; submissive. A born snob, Wilbur was *amenable* to any suggestions from those he looked up to, but he resented advice from his supposed inferiors. Unfortunately, his incorrigible snobbery was not *amenable* to improvement.

ample ADJ. abundant. Bond had *ample* opportunity to escape. Why did he let us catch him?

antagonism N. hostility; active resistance. Barry showed his *antagonism* toward his new stepmother by ignoring her whenever she tried talking to him. antagonistic, ADJ.

apathy N. lack of caring; indifference. A firm believer in democratic government, she could not understand the *apathy* of people who never bothered to vote. She wondered whether they had ever cared or whether they had always been *apathetic.*

apprehension N. fear; discernment; capture. The tourist refused to drive his rental car through downtown Miami because he felt some *apprehension* that he might be carjacked.

apprenticeship N. time spent as a novice learning a trade from a skilled worker. As a child, Pip had thought it would be wonderful to work as Joe's *apprentice;* now he hated his *apprenticeship* and scorned the blacksmith's trade.

appropriate ADJ. fitting or suitable; pertinent. Madonna spent hours looking for a suit that would be *appropriate* to wear at a summer wedding.

appropriate V. acquire; take possession of for one's own use; set aside for a special purpose. The ranchers *appropriated* lands that had originally been intended for Indian use. In response, Congress *appropriated* additional funds for the Bureau of Indian Affairs.

aristocracy N. hereditary nobility; privileged class. Americans have mixed feelings about hereditary *aristocracy:* we say all men are created equal, but we describe people who bear themselves with grace and graciousness as natural *aristocrats.*

aspire V. seek to attain; long for. Because he *aspired* to a career in professional sports, Philip enrolled in a graduate program in sports management. aspiration, N.

assert V. state strongly or positively; insist on or demand recognition of (rights, claims, etc.). When Jill *asserted* that nobody else in the junior class had such an early curfew, her parents *asserted* themselves, telling her that if she didn't get home by nine o'clock she would be grounded for the week. assertion, N.

assumption N. something taken for granted; taking over or taking possession of. The young princess made the foolish *assumption* that the regent would not object to her *assumption* of power. assume, V.

authentic ADJ. genuine. The art expert was able to distinguish the *authentic* van Gogh painting from the forged copy. authenticate, V.

autonomous ADJ. self-governing. This island is a colony; however, in most matters, it is *autonomous* and receives no orders from the mother country. The islanders are an independent lot and would fight to preserve their *autonomy.*

aversion N. firm dislike. Bert had an *aversion* to yuppies; Alex had an *aversion* to punks. Their mutual *aversion* was so great that they refused to speak to one another.

banal ADJ. hackneyed; commonplace; trite; lacking originality. The hack writer's worn-out clichés made his comic sketch seem *banal.* He even resorted to the *banality* of having someone slip on a banana peel!

beneficial ADJ. helpful; advantageous; useful. Tiny Tim's cheerful good nature had a *beneficial* influence on Scrooge's disposition.

benign ADJ. kindly; favorable; not malignant. Though her *benign* smile and gentle bearing made Miss Marple seem a sweet little old lady, in reality she was a tough-minded, shrewd observer of human nature. benignity, N.

betray V. be unfaithful; reveal (unconsciously or unwillingly). The spy *betrayed* his country by selling military secrets to the enemy. When he was taken in for questioning, the tightness of his lips *betrayed* his fear of being caught.

brittle ADJ. easily broken; difficult. My employer's self-control was as *brittle* as an eggshell. Her *brittle* personality made it difficult for me to get along with her.

buoyant ADJ. able to float; cheerful and optimistic. When the boat capsized, her *buoyant* life jacket kept Jody afloat. Scrambling back on board, she was still in a *buoyant* mood, certain that despite the delay she'd win the race. buoyancy, N.

candor N. frankness; open honesty. Jack can carry *candor* too far: when he told Jill his honest opinion of her, she nearly slapped his face. Instead of being so *candid,* try keeping your opinions to yourself.

captivate V. charm; fascinate. Although he was predisposed to dislike Elizabeth, Darcy found himself *captivated* by her charm and wit.

caricature N. distortion; burlesque. The *caricatures* he drew always emphasized a personal weakness of the people he burlesqued. also V.

censor N. inspector overseeing public morals; official who prevents publication of offensive material. Because certain passages in his novel *Ulysses* had been condemned by the *censor,* James Joyce was unable to publish the novel in England for many years.

chronicle V. report; record (in chronological order). The gossip columnist was paid to *chronicle* the latest escapades of the socially prominent celebrities. also N.

circumspect ADJ. prudent; cautious. Investigating before acting, she tried always to be *circumspect.*

cite V. quote; refer to; commend. Because Virginia could *cite* hundreds of biblical passages from memory, her pastor *cited* her for her studiousness. citation, N.

cliché N. phrase dulled in meaning by repetition. High school compositions are often marred by such *clichés* as "strong as an ox."

coalesce V. combine; fuse. The brooks *coalesced* into one large river. When minor political parties *coalesce*, their *coalescence* may create a major coalition.

collaborate V. work together. Two writers *collaborated* in preparing this book.

compliance N. readiness to yield; conformity in fulfilling requirements. Bill was so bullheaded that we never expected his easy *compliance* to our requests. As an architect, however, Bill recognized that his design for the new school had to be in *compliance* with the local building code.

component N. element; ingredient. I wish all the *components* of my stereo system were working at the same time.

composure N. mental calmness. Even the latest work crisis failed to shake her *composure.*

compromise V. adjust or settle by making mutual concessions; endanger the interests or reputation of. Sometimes the presence of a neutral third party can help adversaries *compromise* their differences. Unfortunately, your presence at the scene of the dispute *compromises* our claim to neutrality in this matter. also N.

condone V. overlook voluntarily; forgive. Although she had excused Huck for his earlier escapades, Widow Douglas refused to *condone* his latest prank.

confirm V. corroborate; verify; support. I have several witnesses who will *confirm* my account of what happened.

conformity N. agreement or compliance; actions in agreement with prevailing social customs. In *conformity* with the bylaws of the Country Dance and Song Society, I am submitting a petition nominating Susan Murrow as president of the society. Because Kate had always been a rebellious child, we were surprised by her *conformity* to the standards of behavior prevalent at her new school.

confront V. face someone or something; encounter, often in a hostile way. Fearing his wife's hot temper, Stanley was reluctant to *confront* her about her skyrocketing credit card bills.

congenial ADJ. pleasant; friendly. My father loved to go out for a meal with *congenial* companions.

consistency N. harmony of parts; dependability; uniformity; degree of thickness. Holmes judged puddings and explanations on their *consistency:* he liked his puddings without lumps and his explanations without contradictions or improbabilities. consistent, ADJ.

consolidation N. unification; process of becoming firmer or stronger. The recent *consolidation* of several small airlines into one major company has left observers of the industry wondering whether room still exists for the "little guy" in aviation. consolidate, V.

contentious ADJ. quarrelsome. Disagreeing violently with the referees' ruling, the coach became so *contentious* that they threw him out of the game.

convention N. social or moral custom; established practice. Flying in the face of *convention,* George Sand shocked society by taking lovers and wearing men's clothes.

convoluted ADJ. complex and involved; intricate; winding; coiled. Talk about twisted! The new tax regulations are so *convoluted* that even my accountant can't unravel their mysteries.

corrosion N. destruction by chemical action. The *corrosion* of the girders supporting the bridge took place so gradually that no one suspected any danger until the bridge suddenly collapsed. corrode, V.

curtail V. shorten; reduce. When Elton asked Cher for a date, she said she was really sorry she couldn't go out with him, but her dad had ordered her to *curtail* her social life.

dawdle V. loiter; waste time. At the mall, Mother grew impatient with Jo and Amy because they tended to *dawdle* as they went from store to store.

dearth N. scarcity. The *dearth* of skilled labor compelled the employers to open trade schools.

debilitate V. weaken; enfeeble. Michael's severe bout of the flu *debilitated* him so much that he was too tired to go to work for a week.

decorous ADJ. proper. Prudence's *decorous* behavior was praised by her teachers, who wished they had a classroom full of such polite and proper little girls. decorum, N.

decry V. express strong disapproval of; disparage. The founder of the Children's Defense Fund, Marian Wright Edelman, strongly *decries* the lack of financial and moral support for children in America today.

defamation N. harming a person's reputation. *Defamation* of character may result in a slander suit. If rival candidates persist in *defaming* one another, the voters may conclude that all politicians are crooks.

deference N. courteous regard for another's wish. In *deference* to the minister's request, please do not take photographs during the wedding service.

defiance N. opposition; willingness to resist. In learning to read and write in *defiance* of his master's orders, Frederick Douglass showed exceptional courage. defy, V.

degenerate V. become worse; deteriorate. As the fight dragged on, the champion's style *degenerated* until he could barely keep on his feet.

demean V. degrade; humiliate. Standing on his dignity, he refused to *demean* himself by replying to the offensive letter. If you truly believed in the dignity of labor, you would not think it would *demean* you to work as a janitor.

denounce V. condemn; criticize. The reform candidate *denounced* the corrupt city officials for having betrayed the public's trust. denunciation, N.

depict V. portray. In this sensational exposé, the author *depicts* John Lennon as a drug-crazed neurotic. Do you question the accuracy of this *depiction* of Lennon?

deplete V. reduce; exhaust. We must wait until we *deplete* our present inventory before we order replacements.

deplore V. regret strongly; express grief over. Although Ann Landers *deplored* the disintegration of the modern family, she recognized that not every marriage could be saved.

derision N. ridicule; mockery. Greeting his pretentious dialogue with *derision,* the critics refused to consider his play seriously. deride, V.

derivative ADJ. unoriginal; derived from another source. Although her early poetry was clearly *derivative* in nature, the critics felt she had promise and eventually would find her own voice.

detached ADJ. emotionally removed; calm and objective; indifferent. A psychoanalyst must maintain a *detached* point of view and stay uninvolved with her patients' personal lives. detachment, N (secondary meaning)

deterrent N. something that discourages; hindrance. Does the threat of capital punishment serve as a *deterrent* to potential killers? deter, V.

didactic ADJ. teaching; instructional. Pope's lengthy poem *An Essay on Man* is too *didactic* for my taste: I dislike it when poets turn preachy and moralize.

diffident ADJ. shy; lacking confidence; reserved. Can a naturally *diffident* person become a fast-talking, successful used car salesman?

digression N. wandering away from the subject. Nobody minded when Professor Renoir's lectures wandered away from their official theme; his *digressions* were always more fascinating than the topic of the day. digress, V.

discernible ADJ. distinguishable; perceivable. The ships in the harbor were not *discernible* in the fog.

disclaimer N. denial of a legal claim or right; disavowal. Though reporter Joe Klein issued a *disclaimer* stating that he was *not* "Anonymous," the author of *Primary Colors,* eventually he admitted that he had written the controversial novel. disclaim, V.

disclose V. reveal. Although competitors offered him bribes, he refused to *disclose* any information about his company's forthcoming product. disclosure, N.

discord N. lack of harmony; conflict; Watching Tweedledum battle Tweedledee, Alice wondered what had caused this pointless *discord.*

discrepancy N. lack of consistency; contradiction; difference. "Observe, Watson, the significant *discrepancies* between Sir Percy's original description of the crime and his most recent testimony. What do these contradictions suggest?"

disgruntled ADJ. discontented; sulky and dissatisfied. The numerous delays left the passengers feeling *disgruntled.* disgruntle, V.

disinterested ADJ. unprejudiced. Given the judge's political ambitions and the lawyers' financial interest in the case, the only *disinterested* person in the courtroom may have been the court reporter.

dismiss V. put away from consideration; reject. Believing in John's love for her, she *dismissed* the notion that he might be unfaithful. (secondary meaning)

disparage V. belittle. A doting mother, Emma was more likely to praise her son's crude attempts at art than to *disparage* them.

disparate ADJ. basically different; unrelated. Unfortunately, Tony and Tina have *disparate* notions of marriage: Tony sees it as a carefree extended love affair, while Tina sees it as a solemn commitment to build a family and a home.

dispatch N. speediness; prompt execution; message sent with all due speed. Young Napoleon defeated the enemy with all possible *dispatch;* he then sent a *dispatch* to headquarters, informing his commander of the great victory. also V.

dispel V. scatter; cause to vanish. The bright sunlight eventually *dispelled* the morning mist.

disperse V. scatter. The police fired tear gas into the crowd to *disperse* the protesters.

dissent V. disagree. In the recent Supreme Court decision, Justice O'Connor *dissented* from the majority opinion. also N.

dissipate V. squander; waste; scatter. He is a fine artist, but we fear he may *dissipate* his gifts if he keeps wasting his time doodling on napkins.

distinction N. honor; contrast; discrimination. A holder of the Medal of Honor, George served with great *distinction* in World War II. He made a *distinction,* however, between World War II and Vietnam, which he considered an immoral conflict.

divulge V. reveal. No lover of gossip, Charlotte would never *divulge* anything that a friend told her in confidence.

docile ADJ. obedient; easily managed. As *docile* as he seems today, that old lion was once a ferocious, snarling beast.

doctrine N. teachings, in general; particular principle (religious, legal, etc.) taught. He was so committed to the *doctrines* of his faith that he was unable to evaluate them impartially.

dogmatic ADJ. opinionated; arbitrary; doctrinal. We tried to discourage Doug from being so *dogmatic,* but never could convince him that his opinions might be wrong.

eclectic ADJ. composed of elements drawn from disparate sources. His style of interior decoration was *eclectic:* bits and pieces of furnishings from widely divergent periods, strikingly juxtaposed to create a unique decor. eclecticism, N.

eclipse V. darken; extinguish; surpass. The new stock market high *eclipsed* the previous record set in 1995.

elated ADJ. overjoyed; in high spirits. Grinning from ear to ear, Carl Lewis was clearly *elated* by his ninth Olympic gold medal. elation, N.

elicit V. draw out (by discussion); call forth. The camp counselor's humorous remarks finally *elicited* a smile from the shy new camper.

elusive ADJ. evasive; baffling; hard to grasp. Trying to pin down exactly when the contractors would be done remodeling the house, Nancy was frustrated by their *elusive* replies. elude, V.

embellish V. adorn. We enjoyed my mother-in-law's stories about how she came here from Russia, in part because she *embellished* the bare facts of the journey with humorous anecdotes and vivid descriptive details.

endorse V. approve; support. Everyone waited to see which one of the rival candidates for the city council the mayor would *endorse.* endorsement, N. (secondary meaning).

enhance V. increase; improve. You can *enhance* your chances of being admitted to the college of your choice by learning to write well; an excellent essay can *enhance* any application.

enigma N. puzzle; mystery. "What *do* women want?" asked Dr. Sigmund Freud. Their behavior was an *enigma* to him.

entice V. lure; attract; tempt. She always tried to *entice* her baby brother into mischief.

enumerate V. list; mention one by one. Huck hung his head in shame as Miss Watson *enumerated* his many flaws.

ephemeral ADJ. short-lived; fleeting. The mayfly is an *ephemeral* creature: its adult life lasts little more than a day.

erode V. eat away. The limestone was *eroded* by the dripping water until only a thin shell remained. erosion, N.

erratic ADJ. odd; unpredictable. Investors become anxious when the stock market appears *erratic.*

erroneous ADJ. mistaken; wrong. I thought my answer was correct, but it was *erroneous.*

esoteric ADJ. hard to understand; known only to the chosen few. *New Yorker* short stories often included *esoteric* allusions to obscure people and events; the implication was, if you were in the in-crowd, you'd get the reference; if you came from Cleveland, you would not.

espouse V. adopt; support. She was always ready to *espouse* a worthy cause.

esteem V. respect; value; Jill *esteemed* Jack's taste in music, but she deplored his taste in clothes.

excerpt N. selected passage (written or musical). The cinematic equivalent of an *excerpt* from a novel is a clip from a film.

exemplary ADJ. serving as a model; outstanding. At commencement the dean praised Ellen for her *exemplary* behavior as class president.

exonerate V. acquit; exculpate. The defense team feverishly sought fresh evidence that might *exonerate* its client.

expedite V. hasten. Because we are on a tight schedule, we hope you will be able to *expedite* the delivery of our order. expeditious, ADJ.

exploit N. deed or action, particularly a brave deed. Raoul Wallenberg was noted for his *exploits* in rescuing Jews from Hitler's forces.

exploit V. make use of, sometimes unjustly. Cesar Chavez fought attempts to *exploit* migrant farm workers in California. exploitation, N.

facilitate V. help bring about; make less difficult. Rest and proper nourishment should *facilitate* the patient's recovery.

fallacious ADJ. false; misleading. Paradoxically, *fallacious* reasoning does not always yield erroneous results: even though your logic may be faulty, the answer you get may nevertheless be correct. fallacy, N.

farce N. broad comedy; mockery. Nothing went right; the entire interview degenerated into a *farce*. farcical, ADJ.

fastidious ADJ. difficult to please; squeamish. Bobby was such a *fastidious* eater that he would eat a sandwich only if his mother first cut off every scrap of crust.

fawning ADJ. seeking favor by cringing and flattering; obsequious. "Stop crawling around like a boot-licker, Uriah! I can't stand your sweet talk and *fawning* ways." fawn, V.

feasible ADJ. practical. Is it *feasible* to build a new stadium for the Yankees on New York's West Side? Without additional funding, the project is clearly unrealistic.

fervor N. glowing ardor; intensity of feeling. At the protest rally, the students cheered the strikers and booed the dean with equal *fervor.* fervent, fervid, ADJ.

flippant ADJ. lacking proper seriousness. When Mark told Mona he loved her, she dismissed his earnest declaration with a *flippant* "Oh, you say that to all the girls!" flippancy, N.

forthright ADJ. outspoken; frank. Never afraid to call a spade a spade, she was perhaps too *forthright* to be a successful party politician.

frail ADJ. weak. The delicate child seemed too *frail* to lift the heavy carton.

frivolous ADJ. lacking in seriousness; self-indulgently carefree; relatively unimportant. Though Nancy enjoyed Bill's *frivolous,* lighthearted companionship, she sometimes wondered whether he could ever be serious. frivolity, N.

garrulous ADJ. loquacious; wordy; talkative. My Uncle Henry can out-talk any three people I know. He is the most *garrulous* person in Cayuga County. garrulity, N.

generate V. cause; produce; create. In his first days in office, President Clinton managed to *generate* a new mood of optimism; we hoped he could *generate* a few new jobs.

genre N. particular variety of art or literature. Both a short story writer and a poet, Langston Hughes proved himself equally skilled in either *genre.*

gluttonous ADJ. greedy for food. The *gluttonous* boy ate all the cookies.

gratify V. please. Amy's success in her new job *gratified* her parents.

gregarious ADJ. sociable. Typically, party-throwers are *gregarious;* hermits are not.

hackneyed ADJ. commonplace; trite. When the reviewer criticized the movie for its *hackneyed* plot, we agreed; we had seen similar stories hundreds of times before.

halting ADJ. hesitant; faltering. Novice extemporaneous speakers often talk in a *halting* fashion as they grope for the right words.

hamper V. obstruct. The new mother didn't realize how much the effort of caring for an infant would *hamper* her ability to keep an immaculate house.

hindrance N. block; obstacle. Stalled cars along the highway are a *hindrance* to traffic that tow trucks should remove without delay. hinder, V.

hostility N. unfriendliness; hatred. Children who have been the sole objects of their parents' attention often feel *hostility* toward a new baby in the family, resenting the newcomer who has taken their place.

hypocritical ADJ. pretending to be virtuous; deceiving. It was *hypocritical* of Martha to say such nice things about my poetry to me and then make fun of my verses behind my back. hypocrisy, N.

hypothetical ADJ. based on assumptions or hypotheses; supposed. Suppose you are accepted by Harvard, Stanford, and Brown. Which one would you choose to attend? Remember, this is only a *hypothetical* situation. hypothesis, N.

iconoclastic ADJ. attacking cherished traditions. Deeply *iconoclastic,* Jean Genet deliberately set out to shock conventional theatergoers with his radical plays.

immutable ADJ. unchangeable. All things change over time; nothing is *immutable.*

impede v. hinder; block; delay. A series of accidents *impeded* the launching of the space shuttle.

imperceptible ADJ. unnoticeable; undetectable. Fortunately, the stain on the blouse was *imperceptible* after the blouse had gone through the wash.

implacable ADJ. incapable of being pacified. Madame Defarge was the *implacable* enemy of the Evremonde family.

implement V. put into effect; supply with tools. The mayor was unwilling to *implement* the plan until she was sure it had the governor's backing. also N.

implication N. something hinted at or suggested. When Miss Watson said she hadn't seen her purse since the last time Jim was in the house, the *implication* was that she suspected Jim had taken it. imply, V.

impromptu ADJ. without previous preparation; off the cuff; on the spur of the moment. The judges were amazed that she could make such a thorough, well-supported presentation in an *impromptu* speech.

incarcerate V. imprison. The civil rights workers were willing to be arrested and even *incarcerated* if by their imprisonment they could serve the cause.

incongruity N. lack of harmony; absurdity. The *incongruity* of his wearing sneakers with formal attire amused the observers. incongruous, ADJ.

inconsequential ADJ. insignificant; unimportant. Brushing off Ali's apologies for having broken the wine glass, Tamara said, "Don't worry about it; it's *inconsequential.*"

inconsistency N. state of being self-contradictory; lack of uniformity or steadiness. How are lawyers different from agricultural inspectors? While lawyers check *inconsistencies* in witnesses' statements, agricultural inspectors check *inconsistencies* in Grade A eggs. inconsistent, ADJ.

incorporate V. introduce something into a larger whole; combine; unite. Breaking with precedent, President Truman ordered the military to *incorporate* blacks into every branch of the armed services. also ADJ.

indict V. charge. The district attorney didn't want to *indict* the suspect until she was sure she had a strong enough case to convince a jury. indictment, N.

indifferent ADJ. unmoved or unconcerned by; mediocre. Because Consuela felt no desire to marry, she was *indifferent* to Edward's constant proposals. Not only was she *indifferent* to him personally, but she felt that, given his general silliness, he would make an *indifferent* husband.

induce V. persuade; bring about. After the quarrel, Tina said nothing could *induce* her to talk to Tony again. inducement, N.

industrious ADJ. diligent; hard-working. Look busy when the boss walks past your desk; it never hurts to appear *industrious.* industry, N.

inept ADJ. lacking skill; unsuited; incompetent. The *inept* glovemaker was all thumbs. ineptitude, ineptness, N.

infallible ADJ. unerring; faultless. Jane refused to believe the pope was *infallible,* reasoning: "All human beings are capable of error. The pope is a human being. Therefore, the pope is capable of error."

ingenious ADJ. clever; resourceful. Kit admired the *ingenious* way that her computer keyboard opened up to reveal the built-in CD-ROM below. ingenuity, N.

ingenuous ADJ. naive and trusting; young; unsophisticated. The woodsman had not realized how *ingenuous* Little Red Riding Hood was until he heard that she had gone off for a walk in the woods with the Big Bad Wolf.

ingrate N. ungrateful person. That *ingrate* Bob sneered at the tie I gave him.

inherent ADJ. firmly established by nature or habit. Katya's *inherent* love of justice caused her to champion anyone she considered treated unfairly by society.

initiate V. begin; originate; receive into a group. The college is about to *initiate* a program in reducing math anxiety among students.

innate ADJ. inborn. Mozart's parents soon recognized young Wolfgang's *innate* talent for music.

innocuous ADJ. harmless. An occasional glass of wine with dinner is relatively *innocuous* and should have no ill effect on you.

inscrutable ADJ. impenetrable; not readily understood; mysterious. Experienced poker players try to keep their expressions *inscrutable,* hiding their reactions to the cards behind a so-called "poker face."

insightful ADJ. discerning; perceptive. Sol thought he was very *insightful* about human behavior, but he was actually clueless as to why people acted the way they did.

intangible ADJ. not able to be perceived by touch; vague. Though the financial benefits of his Oxford post were meager, Lewis was drawn to it by its *intangible* rewards: prestige, intellectual freedom, the fellowship of his peers.

integrity N. uprightness; wholeness. Lincoln, whose personal *integrity* has inspired millions, fought a civil war to maintain the *integrity* of the Republic, that these United States might remain undivided for all time.

intricacy N. complexity; knottiness. Philip spent many hours designing mazes of such great *intricacy* that none of his classmates could solve them. intricate, ADJ.

introspective ADJ. looking within oneself. Though young Francis of Assisi led a wild and worldly life, even he had *introspective* moments during which he examined his soul.

irony N. hidden sarcasm or satire; use of words that seem to mean the opposite of what they actually mean. Gradually his listeners began to realize that the excessive praise he was lavishing on his opponent was actually *irony;* he was in fact ridiculing the poor fool.

judicious ADJ. sound in judgment; wise. At a key moment in his life, he made a *judicious* investment that was the foundation of his later wealth.

languid ADJ. weary; feeble; listless; apathetic. The chronic invalid's most recent siege of illness left her *languid* and drooping. languor, N. languish, V.

larceny N. theft. Because of the prisoner's long record of thefts, the district attorney refused to reduce the charge from grand *larceny* to petty *larceny.*

lethargic ADJ. drowsy; dull. The stuffy room made her *lethargic:* she felt as if she was about to nod off.

loathe V. detest. Booing and hissing, the audience showed how much they *loathed* the wicked villain.

malice N. hatred; spite. Jealous of Cinderella's beauty, her wicked stepsisters expressed their *malice* by forcing her to do menial tasks.

meek ADJ. quiet and obedient; spiritless. Can Lois Lane see through Superman's disguise and spot the superhero masquerading as the *meek,* timorous Clark Kent?

meticulous ADJ. excessively careful; painstaking; scrupulous. Martha Stewart is a *meticulous* housekeeper, fussing about each and every detail that goes into making up her perfect home.

misconception N. misunderstanding; misinterpretation. I'm afraid you are suffering from a *misconception,* Mr. Collins: I do not want to marry you at all.

misrepresent V. give a false or incorrect impression, usually intentionally. The ad "Lovely Florida building site with water view" *misrepresented* the property, which was actually ten acres of bottomless swamp.

mock V. ridicule; imitate, often in derision. It is unkind to *mock* anyone; it is stupid to *mock* anyone significantly bigger than you. mockery, N.

monarchy N. government under a single ruler. Though England today is a *monarchy,* there is some question whether it will be one in 20 years, given the present discontent at the prospect of Prince Charles as king.

monotony N. sameness leading to boredom. What could be more deadly dull than the *monotony* of punching numbers into a computer hour after hour?

mutability N. ability to change in form; fickleness. Going from rags to riches, and then back to rags again, the bankrupt financier was a victim of the *mutability* of fortune.

naiveté N. quality of being unsophisticated; simplicity; artlessness; gullibility. Touched by the *naiveté* of sweet, convent-trained Cosette, Marius pledges himself to protect her innocence. naive, ADJ.

nocturnal ADJ. relating to, occurring, or active in the night. Mr. Jones obtained a watchdog to prevent the *nocturnal* raids on his chicken coops.

nonchalance N. indifference; lack of concern; composure. Cool, calm, and collected under fire, James Bond shows remarkable *nonchalance* in the face of danger.

nostalgia N. homesickness; longing for the past. My grandfather seldom spoke of life in the old country; he had little patience with *nostalgia.* nostalgic, ADJ.

notorious ADJ. disreputable; widely known; scandalous. To the starlet, any publicity was good publicity: if she couldn't have a good reputation, she'd settle for being *notorious.* notoriety, N.

nurture V. nourish; educate; foster. The Head Start program attempts to *nurture* pre-kindergarten children so that they will do well when they enter public school. also N.

obnoxious ADJ. offensive; objectionable. A sneak and a tattletale, Sid was an *obnoxious* little brat.

obscure ADJ. dark; vague; unclear. Even after I read the poem a fourth time, its meaning was still *obscure.* obscurity, N.

obscure V. darken; make unclear. At times he seemed purposely to *obscure* his meaning, preferring mystery to clarity.

opaque ADJ. not transparent; impenetrable to light. The *opaque* window shade kept the sunlight out of the room. opacity, N.

optimist N. person who looks on the good side. The pessimist says the glass is half-empty; the *optimist* says it is half-full.

orator N. public speaker. The abolitionist Frederick Douglass was a brilliant *orator* whose speeches brought home to his audience the evils of slavery.

ostentatious ADJ. showy; pretentious; trying to attract attention. Trump's latest casino in Atlantic City is the most *ostentatious* gambling palace in the East: it easily outglitters its competitors. ostentation, N.

outmoded ADJ. no longer stylish; old-fashioned. Unconcerned about keeping in style, Lenore was perfectly happy to wear *outmoded* clothes as long as they were clean and unfrayed.

pacifist N. one opposed to force; antimilitarist. Shooting his way through the jungle, Rambo was clearly not a *pacifist.*

pacify V. soothe; make calm or quiet; subdue. Dentists criticize the practice of giving fussy children sweets to *pacify* them.

paradox N. something apparently contradictory in nature; statement that looks false but is actually correct. Richard presents a bit of a *paradox,* for he is a card-carrying member of both the National Rifle Association and the relatively pacifist American Civil Liberties Union.

patronize V. support; act superior toward; be a customer of. Penniless artists hope to find some wealthy art lover who will *patronize* them. If a wine steward *patronized* me because he saw I knew nothing about fine wine, I'd refuse to *patronize* his restaurant.

pedantic ADJ. showing off learning; bookish. Leavening his decisions with humorous, down-to-earth anecdotes, Judge Walker was not at all the *pedantic* legal scholar. pedant, N.

perjury N. false testimony while under oath. Rather than lie under oath and perhaps be indicted for *perjury,* the witness chose to take the Fifth Amendment, refusing to answer any questions on the grounds that he might incriminate himself.

perpetual ADJ. everlasting. Ponce de Leon hoped to find the legendary fountain of *perpetual* youth. perpetuity, N.

pervasive ADJ. pervading; spread throughout every part. Despite airing them for several hours, she could not rid her clothes of the *pervasive* odor of mothballs that clung to them. pervade, V.

pessimism N. belief that life is basically bad or evil; gloominess. Considering how well you have done in the course so far, you have no real reason for such *pessimism* about your final grade.

petulant ADJ. touchy; peevish. If you'd had hardly any sleep for three nights and people kept on phoning and waking you up, you'd sound pretty *petulant*, too.

phenomena N. Pl. observable facts or events. We kept careful records of the *phenomena* we noted in the course of these experiments.

philanthropist N. lover of mankind; doer of good. In his role as *philanthropist* and public benefactor, John D. Rockefeller, Sr., donated millions to charity; as an individual, however, he was a tight-fisted old man.

plagiarize V. steal another's ideas and pass them off as one's own. The teacher could tell that the student had *plagiarized* parts of his essay; she could recognize whole paragraphs straight from *Barron's Book Notes*.

potency N. power; effectiveness; influence. Looking at the expiration date on the cough syrup bottle, we wondered whether the medication still retained its *potency.* potent, ADJ.

pragmatic ADJ. practical (as opposed to idealistic); concerned with the practical worth or impact of something. This coming trip to France should provide me with a *pragmatic* test of the value of my conversational French class.

precedent N. something preceding in time that may be used as an authority or guide for future action. If I buy you a car for your sixteenth birthday, your brothers will want me to buy them cars when they turn sixteen, too; I can't afford to set such an expensive *precedent.*

predator N. creature that seizes and devours another animal; person who robs or exploits others. Not just cats, but a wide variety of *predators*—owls, hawks, weasels, foxes—catch mice for dinner. A carnivore is by definition *predatory,* for it *preys* on weaker creatures.

premise N. assumption; postulate. Based on the *premise* that there's no fool like an old fool, P. T. Barnum hired a 90-year-old clown for his circus.

premonition N. forewarning. We ignored these *premonitions* of disaster because they appeared to be based on childish fears.

presumptuous ADJ. taking liberties; overstepping bounds; nervy. I thought it was *presumptuous* of Mort to butt into Bishop Tutu's talk with Mrs. Clinton and ask them for their autographs; I wouldn't have had the nerve.

prevail V. triumph; predominate; prove superior in strength, power, or influence; be current. A radical committed to social change, Reed had no patience with the conservative views that *prevailed* in the America of his day. prevalent, ADJ., prevailing, ADJ.

prey N. target of a hunt; victim. In *Stalking the Wild Asparagus*, Euell Gibbons has as his *prey* not wild beasts but wild plants. also V.

profound ADJ. deep; not superficial; complete. Freud's remarkable insights into human behavior caused his fellow scientists to honor him as a *profound* thinker. profundity, N.

proliferation N. rapid growth; spread; multiplication. Times of economic hardship inevitably encourage the *proliferation* of countless get-rich-quick schemes. proliferate, V.

prolific ADJ. abundantly fruitful. My editors must assume I'm a *prolific* writer: they expect me to revise six books this year!

prologue N. introduction (to a poem or play). In the *prologue* to *Romeo and Juliet*, Shakespeare introduces the audience to the feud between the Montagues and the Capulets.

prominent ADJ. conspicuous; notable; sticking out. Have you ever noticed that Prince Charles's *prominent* ears make him resemble the big-eared character in *Mad* comics?

promote V. help to flourish; advance in rank; publicize. Founder of the Children's Defense Fund, Marian Wright Edelman ceaselessly *promotes* the welfare of young people everywhere.

prophetic ADJ. foretelling the future. I have no magical *prophetic* powers; when I predict what will happen, I base my predictions on common sense. prophesy, V.

prosperity N. good fortune; financial success; physical well-being. Promising to stay together "for richer, for poorer," the newlyweds vowed to be true to one another in *prosperity* and hardship alike.

provocative ADJ. arousing anger or interest; annoying. In a typically *provocative* act, the bully kicked sand into the weaker man's face.

prudent ADJ. cautious; careful. A miser hoards money not because he is *prudent* but because he is greedy. prudence, N.

ramble V. wander aimlessly (physically or mentally). Listening to the teacher *ramble*, Shelby wondered whether he'd ever get to the point. also N.

random ADJ. without definite purpose, plan, or aim; haphazard. Although the sponsor of the raffle claimed all winners were chosen at *random*, people had their suspicions when the grand prize went to the sponsor's brother-in-law.

recluse N. hermit; loner. Disappointed in love, Miss Emily became a *recluse;* she shut herself away in her empty mansion and refused to see another living soul. reclusive, ADJ.

refute V. disprove. The defense called several respectable witnesses who were able to *refute* the false testimony of the prosecution's only witness.

rejuvenate V. make young again. The charlatan claimed that his elixir would *rejuvenate* the aged and weary.

relinquish V. give up something with reluctance; yield. Once you get used to fringe benefits like expense account meals and a company car, it's very hard to *relinquish* them.

renown N. fame. For many years an unheralded researcher, Barbara McClintock gained international *renown* when she won the Nobel Prize in Physiology and Medicine.

reprehensible ADJ. deserving blame. Shocked by the viciousness of the bombing, politicians of every party uniformly condemned the terrorists' *reprehensible* deed.

repudiate V. disown; disavow. On separating from Tony, Tina announced that she would *repudiate* all debts incurred by her soon-to-be ex-husband.

reserved ADJ. self-controlled; careful in expressing oneself. They made an odd couple: she was outspoken and uninhibited; he was cautious and *reserved*. (secondary meaning)

resignation N. patient submissiveness; statement that one is quitting a job. If Bob Cratchit had not accepted Scrooge's bullying with such *resignation,* he might have gotten up the nerve to hand in his *resignation*. resigned, ADJ.

resolution N. determination. Nothing could shake his *resolution* to succeed despite all difficulties. resolved, ADJ.

resolve V. decide; settle; solve. "I have *resolved,* Watson, to travel to Bohemia to *resolve* the dispute between Irene Adler and the King. In my absence, do your best to *resolve* any mysteries that arise."

restraint N. moderation or self-control; controlling force; restriction. Control yourself, young lady! Show some *restraint!*

retain V. keep; employ. Fighting to *retain* his seat in Congress, Senator Foghorn *retained* a new manager to head his reelection campaign.

reticent ADJ. reserved; uncommunicative; inclined to be silent. Fearing his competitors might get advance word about his plans from talkative staff members, Hughes preferred *reticent* employees to loquacious ones.

reverent ADJ. respectful; worshipful. Though I bow my head in church and recite the prayers, sometimes I don't feel properly *reverent*. revere, V.

ruthless ADJ. pitiless; cruel. Captain Hook was a dangerous, *ruthless* villain who would stop at nothing to destroy Peter Pan.

satirize V. mock. Cartoonist Gary Trudeau often *satirizes* contemporary politicians; through the comments of the *Doonesbury* characters, Trudeau ridicules political corruption and folly. satirical, ADJ.

scrutinize V. examine closely and critically. Searching for flaws, the sergeant *scrutinized* every detail of the private's uniform.

seclusion N. isolation; solitude. One moment she loved crowds; the next, she sought *seclusion*.

serenity N. calmness; placidity. The *serenity* of the sleepy town was shattered by a tremendous explosion.

sever V. cut; separate. Dr. Guillotin invented a machine that could neatly *sever* an aristocratic head from its equally aristocratic body.

severity N. harshness; intensity; austerity; rigidity. The *severity* of Jane's migraine attack was so great that she took to her bed for a week.

singular ADJ. unique; extraordinary; odd. Though the young man tried to understand Father William's *singular* behavior, he still found it odd that the old man incessantly stood on his head. singularity, N.

skeptical ADJ. doubting; suspending judgment until having examined the evidence supporting a point of view. I am *skeptical* about this project; I want some proof that it can work. skepticism, N.

steadfast ADJ. loyal; unswerving. Penelope was *steadfast* in her affections, faithfully waiting for Ulysses to return from his wanderings.

stoic ADJ. impassive; unmoved by joy or grief. I wasn't particularly *stoic* when I had my flu shot; I squealed like a stuck pig. also N.

stratagem N. deceptive scheme. Though Wellington's forces seemed to be in full retreat, in reality their withdrawal was a *stratagem* intended to lure the enemy away from its sheltered position.

subdued ADJ. less intense; quieter. Bob liked the *subdued* lighting at the restaurant because he thought it was romantic. I just thought it was dimly lit.

subversive ADJ. tending to overthrow or destroy. At first glance, the notion that Styrofoam cups may actually be more ecologically sound than paper cups strikes most environmentalists as *subversive*.

superficial ADJ. trivial; shallow. Since your report gave only a *superficial* analysis of the problem, I cannot give you more than a passing grade.

superfluous ADJ. excessive; unnecessary. Please try not to include so many *superfluous* details in your report; just give me the bare facts. superfluity, N.

suppress V. crush; subdue; inhibit. Too polite to laugh in anyone's face, Roy did his best to *suppress* his amusement at Ed's inane remark.

surpass V. exceed. Her PSAT scores *surpassed* our expectations.

susceptible ADJ. impressionable; easily influenced; having little resistance, as to a disease; receptive to. Said the patent medicine man to the extremely *susceptible* customer: "Buy this new miracle drug, and you will no longer be *susceptible* to the common cold."

suspend V. defer or postpone; expel or eject; halt or discontinue; hang from above. When the judge *suspended* his sentence, Bill breathed a sigh of relief. When the principal *suspended* her from school, Wanda tried to look as if she didn't care. When the trapeze artist broke her arm, she had to *suspend* her activities: she no longer could be *suspended* from her trapeze.

sustain V. experience; support; nourish. Stuart *sustained* such a severe injury that the doctors feared he would be unable to work to *sustain* his growing family.

symmetry N. arrangement of parts so that balance is obtained; congruity. Something lopsided by definition lacks *symmetry*.

synthesis N. combining parts into a whole. Now that we have succeeded in isolating this drug, our next problem is to plan its *synthesis* in the laboratory. synthesize, V.

taciturn ADJ. habitually silent; talking little. The stereotypical cowboy is a *taciturn* soul, answering lengthy questions with a "Yep" or "Nope."

tedious ADJ. boring; tiring. The repetitious nature of work on the assembly line made Martin's job very *tedious*. tedium, N.

temper V. moderate; tone down or restrain; toughen (steel). Not even her supervisor's grumpiness could *temper* Nancy's enthusiasm for her new job.

temperament N. characteristic frame of mind; disposition; emotional excess. Although the twins look alike, they differ markedly in *temperament:* Todd is calm, but Rod is excitable. Racket-throwing tennis star John McEnroe was famed for his displays of *temperament*.

termination N. end. Though the time for *termination* of the project was near, we still had a lot of work to finish before we shut up shop.

thwart V. baffle; frustrate. He felt that everyone was trying to *thwart* his plans and prevent his success.

toxic ADJ. poisonous. We must seek an antidote for whatever *toxic* substance he has eaten. toxicity, N.

transcendent ADJ. surpassing; exceeding ordinary limits; superior. Standing on the hillside watching the sunset through the Golden Gate was a *transcendent* experience for Lise: it was so beautiful it surpassed her wildest dreams.

transparent ADJ. easily detected; permitting light to pass through freely. Bobby managed to put an innocent look on his face; to his mother, however, his guilt was *transparent*.

trepidation N. fear; nervous apprehension. As she entered the office of the dean of admissions, Sharon felt some *trepidation* about how she would do in her interview.

turbulence N. state of violent agitation. Warned of approaching *turbulence* in the atmosphere, the pilot told the passengers to fasten their seat belts.

urbane ADJ. suave; refined; elegant. The courtier was *urbane* and sophisticated. urbanity, N.

utopia N. ideal place, state, or society. Fed up with this imperfect universe, Don would have liked to run off to Shangri-la or some other fictitious *utopia*. utopian, ADJ.

vacillate V. waver; fluctuate. Uncertain which suitor she ought to marry, the princess *vacillated,* saying now one, now the other. vacillation, N.

versatile ADJ. having many talents; capable of working in many fields. She was a *versatile* athlete, earning varsity letters in basketball, hockey, and track.

volatile ADJ. changeable; explosive; evaporating rapidly. The political climate today is extremely *volatile:* no one can predict what the electorate will do next. Maria Callas's temper was extremely *volatile:* the only thing you could predict was that she was sure to blow up. Ethyl chloride is an extremely *volatile* liquid: it evaporates instantly.

voracious ADJ. ravenous. The wolf is a *voracious* animal, its hunger never satisfied.

wary ADJ. very cautious. The spies grew *wary* as they approached the sentry.

5 The Mathematics Sections: Strategies, Tips, and Practice

The College Board considers the PSAT to be "a test of general reasoning abilities." It attempts to use basic concepts of arithmetic, algebra, and geometry as a method of testing your ability to think logically. The College Board is not testing whether you know how to calculate an average, find the area of a circle, use the Pythagorean theorem, or read a bar graph. *It assumes you can.* In fact, because the Board is not even interested in testing your memory, most of the formulas you will need are listed at the beginning of each math section. In other words, the College Board's objective is to use your familiarity with numbers and geometric figures as a way of testing your *logical thinking skills.*

Most of the arithmetic that you need to know for the PSAT is taught in elementary school, and much of the other material is taught in middle school or junior high school. The only high school math that you need is some elementary algebra and a little basic geometry. To do well on the PSAT, you must know this basic material. But that's not enough. You have to be able to use these concepts in ways that may be unfamiliar to you. That's where the test-taking tactics come in.

An Important Symbol

Throughout the book, the symbol $\Rightarrow$ is used to indicate that one step in the solution of a problem follows immediately from the preceding one, and that no explanation is necessary. You should read

$2x = 12 \Rightarrow x = 6$ as
$2x = 12$, *which implies that* $x = 6$, or, *since* $2x = 12$, *then* $x = 6$.

Here is a sample solution to the following problem using $\Rightarrow$:

What is the value of $3x^2 - 7$ when $x = -5$?

$x = -5 \Rightarrow x^2 = (-5)^2 = 25 \Rightarrow 3x^2 = 3(25) = 75 \Rightarrow 3x^2 - 7 = 75 - 7 = 68.$

When the reason for a step is not obvious, $\Rightarrow$ is not used; rather, an explanation is given, often including a reference to a fact from the list on pages 98–107. In many solutions, some steps are explained, while others are linked by the $\Rightarrow$ symbol, as in the following example:

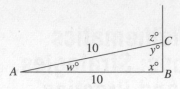

In the diagram above, if $w = 10$, what is the value of z?

- By **Fact 41**, $w + x + y = 180$.
- Since $\triangle ABC$ is isosceles, $x = y$ [**Fact 43**].
- Therefore, $w + 2y = 180 \Rightarrow 10 + 2y = 180 \Rightarrow 2y = 170 \Rightarrow y = 85$.
- Finally, since $y + z = 180$ [Fact 36], $85 + z = 180 \Rightarrow z = 95$.

Use of the Calculator

There isn't a single question on the PSAT for which a calculator is required. In fact, for most questions a calculator is completely useless. There are several questions, however, for which a calculator *could* be used, and since calculators are permitted, you should definitely bring one with you when you take the PSAT. As you go through the hundreds of practice math questions in this book, you should have available the calculator you intend to take to the test, and you should use it whenever you think it is appropriate. You will probably use it more at the beginning of your review because, as you go through this book, you will learn more and more strategies to help you solve problems easily without doing tedious calculations.

If you forget to bring a calculator to the actual test, you will not be able to use one, since none will be provided, and you will not be allowed to share one with a friend. For exactly the same reason, be sure that you have new batteries in your calculator or that you bring a spare, because if your calculator fails during the test, you will have to finish without one.

What Calculator Should You Use?

Almost any four-function, scientific, or graphing calculator is acceptable. Since you don't "need" a calculator at all, you don't "need" any particular type. There is absolutely no advantage to having a graphing calculator, but we do recommend a scientific calculator, since it is occasionally useful to have parentheses keys, ( ); a reciprocal key, $\frac{1}{x}$; and an exponent key, y^x or $\wedge$. All scientific calculators have these features. If you tend to make mistakes working with fractions, you might want to get a calculator that can do fractional arithmetic. With such a calculator, for example, you can add $\frac{1}{3}$ and $\frac{1}{5}$ by entering 1/3 + 1/5; the readout will be 8/15, not the decimal 0.5333333.

CAUTION: Do not buy a new calculator right before you take the PSAT. The best advice is to use a calculator you are completely familiar with—the one you always use in your math class. If you don't have one or want to get a different one, *buy it now* and become familiar with it. Do all the practice exams in this book with the same calculator you intend to bring to the test.

When Should Calculators Be Used?

If you have strong math skills and are a good test-taker, you will probably use your calculator infrequently, if at all, since, for one thing, strong math students can do a lot of basic arithmetic just as accurately, and faster, in their heads or on paper than with a calculator. A less obvious but more important point is that students who are good test-takers will realize that many problems can be solved without doing any calculations at all (mental, written, or with a calculator); they will solve those problems in less time than it takes to pick a calculator up. On the other hand, if you are less confident about your mathematical ability or your test-taking skills, you will probably find your calculator a useful tool.

NOTE: Throughout this book, this icon will be placed next to a problem where the use of a calculator is recommended. As you will see, this judgment is very subjective. Sometimes a question can be answered in a few seconds with no calculations whatsoever, *if* you see the best approach. In that case, the use of a calculator would *not* be recommended. If you don't see the easy way, however, and have to do some arithmetic, you may prefer to use a calculator.

Let's look at two sample questions on which some students would use calculators frequently, others less frequently, and still others not at all.

EXAMPLE 1

If $16 \times 25 \times 36 = (4a)^2$, what is the value of a?

(A) 6   (B) 15   (C) 30   (D) 36   (E) 60

(i) Heavy calculator use: WITH A CALCULATOR multiply: $16 \times 25 \times 36 = 14400$. Observe that $(4a)^2 = 16a^2$, and so $16a^2 = 14,400$. WITH A CALCULATOR divide:
$a^2 = 14,400 \div 16 = 900$. Finally, WITH A CALCULATOR take the square root: $a = \sqrt{900} = 30$. The answer is C.

(ii) Light calculator use: Immediately notice that you can "cancel" the 16 on the left-hand side with the 4^2 on the right-hand side. WITH A CALCULATOR: multiply $25 \times 36 = 900$, and WITH A CALCULATOR take the square root of 900.

(iii) No calculator use: Cancel the 16 and the 4^2. Notice that $25 = 5^2$ and $36 = 6^2$; so $a^2 = 5^2 \times 6^2 = 30^2$, and $a = 30$.

EXAMPLE 2 (GRID-IN)

If the length of a diagonal of a rectangle is 15, and if one of the sides is 9, what is the perimeter?

Whether or not you intend to use your calculator, the first thing to do is to draw a diagram.

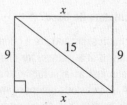

 (i) Heavy calculator use: By the Pythagorean theorem, $x^2 + 9^2 = 15^2$. Observe that $9^2 = 81$, and WITH A CALCULATOR evaluate: $15^2 = 225$. Then WITH A CALCULATOR subtract: $225 - 81 = 144$. So, $x^2 = 144$. Hit the square root key on your calculator to get $x = 12$. Finally, WITH A CALCULATOR add to find the perimeter: $9 + 12 + 9 + 12 = 42$.

 (ii) Light calculator use: Everything is the same as in (i) except *some* of the calculations can be done mentally: finding the square root of 144 and adding to find the perimeter.

(iii) No calculator use: *All of the calculations* are done mentally, or, better yet, *no calculations are done at all*, because you immediately see that each half of the rectangle is a 9-12-15 right triangle (a 3-4-5 right triangle in which each side was multiplied by 3), and you add up the sides in your head.

Here are three final comments on the use of calculators:

1. The reason that calculators are of limited value on the PSAT is that no calculator can *do* mathematics. *You* have to know the mathematics and the way to apply it. A calculator cannot tell you whether to multiply or divide or that on a particular question you should use the Pythagorean theorem.

2. No PSAT problem ever requires tedious calculations. However, if you don't see how to avoid calculating, just do it—*don't spend a lot of time looking for a shortcut that will save you a little time!*

3. Most students use calculators more than they should, but if you can solve a problem with a calculator that you might otherwise miss, use the calculator.

Helpful Hint

In general, you should do very little arithmetic using paper and pencil. If you can't do it mentally, use your calculator. In particular, avoid long division and multiplication in which the factors have two or more digits. If you know that $15^2 = 225$, terrific; if not, it is better to use your calculator than to multiply with paper and pencil.

DIRECTIONS FOR MATHEMATICS SECTIONS

On the first page of Section 2 (the first math section) you will see the following instructions for multiple-choice questions.

> For each problem in this section, determine which of the five choices is correct and blacken that choice on your answer sheet. You may use any blank space on the page for your work.

Notes:

- You may use a calculator whenever you believe it will be helpful.
- Use the diagrams provided to help you solve the problems. Unless you see the phrase "Note: Figure not drawn to scale" under a diagram, it has been drawn as accurately as possible. Unless it is stated that a figure is three-dimensional, you may assume that it lies in a plane.

On the first page of Section 4 (the second math section) you will see these exact same directions for questions 21–28.

In the middle of Section 4 of your PSAT you will see the following directions for handling questions 29–38, the student-produced response questions, the only questions on the PSAT that are not multiple-choice. Because the answers to these questions are entered in special grids, they are usually referred to as grid-in questions.

Directions for Student-Produced Response Questions (Grid-ins)

In questions 29–38, first solve the problem, and then enter your answer on the grid provided on the answer sheet. The instructions for entering your answers follow.

- First, write your answer in the boxes at the top of the grid.
- Second, grid your answer in the columns below the boxes.
- Use the fraction bar in the first row or the decimal point in the second row to enter fractions and decimals.

Answer: $\frac{8}{15}$ Answer: 1.75

Write your answer in the boxes

Grid in your answer

Answer: 100

Either position is acceptable

- Grid only one space in each column.
- Entering the answer in the boxes is recommended as an aid in gridding, but is not required.
- The machine scoring your exam can read only what you grid, so you **must grid in your answers correctly to get credit.**
- If a question has more than one correct answer, grid in only one of them.
- The grid does not have a minus sign, so **no answer can be negative.**
- A mixed number *must* be converted to an improper fraction or a decimal before it is gridded. Enter $1\frac{1}{4}$ as $\frac{5}{4}$ or 1.25; the machine will interpret 1 1/4 as $\frac{11}{4}$ and mark it wrong.

- **All decimals must be entered as accurately as possible.** Here are the three acceptable ways of gridding

$$\frac{3}{11} = 0.272727...$$

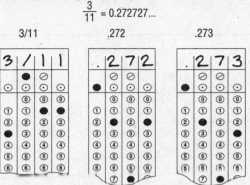

- Note that rounding to .273 is acceptable, because you are using the full grid, but you would receive **no credit** for .3 or .27, because they are less accurate.

Helpful Hint

As you prepare for this test, learn the directions for each section. When you take the PSAT, do not waste even one second reading directions.

In addition to the directions for multiple-choice questions, the first page of each math section has a box labeled "Reference Information" that contains the following mathematical facts:

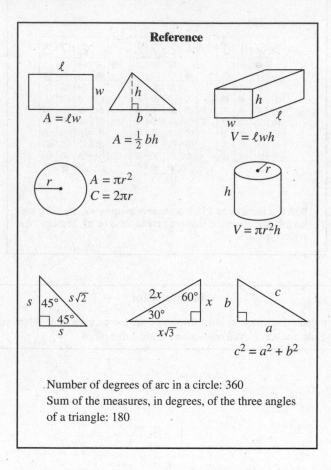

Reference

$A = \ell w$

$A = \frac{1}{2}bh$

$V = \ell wh$

$A = \pi r^2$
$C = 2\pi r$

$V = \pi r^2 h$

$c^2 = a^2 + b^2$

Number of degrees of arc in a circle: 360
Sum of the measures, in degrees, of the three angles
of a triangle: 180

Many books advise that since these formulas are printed in the exam booklet, students can always look them up as needed and, therefore, don't have to learn or review them. Even the College Board's official guide, *SAT Preparation Booklet,* states:

The test doesn't require you to memorize formulas. Commonly used formulas are provided in the test booklet at the beginning of each mathematical section.

This is very poor advice. During the test, you don't want to spend any of your valuable time looking up facts that you can learn now. Each of these "commonly used formulas," as well as many other important facts, is presented on pages 98–107. As you learn and review these facts, you should commit them to memory.

Instructions for Grid-In Questions

On the math part of the PSAT, questions 29–38 are the student-produced response questions. This is the type of question that is most familiar—you solve a problem and then write the answer on your answer sheet. The only difference is that on the PSAT, after you write the answer on your answer sheet, you must then enter the answer on a special grid that can be read by a computer. For this reason, these questions are usually referred to as grid-ins.

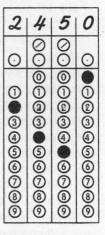

To be sure you get credit for these questions, you need to know the guidelines for gridding in your answers. Not all of this information is given in the directions printed in the exam booklet, so you should carefully read each of the ten rules below.

Your answer sheet will have ten grids, one for each question. Each one will look like the grid shown here. After solving a problem, the first step is to write the answer in the four boxes at the top of the grid. You then blacken the appropriate space under each box. For example, if your answer to a question is 2450, you write 2450 at the top of the grid, one digit in each box, and then in each column blacken the space that contains the number you wrote at the top of the column. This is not difficult, but there are some special rules concerning grid-in questions, so let's go over them before you practice gridding in some numbers.

1. The only symbols that appear in the grid are the digits 0 to 9, a decimal point, and a slash (/), used to write fractions. Keep in mind that, since there is no negative sign, *the answer to every grid-in question must be a positive number or 0.*

2. You will receive credit for a correct answer no matter where you grid it. For example, the answer 17 could be gridded in any of three positions:

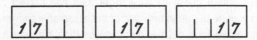

Nevertheless, we suggest that you consistently *write all your answers* the way numbers are usually displayed—*to the right, with blank spaces at the left.*

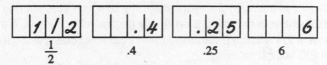

$\frac{1}{2}$ .4   .25   6

3. *Never round off your answers.* If a decimal answer will fit in the grid and you round it off, your answer will be marked wrong. For example, if the answer were .148 and you rounded it to the nearest hundredth, and entered .15, you would receive no credit. If a decimal answer will not fit in the grid, enter a decimal point in the first column, followed by the first three digits. For example, if your answer is 0.373737 . . . , enter it as .373. You would receive credit if you rounded it to .374, but don't. You might occasionally make a mistake in rounding, whereas you'll never make a mistake if you just copy the first three digits. **Note:** If the correct answer has more than two decimal digits, *you must use all four columns of the grid.*

4. *Never write a 0 before the decimal point.* The first column of the grid doesn't even have a 0 in it. If the correct answer is 0.3333 . . . , you must grid it as .333. You can't grid 0.33, and 0.3 is not accurate enough.

5. Never simplify fractions.
   - If your answer is a fraction that will fit in the grid, such as $\frac{2}{3}$ or $\frac{4}{18}$ or $\frac{6}{34}$, just enter it. Don't waste time reducing it or converting it to a decimal.
   - If your answer is a fraction that won't fit in the grid, do not attempt to reduce it; *use your calculator to convert it to a decimal.* For example, $\frac{24}{65}$ won't fit in a grid; it would require five spaces: 2 4 / 6 5. Do not waste even a few seconds trying to reduce it; just divide on your calculator, and enter .369. Unlike $\frac{24}{65}$, the fraction $\frac{24}{64}$ can be reduced—to $\frac{12}{32}$, which doesn't help, or to $\frac{6}{16}$ or $\frac{3}{8}$, both of which could be entered. *Don't do it!* It takes time and you might make a mistake. You won't make a mistake if you just use your calculator: $24 \div 64 = .375$.

6. *Be aware that you can never enter a mixed number.* If your answer is $2\frac{1}{2}$, you cannot leave a space and enter it as 2 1/2. Also if you enter $\boxed{2\,1\,/\,2}$, the machine will read it as $\frac{21}{2}$ and mark it wrong. You must enter $2\frac{1}{2}$ as the improper fraction $\frac{5}{2}$ or as the decimal 2.5.

7. Sometimes grid-in questions have more than one correct answer. On these questions you are to *grid-in only one of the acceptable answers.* For example, if a question asked for a positive number less than 100 which was divisible by both 5 and 7, you could enter *either* 35 *or* 70, but not both.

8. There is no penalty for a wrong answer to a grid-in question. Therefore, you might as well guess.

9. *Be sure to grid every answer carefully.* The computer does not read what you have written in the boxes; it reads only the answer in the grid. If the correct answer to a question is 100 and you write 100 in the boxes, but accidentally grid in 200, you get no credit.

10. If you know that the answer to a question is 100, can you just grid it in and not bother writing it on top? Yes, you will get full credit, and so some books rec-

ommend that you don't waste time writing the answer. This is terrible advice. Instead, *write each answer in the boxes.* It takes less than two seconds per answer to do this, and it definitely cuts down on careless errors in gridding. More important, if you go back to check your work, it is much easier to read what's in the boxes than what's in the grid.

Now, check your understanding of these guidelines. Use the empty grids below to enter each of the following numbers.

1. 123   **2.** $\frac{7}{11}$ **3.** $2\frac{3}{4}$ **4.** $\frac{8}{30}$

5. 0   **6.** $\frac{48}{80}$ **7.** 1.1111 . . .   **8.** $\frac{19}{15}$

7.

8.

Solutions. Each grid contains the answer we recommend. Other acceptable answers, if any, are written below each grid.

1.

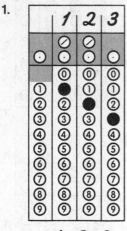

or *1 2 3*

2.

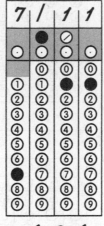

or *. 6 3 6*

3.

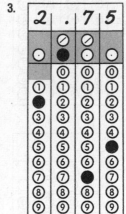

or *1 1 / 4*

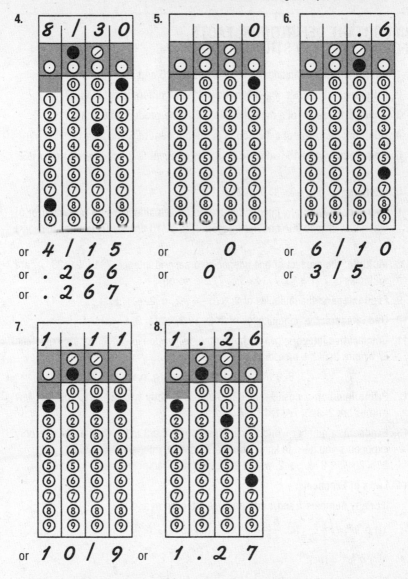

4. or 4 / 1 5
   or . 2 6 6
   or . 2 6 7

5. or 0
   or 0

6. or 6 / 1 0
   or 3 / 5

7. or 1 0 / 9   8. or 1 . 2 7

If you missed even one of these, go back and reread the rules on gridding. *You never want to have a correct answer and get no credit because you didn't grid it properly.* When you do the grid-in problems on the practice PSATs in this book, actually grid in the answers. Make sure you understand all of these rules *now.* When you actually take the PSAT, don't even look at the gridding instructions.

IMPORTANT DEFINITIONS, FACTS, FORMULAS, AND STRATEGIES

1. **Sum:** the result of an addition: 8 is the sum of 6 and 2

2. **Difference:** the result of a subtraction: 4 is the difference of 6 and 2

3. **Product:** the result of a multiplication: 12 is the product of 6 and 2

4. **Quotient:** the result of a division: 3 is the quotient of 6 and 2

5. **Remainder:** when 15 is divided by 6, the quotient is 2 and the remainder is 3: $15 = 6 \times 2 + 3$

6. **Integers:** $\{..., -3, -2, -1, 0, 1, 2, 3, ...\}$

7. **Factor** or **Divisor:** any integer that leaves no remainder (i.e., a remainder of 0) when it is divided into another integer: 1, 2, 5, 10 are the factors (or divisors) of 10

8. **Multiple:** the product of one integer by a second integer: 7, 14, 21, 28, ... are multiples of 7 ($7 = 1 \times 7$, $14 = 2 \times 7$, and so on)

9. **Even integers:** the multiples of 2: $\{..., -4, -2, 0, 2, 4, ...\}$

10. **Odd integers:** the nonmultiples of 2: $\{..., -3, -1, 1, 3, 5, ...\}$

11. **Consecutive integers:** two or more integers, written in sequence, each of which is 1 more than the preceding one. For example:

$$7, 8, 9 \qquad -2, -1, 0, 1, 2 \qquad n, n+1, n+2$$

12. **Prime number:** a positive integer that has exactly two divisors. The first few primes are 2, 3, 5, 7, 11, 13, 17. (*not* 1)

13. **Exponent:** a number written as a superscript: the 3 in 7^3. On the SAT, the only exponents you need to know about are positive integers: $2^n = 2 \times 2 \times 2 \times ... \times 2$, where 2 appears as a factor n times.

14. **Laws of Exponents:**

    For any numbers b and c and positive integers m and n:

    (i) $b^m b^n = b^{m+n}$ (ii) $\dfrac{b^m}{b^n} = b^{m-n}$ (iii) $(b^m)^n = b^{mn}$

    (iv) $b^m c^m = (bc)^m$

15. **Square root of a positive number:** if a is positive, $\sqrt{a}$ is the only positive number whose square is a: $(\sqrt{a})^2 = \sqrt{a} \times \sqrt{a} = a$

16. The product and the quotient of two positive numbers or two negative numbers are positive; the product and the quotient of a positive number and a negative number are negative.

17. • The product of an *even* number of negative factors is positive.
   • The product of an *odd* number of negative factors is negative.

18. For any positive numbers *a* and *b*:

$$\sqrt{ab} = \sqrt{a} \times \sqrt{b} \quad \text{and} \quad \sqrt{\frac{a}{b}} = \frac{\sqrt{a}}{\sqrt{b}}$$

19. For any real numbers *a*, *b*, and *c*:

   • $a(b + c) = ab + ac$ • $a(b - c) = ab - ac$

   and, if a ≠ 0,

   • $\dfrac{b+c}{a} = \dfrac{b}{a} + \dfrac{c}{a}$ • $\dfrac{b-c}{a} = \dfrac{b}{a} - \dfrac{c}{d}$

20. To compare two fractions, use your calculator to convert them to decimals.

21. To multiply two fractions, multiply their numerators and multiply their denominators:

$$\frac{3}{5} \times \frac{4}{7} = \frac{3 \times 4}{5 \times 7} = \frac{12}{35}$$

22. To divide any number by a fraction, multiply that number by the reciprocal of the fraction.

$$\frac{3}{5} \div \frac{2}{3} = \frac{3}{5} \times \frac{3}{2} = \frac{9}{10}$$

23. To add or subtract fractions with the same denominator, add or subtract the numerators and keep the denominator:

$$\frac{4}{9} + \frac{1}{9} = \frac{5}{9} \quad \text{and} \quad \frac{4}{9} - \frac{1}{9} = \frac{3}{9} = \frac{1}{3}$$

24. To add or subtract fractions with different denominators, first rewrite the fractions as equivalent fractions with the same denominator:

$$\frac{1}{6} + \frac{3}{4} = \frac{2}{12} + \frac{9}{12} = \frac{11}{12}$$

25. **Percent:** a fraction whose denominator is 100:

$$15\% = \frac{15}{100} = .15$$

26. The *percent increase* of a quantity is

$$\frac{\text{actual increase}}{\text{original amount}} \times 100\%.$$

   The *percent decrease* of a quantity is

$$\frac{\text{actual decrease}}{\text{original amount}} \times 100\%.$$

27. **Ratio:** a fraction that compares two quantities that are measured in the same units. The ratio *2 to 3* can be written $\frac{2}{3}$ or 2:3.

28. In any ratio problem, write the letter x after each number and use some given information to solve for x.

29. **Proportion:** an equation that states that two ratios (fractions) are equal. Solve proportions by cross-multiplying: if $\dfrac{a}{b} = \dfrac{c}{d}$, then $ad = bc$.

30. **Average of a set of n numbers:** the sum of those numbers divided by n:

$$\text{average} = \frac{\text{sum of the } n \text{ numbers}}{n} \quad \text{or simply}$$

$$A = \frac{\text{sum}}{n}$$

31. If you know the average, A, of a set of n numbers, multiply A by n to get their sum: sum = nA.

32. To multiply two binomials, use the FOIL method: multiply each term in the first parentheses by each term in the second parentheses and simplify by combining terms, if possible.

$$(2x - 7)(3x + 2) = (2x)(3x) + (2x)(2) + (-7)(3x) + (-7)(2) =$$

First terms   Outer terms   Inner terms   Last terms

$$6x^2 + 4x - 21x - 14 = 6x^2 - 17x - 14$$

33. The three most important binomial products on the PSAT are these:
    - $(x - y)(x + y) = x^2 - y^2$
    - $(x - y)^2 = (x - y)(x - y) = x^2 - 2xy + y^2$
    - $(x + y)^2 = (x + y)(x + y) = x^2 + 2xy + y^2$

34. All distance problems involve one of three variations of the same formula:

$$\text{distance} = \text{rate} \times \text{time} \qquad \text{rate} = \frac{\text{distance}}{\text{time}}$$

$$\text{time} = \frac{\text{distance}}{\text{rate}}$$

35.

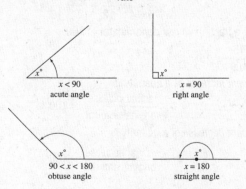

$x < 90$
acute angle

$x = 90$
right angle

$90 < x < 180$
obtuse angle

$x = 180$
straight angle

36. If two or more angles form a straight angle, the sum of their measures is 180°.

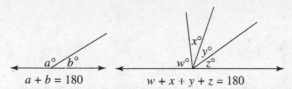

$$a + b = 180 \qquad w + x + y + z = 180$$

37. The sum of all the measures of all the angles around a point is 360°.

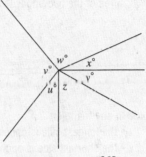

$$u + v + w + x + y + z = 360$$

38.

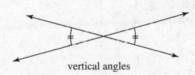

vertical angles

39. Vertical angles have equal measures.

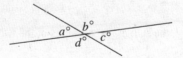

$$a = c \text{ and } b = d.$$

40. If a pair of parallel lines is cut by a transversal that is *not* perpendicular to the parallel lines:
    • Four of the angles are acute, and four are obtuse.
    • All four acute angles are equal: $a = c = e = g$.
    • All four obtuse angles are equal: $b = d = f = h$.
    • The sum of any acute angle and any obtuse angle is 180°: for example, $d + e = 180$, $c + f = 180$, $b + g = 180$, ...

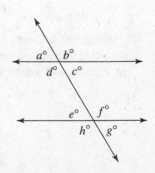

41. In any triangle, the sum of the measures of the three angles is 180°: $x + y + z = 180$.

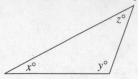

42. The measure of an exterior angle of a triangle is equal to the sum of the measures of the two opposite interior angles.

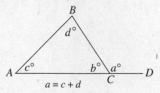

43. In any triangle:
    - the longest side is opposite the largest angle;
    - the shortest side is opposite the smallest angle;
    - sides with the same length are opposite angles with the same measure.

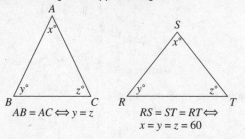

44. In any right triangle, the sum of the measures of the two acute angles is 90°.

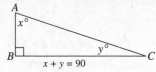

45. **Pythagorean theorem:**
    In a right triangle (and *only* in a right triangle), if the two lengths of the sides are *a*, *b*, and *c*, with *a* and *b* each less than *c*:
    $$a^2 + b^2 = c^2$$

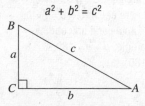

46. In a 45-45-90 right triangle, the sides are x, x, and $x\sqrt{2}$.

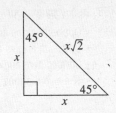

47. In a 30-60-90 right triangle the sides are x, $x\sqrt{3}$, and $2x$.

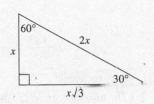

48. **Triangle inequality:**
The sum of the lengths of any two sides of a triangle is greater than the length of the third side.

The difference between the lengths of any two sides of a triangle is less than the length of the third side.

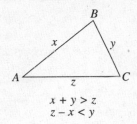

$$x + y > z$$
$$z - x < y$$

49. The area of a triangle is given by $A = \dfrac{1}{2}bh$, where b = base and h = height.

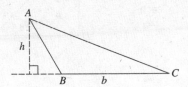 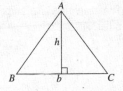

50. If A represents the area of an equilateral triangle with side s, then $A = \dfrac{s^2\sqrt{3}}{4}$.

51. In any quadrilateral, the sum of the measures of the four angles is 360°.

52. A **parallelogram** is a quadrilateral in which both pairs of opposite sides are parallel. A **rectangle** is a parallelogram in which all four angles are right angles. A **square** is a rectangle in which all four sides have the same length.

53. In any parallelogram:

- Opposite sides are congruent: $AB = CD$ and $AD = BC$.
- Opposite angles are congruent: $a = c$ and $b = d$.
- Consecutive angles add up to 180°: $a + b = 180$, $b + c = 180$, and so on.
- The two diagonals bisect each other: $AE = EC$ and $BE = ED$.

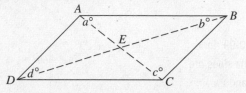

54. In any rectangle:

- The measure of each angle in a rectangle is 90°.
- The diagonals of a rectangle have the same length: $AC = BD$.

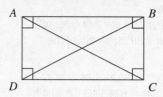

55. In any square:

- All four sides have the same length.
- Each diagonal divides the square into two 45-45-90 right triangles.
- The diagonals are perpendicular to each other: $AC \perp BD$.

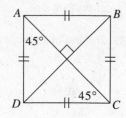

56. **Formulas for perimeter and area:**

   • For a parallelogram: $A = bh$ and $P = 2(a + b)$.
   • For a rectangle: $A = \ell w$ and $P = 2(\ell + w)$.
   • For a square: $A = s^2$ or $A = \dfrac{1}{2}d^2$ and $P = 4s$.

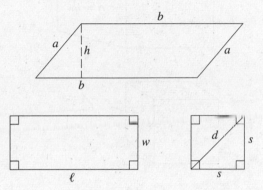

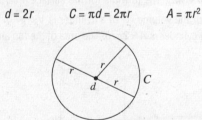

57. Let r be the radius, d the diameter, C the circumference, and A the area of a circle, then

$$d = 2r \qquad C = \pi d = 2\pi r \qquad A = \pi r^2$$

58. The formula for the volume of a rectangular solid is $V = \ell wh$.

    In a cube, all the edges are equal. Therefore, if e is the edge, the formula for the volume is $V = e^3$.

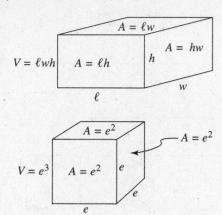

59. The formula for the surface area of a rectangular solid is $A = 2(\ell w + \ell h + wh)$. The formula for the surface area of a cube is $A = 6e^2$.

60. The formula for the volume, V, of a cylinder is $V = \pi r^2 h$. The surface area, A, of the side of the cylinder is $A = 2\pi rh$. The area of the top and bottom are each πr^2.

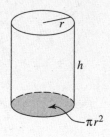

61. The distance, d, between two points, $A(x_1, y_1)$ and $B(x_2, y_2)$, can be calculated using the distance formula:

$$d = \sqrt{(x_2 - x_1)^2 + (y_2 - y_1)^2}$$

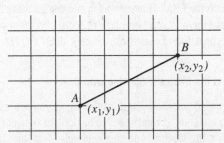

02. The formula for the slope of the line that passes through (x_1, y_1) and (x_2, y_2) is:

$$\text{slope} = \frac{y_2 - y_1}{x_2 - x_1}$$

63. • The slope of any horizontal line is 0.
    • The slope of any line that goes up as you move from left to right is positive.
    • The slope of any line that goes down as you move from left to right is negative.

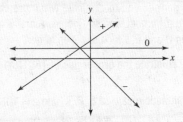

64. **The Counting Principle:** If two jobs need to be completed and there are m ways to do the first job and n ways to do the second job, then there are $m \times n$ ways to do one job followed by the other. This principle can be extended to any number of jobs.

65. If E is any event, the **probability** that E will occur is given by

$$P(E) = \frac{\text{number of favorable outcomes}}{\text{total number of possible outcomes}},$$

assuming that all of the possible outcomes are equally likely.

66.–69. Let E be an event, and let $P(E)$ be the probability that it will occur.

66. If E is *impossible,* then $P(E) = 0$.

67. If it is *certain* that E will occur, then $P(E) = 1$.

68. In all other cases, $0 < P(E) < 1$.

69. The probability that event E will *not* occur is $1 - P(E)$.

70. If an experiment is done 2 (or more) times, the probability that first one event will occur, and then a second event will occur, is the product of the probabilities.

Math Tactics and Strategies

You will now learn important strategies to help you answer both the multiple-choice and grid-in questions on the PSAT. However, as invaluable as these tactics are, use them only when you need them. *If you know how to solve a problem and are confident that you can do so accurately and reasonably quickly, JUST DO IT!*

1 / Test the Choices, Starting with C

TACTIC 1, often called *backsolving*, is useful when you are asked to solve for an unknown and you understand what needs to be done to answer the question, but you want to avoid doing the algebra. The idea is simple: Test the various choices to see which one is correct.

   NOTE: On the PSAT the answers to virtually all numerical multiple-choice questions are listed in either increasing or decreasing order. Consequently, Choice C is the middle value, and in applying **TACTIC 1**, *you should always start with Choice C*. For example, assume that Choices A, B, C, D, and E are given in increasing order. Try Choice C. If it works, you've found the answer. If Choice C doesn't work, you almost always will know whether you need to test a larger number or a smaller one, and that information permits you to eliminate two more choices. If Choice C is too small, you need a larger number, and so Choices A and B are out; if Choice C is too big, eliminate Choices D and E, which are even larger.

   Examples 1 and 2 illustrate the proper use of **TACTIC 1**.

Example 1

   If the average (arithmetic mean) of 5, 6, 7, and x is 10, what is the value of x?

   (A) 8   (B) 13   (C) 18   (D) 22   (E) 28

Solution. Use **TACTIC 1**. Test Choice C: $x = 18$.

- Is the average of 5, 6, 7, and 18 equal to 10?
- No: $\dfrac{5 + 6 + 7 + 18}{4} = \dfrac{36}{4} = 9$, which is *too small*.
- Eliminate Choice C, and, since for the average to be 10, x must be *greater* than 18, eliminate Choices A and B, as well.
- Try Choice D: $x = 22$. Is the average of 5, 6, 7, and 22, equal to 10?
- Yes: $\dfrac{5 + 6 + 7 + 22}{4} = \dfrac{40}{4} = 10$. The answer is Choice D.

   Remember that every problem that can be solved using **TACTIC 1** can be solved directly, usually in less time. Therefore, we again stress: *If you are confident that you can solve a problem quickly and accurately, just do so.*

Example 2

Judy is now twice as old as Adam, but 6 years ago, she was 5 times as old as he was. How old is Judy now?

(A) 8   (B) 16   (C) 20   (D) 24   (E) 32

Solution. Use **TACTIC 1** and backsolve starting with Choice C. If Judy is now 20, Adam is 10, and 6 years ago, they would have been 14 and 4. Since Judy would have been less than 5 times as old as Adam, eliminate Choices C, D, and E, and try a smaller value. If Judy is now 16, Adam is 8; 6 years ago, they would have been 10 and 2. That's it; 10 *is* 5 times 2. The answer is Choice B.

Some tactics allow you to eliminate a few choices so you can make an educated guess. On those problems where it can be used, **TACTIC 1** *always* gets you the right answer. The only reason not to use it on a particular problem is that you can *easily* solve the problem directly.

2 / Replace Variables with Numbers

Mastery of **TACTIC 2** is critical for anyone developing good test-taking skills. This tactic can be used whenever the five choices involve the variables in the question. There are three steps:

1. Replace each letter with an easy-to-use number.
2. Solve the problem using those numbers.
3. Evaluate each of the five choices with the numbers you chose to see which choice is equal to the answer you obtained.

Examples 3 and 4 illustrate the proper use of **TACTIC 2**.

Example 3

If a is equal to the sum of b and c, which of the following is equal to the difference of b and c?

(A) $a - b - c$ (B) $a - b + c$ (C) $a - c$ (D) $a - 2c$ (E) $a - b - 2c$

Solution.

- Choose three easy-to-use numbers that satisfy $a = b + c$: for example, $a = 5$, $b = 3$, $c = 2$.
- Then, solve the problem with these numbers: the difference of b and c is $3 - 2 = 1$.
- Finally, check each of the five choices to see which one is equal to 1:

    (A) Does $a - b - c = 1$?   No. $5 - 3 - 2 = 0$
    (B) Does $a - b + c = 1$?   No. $5 - 3 + 2 = 4$
    (C) Does $a - c = 1$?   No. $5 - 2 = 3$
    (D) Does $a - 2c = 1$?   Yes! $5 - 2(2) = 5 - 4 = 1$
    (E) Does $a - b - 2c = 1$?   No. $5 - 3 - 2(2) = 2 - 4 = -2$

- The answer is Choice D.

Example 4

If the sum of five consecutive even integers is t, then, in terms of t, what is the greatest of these integers?

(A) $\dfrac{t-20}{5}$ (B) $\dfrac{t-10}{5}$ (C) $\dfrac{t}{5}$ (D) $\dfrac{t+10}{5}$ (E) $\dfrac{t+20}{5}$

Solution.

- Choose five easy-to-use consecutive even integers: 2, 4, 6, 8, 10. Then their sum, t, is 30.
- Solve the problem with these numbers: the greatest of these integers is 10.
- When $t = 30$, the five choices are $\dfrac{10}{5}, \dfrac{20}{5}, \dfrac{30}{5}, \dfrac{40}{5}, \dfrac{50}{5}$.
- Only $\dfrac{50}{5}$, Choice E, is equal to 10.

Of course, if your algebra skills are good, Examples 3 and 4 can be solved without using **TACTIC 2**. The important point is that if you are uncomfortable with the correct algebraic solution, you don't have to omit these questions. You can use **TACTIC 2** and *always* get the correct answer.

Example 5 is somewhat different. You are asked to reason through a word problem involving only variables. Most students find problems like this one mind-boggling. Here, the use of **TACTIC 2** is essential. Without it, most students would find Example 5 very difficult, if not impossible.

Helpful Hint

Replace the letters with numbers that are easy to use, not necessarily ones that make sense. It is perfectly OK to ignore reality. A school can have 2 students, apples can cost 10 dollars each, trains can go 5 miles per hour or 1000 miles per hour—it doesn't matter.

Example 5

A vendor sells h hot dogs and s sodas. If a hot dog costs twice as much as a soda, and if the vendor takes in a total of d dollars, how many *cents* does a soda cost?

(A) $\dfrac{100d}{s+2h}$ (B) $\dfrac{s+2h}{100d}$ (C) $\dfrac{100}{d(s+2h)}$

(D) $100d(s+2h)$ (E) $\dfrac{d}{100(s+2h)}$

Solution.

- Replace h, s, and d with three easy-to-use numbers. Suppose a soda costs 50¢ and a hot dog $1.00. Then if he sold 2 sodas and 3 hot dogs, he took in 4 dollars.

- Which of the choices equals 50 when $s = 2$, $h = 3$ and $d = 4$?
- Only Choice A: $\dfrac{100(4)}{2+2(3)} = \dfrac{400}{8} = 50$.

Helpful Hint

Of course, when you check the choices, you should use your calculator whenever necessary. However, you do not need to determine the value of each choice; you only need to know if it is the correct choice. In Example 5, Choices B and E are small fractions, and could not possibly equal 50, and Choice D is clearly greater than 50, so don't waste your time evaluating them. Only Choices A and C are even possible.

---

3 / Choooo on Appropriate Number

TACTIC 3 is similar to **TACTIC 2**, in that we pick convenient numbers. However, no variable is given in the problem. **TACTIC 3** is especially useful in problems involving fractions, ratios, and percents.

Helpful Hint

In problems involving fractions, the best number to use is the least common denominator (LCD) of all the fractions. In problems involving percents, the easiest number to use is 100.

Example 6

On a certain college committee, $\dfrac{2}{3}$ of the members are female, and $\dfrac{3}{8}$ of the females are varsity athletes. If $\dfrac{3}{5}$ of the committee members are not varsity athletes, what fraction of the members of the committee are male varsity athletes?

(A) $\dfrac{3}{20}$ (B) $\dfrac{11}{60}$ (C) $\dfrac{1}{4}$ (D) $\dfrac{2}{5}$ (E) $\dfrac{5}{12}$

Solution. Since the LCD of the three fractions is 120, assume that the committee has 120 members. Then there are $\dfrac{2}{3} \times 120 = 80$ females. Of the 80 females, $\dfrac{3}{8} \times 80 = 30$ are varsity athletes. Since $\dfrac{3}{5} \times 120 = 72$ committee members are not varsity athletes, then $120 - 72 = 48$ are varsity athletes; of these, 30 are female and the other 18 are male. Finally, the fraction of the members of the committee who are male varsity athletes is $\dfrac{18}{120} = \dfrac{3}{20}$ (Choice A).

Example 7

From 1994 to 1995 the sales of a book decreased by 80%. If the sales in 1996 were the same as in 1994, by what percent did they increase from 1995 to 1996?

(A) 80%   (B) 100%   (C) 120%   (D) 400%   (E) 500%

Solution. Since this problem involves percents, assume that 100 copies of the book were sold in 1994 (and 1996). Sales dropped by 80 (80% of 100) to 20 in 1995 and then increased by 80, from 20 back to 100, in 1996. The percent increase was

$$\frac{\text{the actual increase}}{\text{the original amount}} \times 100\% = \frac{80}{20} \times 100\% = 400\% \text{ (Choice D)}.$$

4 / Eliminate Absurd Choices and Guess

When you have no idea how to solve a problem, eliminate all the absurd choices and guess from among the remaining ones.

During the course of a PSAT, you will probably find at least a few multiple-choice questions that you read, but have no idea how to solve. *Do not automatically omit these questions!* Often, two or three of the answers are absurd. Eliminate them and *guess*. Occasionally, four of the choices are absurd. When this occurs, your answer is no longer a guess.

What makes a choice absurd? Here are a few things to note. Even if you don't know how to solve a problem you may realize that

- the answer must be positive, but some of the choices are negative.
- the answer must be even, but some of the choices are odd.
- a ratio must be less than 1, but some choices are greater than or equal to 1.

Let's look at five examples. In some of them the information given is intentionally insufficient to solve the problem, but you will still be able to determine that some of the answers are absurd. Even when there is enough information to solve the problem, don't. Rather, see if you can determine which choices are absurd and should, therefore, be eliminated.

Example 8

A region inside a semicircle of radius r is shaded. What is its area?

(A) $\frac{1}{4}\pi r^2$ (B) $\frac{1}{3}\pi r^2$ (C) $\frac{1}{2}\pi r^2$ (D) $\frac{2}{3}\pi r^2$ (E) $\frac{3}{4}\pi r^2$

Solution. Even if you have no idea how to find the area of the shaded region, you should know that since the area of a circle is πr^2, the area of a semicircle is $\frac{1}{2}\pi r^2$.

So the area of the shaded region must be *less than* $\frac{1}{2}\pi r^2$. Eliminate Choices C, D, and E. On an actual problem, if the diagram is drawn to scale, you may be able to make an educated guess between Choices A and B. If not, just choose one or the other.

Example 9

The average of 5, 10, 15, and x is 20. What is x?

(A) 0   (B) 20   (C) 25   (D) 45   (E) 50

Solution. If the average of four numbers is 20, and three of them are less than 20, the other one must be greater than 20. Eliminate Choices A and B and guess. If you further realize that since 5 and 10 are *a lot* less than 20, x will be *a lot* more than 20, then eliminate Choice C, as well.

Example 10

A prize of $27,000 is to be divided in some ratio among 3 people. What is the largest share?

(A) $18,900   (B) $13,500   (C) $8100   (D) $5400   (E) $2700

Solution. If the prize were divided equally, each share would be worth $9000. If it is divided unequally, the largest share must be *more than* $9000, so eliminate Choices C, D, and E. In an actual question, you would be told what the ratio is, and that information might enable you to eliminate Choice A or Choice B. If not, you would just guess.

Example 11

A jar contains only red and blue marbles. The ratio of the number of red marbles to the number of blue marbles is 5:3. What percent of the marbles are blue?

(A) 37.5%   (B) 50%   (C) 60%   (D) 62.5%   (E) 80%

Solution. Since there are 5 red marbles for every 3 blue ones, there are fewer blue ones than red ones. Therefore, *fewer than half* (50%) of the marbles are blue. Eliminate Choices B, C, D, and E. The answer is Choice A.

Example 12

Square $WXYZ$ is divided into two unequal regions. If $WX = 4$, which of the following could be the area of the larger region?

(A) 8π (B) $8\pi - 32$ (C) $16 - 8\pi$ (D) $32 - 8\pi$ (E) $8\pi - 16$

Solution. Since the area of the square is 16, the area of the larger region must be more than 8. Since π is slightly more than 3, 8π (which appears in each choice) is somewhat more than 24, approximately 25. Check the choices:

- (A) $8\pi \approx 25$, which is more than the area of the whole square.
- (B) $8\pi - 32$ is negative. Clearly impossible!
- (C) $16 - 8\pi$ is also negative.
- (D) $32 - 8\pi \approx 7$, which is too small.
- (E) $8\pi - 16 \approx 9$. The answer is E.

5 / Draw a Diagram

On any geometry question for which a figure is not provided, draw one (as accurately as possible) in your test booklet. Often looking at the diagram will lead you to the correct method. Sometimes, as in Example 13 below, a careful examination of the diagram is sufficient to actually determine the correct answer.

Example 13

A rectangle is 7 times as long as it is wide. If the width is w, what is the length of a diagonal?

(A) $2w\sqrt{5}$ (B) $5w\sqrt{2}$ (C) $7w$ (D) $8w$ (E) $50w$

Solution.   First draw a rectangle that is 7 times as large as it is wide. (By marking off 7 widths, you should be able to do this quite accurately.) Then draw in a diagonal.

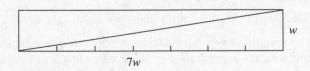

You probably realize that you can use the Pythagorean theorem to find the length of the diagonal; but by looking at the diagram you should see that the diagonal is just slightly larger than the length, $7w$. Now check each answer choice using your calculator when necessary. Clearly, the answer is not $7w$, and $50w$ is way too big. Eliminate choices C and E. Even Choice D, $8w$, is probably too big, but don't eliminate it until you use your calculator to test choices A and B. $2\sqrt{5} \approx 4.5$, which is clearly too small; $5\sqrt{2} \approx 7.07$, which looks just right. Choose B.

6 / Use Diagrams Wisely. If a Diagram is Drawn to Scale, Trust It.

Remember that every diagram that appears on the PSAT has been drawn as accurately as possible, *unless* you see, "<u>Note:</u> Figure not drawn to scale."

In figures that are drawn to scale, the following are true: Line segments that appear to be the same length, *are* the same length; if an angle clearly looks obtuse, it *is* obtuse; and if one angle appears larger than another, you may assume that it *is* larger.

Helpful Hint

On the PSAT, if you know how to solve a geometry problem, just do it directly. However, if you don't, and if there is a diagram that has been drawn to scale, do not leave it out. Trusting the diagram to be accurate, you can always eliminate some of the choices and make an educated guess.

Examples 14, 15, and 16 all contain diagrams that have been drawn to scale. Of course, each of these relatively easy examples has a correct mathematical solution, but try to answer them by eliminating as many choices as possible, based only on the given diagram.

Example 14

If in the figure at the right $AB = AC$, what is the value of x?

(A) 135   (B) 125   (C) 115
(D) 65   (E) 50

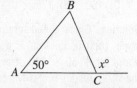

Solution. Clearly, the angle is obtuse, so x is greater than 90, and we can immediately eliminate Choices D and E. If you attempt to "measure" x more accurately, by drawing a few lines in the diagram, you can eliminate Choice A and probably Choice B. Choose Choice C.

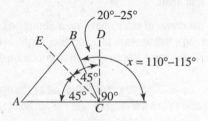

Example 15

In the figure at the right, what is the sum of the measures of all the marked angles?

(A) 360°   (B) 540°   (C) 720°
(D) 900°   (E) 1080°

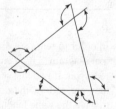

Solution. Make your best estimate of each angle and add them up. The 5 choices are so far apart, that even if you're off by 15° or more on some of the angles, you'll get the right answer. The sum of the estimates shown is 690°, so the correct answer *must* be 720° (Choice C).

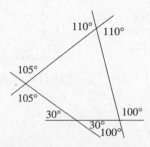

Example 16

In the figure at the right, what is the value of x?

(A) 120   (B) 130   (C) 145
(D) 160   (E) 175

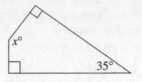

Solution. Since the diagram is drawn to scale, trust it. Look at x: it appears to be *about* $90 + 50 = 140$; it is *definitely* less than 160. Also, y is clearly less than 45, so x is greater than 135. The answer must be 145 (Choice C).

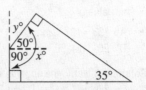

7 / Use Diagrams Wisely. If a Diagram Is Not Drawn to Scale, Redraw It to Scale.

In figures that are not drawn to scale, make *no* assumptions. Lines that look parallel might not be; an angle that appears to be obtuse, might, in fact, be acute; two line segments might have the same length even though one looks twice as long as the other.

In the examples illustrating **TACTIC 6**, all of the diagrams were drawn to scale, and we were able to use the diagrams to our advantage. When diagrams have not been drawn to scale, you must be more careful.

Helpful Hint

In order to redraw a diagram to scale, ask yourself, "What is wrong with the original diagram?" If an angle is marked 45°, but in the figure it looks like a 75° angle, redraw it. If two line segments appear to be parallel, but you have not been told that they are, redraw them so that they are clearly not parallel. If two segments appear to have the same length, but one is marked 5 and the other 10, redraw them so that the second segment is twice as long as the first.

Example 17

In $\triangle ABC$, what is the value of x?

(A) 15   (B) 30   (C) 45
(D) 60   (E) 75

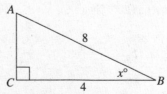

Note: Figure not drawn to scale

Solution. In what way is this figure not drawn to scale? $AB = 8$ and $BC = 4$, but in the figure, AB is not nearly twice as long as BC. Although the figure is not drawn to scale, the square symbol at angle C indicates that angle C is a right angle. So draw a right triangle in which AB *is* twice as long as BC. Now you can see that x is about 60 (Choice D).

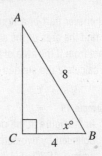

In fact, x is exactly 60. If the hypotenuse of a right triangle is twice the length of one of the legs, then it's a 30-60-90 triangle, and the angle formed by the hypotenuse and that leg is 60°.

Example 18

In the figure at the right, which of the following statements *could* be true?

I. $AB < AC$
II. $AB > AC$
III. Area of $\triangle ABC = 50$

(A) None   (B) I only   (C) II only
(D) I and III only   (E) II and III only

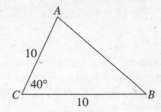

Note: Figure not drawn to scale

Solution. In the given diagram, AB is longer than AC, which is 10. But, we know that we *cannot trust the diagram*. Actually, there are two things wrong: angle C is labeled 40°, but looks much more like 60° or 70°, and AC and BC are each labeled 10, but BC is much longer. Redraw the triangle with a smaller angle and two sides of the same length (see diagram at right).

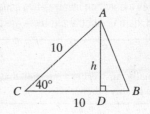

Now just look: $\overline{AB}$ is clearly shorter than $\overline{AC}$. So I is true and II is false. If you draw in altitude $\overline{AD}$, it is also clear that h is less than 10.

$$A = \frac{1}{2}bh = \frac{1}{2}(10)h = 5h < 5 \times 10 = 50$$

The area must be less than 50. III is false. Only I is true (Choice B).

8 / Subtract to Find Shaded Regions

Whenever part of a figure is shaded and part is unshaded, the straightforward way to find the area of the shaded portion is to find the area of the entire figure and subtract from it the area of the unshaded region. Occasionally, you may see an easy way to calculate the shaded area directly, but usually you should subtract.

Example 19

In the figure at the right, the shaded region is bounded by two semicircles and two sides of square *ABCD*. If *AB* = 2, what is the area of the shaded region?

(A) $4 - 2\pi$ (B) $4 - \pi$ (C) $4 + 2\pi$
(D) $16 - 4\pi$ (E) $4\pi - 16$

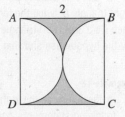

Solution. The entire region is a square whose area is 4. Since each semicircle has a diameter of 2 (hence a radius of 1), together they form a circle of radius 1. The area of such a circle is $\pi(1)^2 = \pi$. So, the area of the shaded region is $4 - \pi$ (Choice B).

9 / Add Equations

When a question involves two equations, almost always the best strategy is to either add them or subtract. If there are three or more equations, just add them.

Helpful Hint

Usually, answering a question that involves two or more equations does not require you to solve them.

Example 20

If $4x + y = 23$ and $x - 2y = 8$, what is the average of *x* and *y*?

(A) 0   (B) 2.5   (C) 3   (D) 3.5   (E) 5

Solution. Add the two equations:

$$
\begin{array}{r}
4x + y = 23 \\
+ \quad x - 2y = 8 \\
\hline
5x - y = 31
\end{array}
$$

This does not appear to help, so try subtracting the two equations:

$$
\begin{array}{r}
4x + y = 23 \\
- \quad x - 2y = 8 \\
\hline
3x + 3y = 15
\end{array}
$$

Divide each side by 3:

$$x + y = 5$$

The average of x and y is their sum divided by 2:

$$\frac{x+y}{2} = \frac{5}{2} = 2.5$$

The answer is Choice B.

NOTE: You *could have* actually solved for x and y [$x = 6$, $y = -1$], and then taken their average. However, that method would have been more time-consuming and unnecessary.

Example 21

If $a - b = 1$, $b - c = 2$, and $c - a = d$, what is the value of d?

(A) -3 (B) -1 (C) 1 (D) 3

(E) It cannot be determined from the information given.

Solution. Since there are more than two equations, add them:

$$\begin{array}{rcl} a - b &=& 1 \\ b - c &=& 2 \\ + \quad c - a &=& d \\ \hline 0 &=& 3 + d \Rightarrow d = -3 \end{array}$$

The answer is Choice A.

10 / Systematically Make Lists

When a question asks "how many," often the best strategy is to make a list. If you do this it is important that you make the list in a *systematic* fashion so that you don't inadvertently leave something out. Often, shortly after starting the list, you can see a pattern developing and can figure out how many more entries there will be without writing them all down.

Listing things systematically means writing them in numerical order (if the entries are numbers) or in alphabetical order (if the entries are letters). If the answer to "how many" is a small number (as in Example 22), just list all possibilities. If the answer is a large number (as in Example 23), start the list and write enough entries until you see a pattern.

Example 22

The sum of three positive integers is 20. If one of them is 5, what is the greatest possible value of the product of the other two?

Solution. Since one of the integers is 5, the sum of the other two is 15. Systematically, list all possible pairs, (a, b), of positive integers whose sum is 15, and check their products. First let $a = 1$, then 2, and so on.

$\underline{a}$	$\underline{b}$	$\underline{ab}$
1	14	14
2	13	26
3	12	36
4	11	44
5	10	50
6	9	54
7	8	56

The answer is 56.

Example 23

A palindrome is a number, such as 74,947, that reads the same forwards and backwards. How many palindromes are there between 200 and 800?

Solution. First, write down the numbers in the 200s that end in 2:

202, 212, 222, 232, 242, 252, 262, 272, 282, 292

Now write the numbers beginning and ending in 3:

303, 313, 323, 333, 343, 353, 363, 373, 383, 393

By now you should see the pattern: there are 10 numbers beginning with a 2, 10 beginning with 3, and there will be 10 beginning with 4, 5, 6, and 7 for a total of $6 \times 10 = 60$ palindromes.

11 / Handle Strange Symbols Properly

On almost all PSATs, there a few questions that use symbols, such as: ⊕ , ☐ , ☺, ✠ , or ♣, that you have never before seen in a mathematics problem. How can you answer such a question? Don't panic! It's easy—you are always told exactly what the symbol means! All you have to do is follow the directions carefully.

When there are two questions using the same symbol, the first question is usually easy and involves only numbers; the second is more difficult and usually contains variables.

Examples 24 and 25 refer to the following definition.

If a and b are unequal positive numbers, $a ☺ b = \dfrac{a+b}{a-b}$

Example 24

What is the value of 6 ☺ 2?

(A) 2   (B) 3   (C) 4   (D) 8   (E) 12

Solution. The definition of ☺ tells us that whenever two numbers surround a "happy face," we are to form a fraction in which the numerator is their sum and the denominator is their difference. So, 6 ☺ 2 is the fraction whose numerator is 6 + 2 = 8 and whose denominator is 6 − 2 = 4: $\frac{8}{4}$ = 2 (Choice A).

Example 25

If c ☺ d = 3, which of the following is true?

(A) $c = 3d$ (B) $c = 2d$ (C) $c = d$ (D) $d = 2c$ (E) $d = 3c$

Solution. $c ☺ d = 3 \Rightarrow \frac{c+d}{c-d} = 3 \Rightarrow c + d = 3c - 3d \Rightarrow 4d = 2c \Rightarrow c = 2d$ (Choice B).

Exercises

None of these exercises *requires* the use of the tactics that you just learned. However, as you try each one, even if you know the correct mathematical solution, before solving it, think about which of the tactics could be used. An answer key follows the questions.

Multiple-Choice Questions

1. If the average (arithmetic mean) of 10, 20, 30, 40, and a is 50, what is the value of a?

    (A) 50   (B) 60   (C) 100   (D) 150   (E) 250

2. Larry has 250 marbles, all red, white, and blue, in the ratio of 1:3:6, respectively. How many blue marbles does he have?

    (A) 25   (B) 75   (C) 100   (D) 125   (E) 150

3. If w whistles cost c cents, how many whistles can you get for d dollars?

    (A) $\frac{100dw}{c}$ (B) $\frac{dw}{100c}$ (C) $100cdw$

    (D) $\frac{dw}{c}$ (E) cdw

4. If x% of w is 10, what is w?

    (A) $\frac{10}{x}$ (B) $\frac{100}{x}$ (C) $\frac{1000}{x}$ (D) $\frac{x}{100}$ (E) $\frac{x}{10}$

5. If 8% of c is equal to 12% of d, which of the following is equal to $c + d$?

    (A) $1.5d$ (B) $2d$ (C) $2.5d$ (D) $3d$ (E) $5d$

6. On a certain legislative committee, $\frac{3}{8}$ of the committee members are Republicans. If $\frac{2}{3}$ of the members are men, and $\frac{3}{5}$ of the men are Democrats, what fraction of the members are Democratic women?

(A) $\frac{3}{20}$ (B) $\frac{9}{40}$ (C) $\frac{1}{4}$ (D) $\frac{2}{5}$ (E) $\frac{5}{12}$

7. Kim receives a commission of $25 for every $2000 worth of merchandise she sells. What percent is her commission?

(A) $1\frac{1}{4}\%$ (B) $2\frac{1}{2}\%$ (C) 5%   (D) 25%   (E) 125%

8. From 1990 to 1995, the value of one share of stock of *XYZ* corporation increased by 25%. If the value was *D* dollars in 1995, what was the value in 1990?

(A) 1.75*D*   (B) 1.25*D*   (C) 1.20*D*   (D) .80*D*   (E) .75*D*

9. What is the value of *p* if *p* is positive and $p \times p \times p = p + p + p$?

(A) $\frac{1}{3}$ (B) $\sqrt{3}$ (C) 3   (D) $3\sqrt{3}$ (E) 9

10. What is 4% of 5%?

(A) .09%   (B) .20%   (C) 2.0%   (D) 9%   (E) 20%

11. In the figure below, *TUVW* is a square and *TUX* is an equilateral triangle. If $VW = 2$, what is the area of the shaded region?

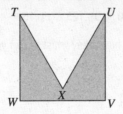

(A) $\sqrt{3}$ (B) 2   (C) 3   (D) $4 - 2\sqrt{3}$ (E) $4 - \sqrt{3}$

12. If $12a + 3b = 1$ and $7b - 2a = 9$, what is the average (arithmetic mean) of *a* and *b*?

(A) 0.1   (B) 0.5   (C) 1   (D) 2.5   (E) 5

13. The map below shows all the roads connecting five towns. How many different ways are there to go from *A* to *E* if you may not return to a town after you leave it and you may not go through both *C* and *D*?

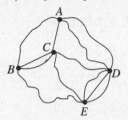

(A) 8   (B) 12   (C) 16   (D) 24   (E) 32

Questions 14–15 refer to the following definition.

For any numbers a, b, c $a \odot b \odot c = abc - (a + b + c)$

14. What is the value of $3 \odot 5 \odot 2$?
   (A) 0   (B) 5   (C) 10   (D) 20   (E) 30

15. For what positive number x is it true that $x \odot 2x \odot 3x = 0$?
   (A) 0   (B) 1   (C) 2   (D) 3   (E) 6

16. In the figure below, if the radius of circle *O* is 10, what is the length of diagonal *AC* of rectangle *OABC*?

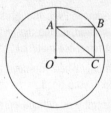

(A) $\sqrt{2}$ (B) $\sqrt{10}$ (C) $5\sqrt{2}$ (D) 10   (E) $10\sqrt{2}$

Grid-in Questions

17. What is the area of a rectangle whose length is twice its width and whose perimeter is equal to the perimeter of a square whose area is 1? _____

18. For how many integers between 1 and 1000 is at least one of the digits a 9?

_____

Answer Key

Next to the answer for each question is the number of the tactic that would be most helpful in answering the question, in the event that you do not see the direct solution.

1. *D* (TACTIC 1)

2. *E* (TACTIC 1)

3. *A* (TACTIC 2)

4. *C* (TACTIC 2)

5. *C* (TACTIC 3)

6. *B* (TACTIC 3)

7. *A* (TACTIC 4)

8. *D* (TACTIC 4)

9. *B* (TACTIC 1)

10. *B* (TACTIC 4)

11. *E* (TACTIC 8)

12. *B* (TACTIC 9)

13. *B* (TACTIC 10)

14. *D* (TACTIC 11)

15. *B* (TACTIC 11)

16. *D* (TACTIC 6)

17. $\frac{8}{9}$ (TACTIC 5)

18. 271 (TACTIC 10)

SUMMARY OF IMPORTANT TIPS AND TACTICS

1. Whenever you know how to answer a question directly, just do it. The tactics given in this chapter should be used only when you need them.

2. Memorize all the formulas you need to know. Even though some of them are printed on the first page of each math section, during the test you do not want to waste any time referring back to that reference material.

3. Be sure to bring a calculator, but use it only when you need it. Don't use it for simple arithmetic that you can easily do in your head.

4. Remember that no problem requires lengthy or difficult computations. If you find yourself doing a lot of arithmetic, stop and reread the question. You are probably not answering the question asked.

5. Answer every question you attempt. Even if you can't solve it, you can almost always eliminate two or more choices. Often you know that an answer must be negative, but two or three of the choices are positive, or an answer must be even, and some of the choices are odd.

6. Unless a diagram is labeled "<u>Note</u>: Figure not drawn to scale," it is perfectly accurate, and you can trust it in making an estimate.

7. When a diagram has not been provided, draw one, especially on any geometry problem.

8. If a diagram has been provided, feel free to label it, mark it up in any way, including adding line segments, if necessary.

9. Answer any question for which you can estimate the answer, even if you are not sure you are correct.

10. Don't panic when you see a strange symbol in a question, It will always be defined. Getting the correct answer just involves following the directions given in the definition.

11. When a question involves two equations, either add them or subtract them. If there are three or more, just add them.

12. Never make unwarranted assumptions. Do not assume numbers are positive or integers. If a question refers to two numbers, do not assume that they have to be different. If you know a figure has four sides, do not assume that it is a rectangle.

13. Be sure to work in consistent units. If the width and length of a rectangle are 8 inches and 2 feet, respectively, either convert the 2 feet to 24 inches or the 8 inches to two-thirds of a foot before calculating the area or perimeter.

Standard Multiple-Choice Questions

1. Whenever you answer a question by backsolving, start with Choice C.

2. When you replace variables with numbers, choose easy-to-use numbers, whether or not they are realistic.

3. Choose appropriate numbers. The best number to use in percent problems is 100. In problems involving fractions, the best number to use is the least common denominator.

4. When you have no idea how to solve a problem, eliminate all of the absurd choices and guess.

Student-Produced Response (Grid-in) Questions

1. Write your answer in the four spaces at the top of the grid, and *carefully* grid in your answer below. No credit is given for a correct answer if it has been gridded improperly.

2. Remember that the answer to a grid-in question can never be negative.

3. You can never grid in a mixed number—you must convert it to an improper fraction or a decimal.

4. Never round off your answers and never reduce fractions. If a fraction can fit in the four spaces of the grid, enter it. If not, use your calculator to convert it to a decimal (by dividing) and enter a decimal point followed by the first three decimal digits.

5. When gridding a decimal, do not write a 0 before the decimal point.

6. If a question has more than one possible answer, only grid in one of them.

7. There is no penalty for wrong answers on grid-in questions, so you should grid in anything that seems reasonable, rather than leave out a question.

6 Improving Written Expression

You definitely want to study hard when you prepare for the writing skills section: a good score on this section of the test may make all the difference between your becoming a National Merit finalist and your coming out a runner up.

The questions test your ability to recognize clear, correct standard written English, the kind of writing your college professors will expect on the papers you write for them. You'll be expected to know basic grammar, such as subject-verb agreement, pronoun-antecedent agreement, correct verb tense, correct sentence structure, and correct diction. You'll need to know how to recognize a dangling participle and how to spot when two parts of a sentence are not clearly connected. You'll also need to know when a paragraph is (or isn't) properly developed and organized.

IMPROVING SENTENCES

The most numerous set of questions in this section involves spotting the form of a sentence that works best. In these improving sentence questions, you will be presented with five different versions of the same sentence; you must choose the best one. Here are the directions:

Some or all parts of the following sentences are underlined. The first answer choice, (A), simply repeats the underlined part of the sentence. The other four choices present four alternate ways to phrase the underlined part. Select the answer that produces the most effective sentence, one that is clear and exact, and blacken the appropriate space on your answer sheet. In selecting your choice, be sure that it is standard written English, and that it expresses the meaning of the original sentence.

EXAMPLE:
The first biography of author Eudora Welty came out in 1998 and she was eighty-nine years old at the time.

- (A)   and she was eighty-nine years old at the time
- (B)   at the time when she was eighty-nine
- (C)   upon becoming an eighty-nine year old
- (D)   when she was eighty-nine
- (E)   at the age of eighty-nine years old

Tips For Handling Improving Sentence Questions

1. If you spot an error in the underlined section, eliminate any answer that contains the same error. If something in the underlined section of a sentence correction question strikes you as an obvious error, you can immediately ignore any answer choices that repeat it. Remember, you still don't have to be able to explain what is wrong. You just need to find a correct equivalent. If the error you found in the underlined section is absent from more than one of the answer choices, look over those choices again to see if they add any new errors.

EXAMPLE 1

Being as I had studied for the test with a tutor, I was confident.

(A) Being as I had studied for the test
(B) Being as I studied for the test
(C) Since I studied for the test
(D) Since I had studied for the test
(E) Because I studied for the test

Being as is not acceptable as a conjunction in standard written English. Therefore, you can eliminate Choices A and B right away. Both *Since* and *Because* are perfectly acceptable conjunctions, so you have to look more closely at Choices C, D, and E. The only other changes these choices make are in the tense of the verb. Since the studying occurred before the taking of the test, the past perfect tense, *had studied*, is correct, so the answer is Choice D.

2. If you don't spot an error in the underlined section, look at the answer choices to see what is changed. Sometimes it's hard to spot what's wrong with the underlined section in a sentence correction question. When that happens, turn to the answer choices. Find the changes in the answers. The changes will tell you what kind of error is being tested. When you substitute the answer choices in the original sentence, ask yourself which of these choices makes the sentence seem clearest to you. That may well be the correct answer choice.

EXAMPLE 2

Even the play's most minor characters work together with extraordinary skill, their interplay creates a moving theatrical experience.

(A) their interplay creates a moving theatrical experience
(B) a moving theatrical experience is created by their interplay
(C) and their interplay creates a moving theatrical experience
(D) and a moving theatrical experience being the creation of their interplay
(E) with their interplay they create a moving theatrical experience

Look at the underlined section of the sentence. Nothing seems wrong with it. It could stand on its own as an independent sentence: *Their interplay creates a moving theatrical experience*. Choices B and E are similar to it, for both could stand as independent sentences. Choices C and D, however, are not independent sentences; both begin with the linking word *and*. The error needing correction here is the common comma splice, in which two sentences are carelessly linked with only a comma. Choice C corrects this error in the simplest way possible, adding the word *and* to tie these sentences together.

3. Make sure that all parts of the sentence are logically connected. Not all parts of a sentence are created equal. Some parts should be subordinated to the rest, connected with subordinating conjunctions or relative pronouns, not just added on with *and*. Overuse of *and* frequently makes sentences sound babyish. Compare "We had dinner at the Hard Rock Cafe, and we went to a concert" with "After we had dinner at the Hard Rock Cafe, we went to a concert."

EXAMPLE 3

The rock star always had enthusiastic fans and they loved him.

(A) and they loved him
(B) and they loving him
(C) what loved him
(D) who loved him
(E) which loved him

The original version of this sentence doesn't have any grammatical errors, but it is a poor sentence because it doesn't connect its two clauses logically. The second clause ("and they loved him") is merely adding information about the fans, so it should be turned into an adjective clause, introduced by a relative pronoun. Choices D and E both seem to work, but you know that *which* should never be used to refer to people, so Choice D is obviously the correct answer.

4. Make sure that all parts of a sentence given in a series are similar in form. If they are not, the sentence suffers from a lack of parallel structure. The sentence "I'm taking classes in algebra, history, and how to speak French" lacks parallel structure. *Algebra* and *history* are nouns, names of subjects. The third subject should also be a noun: *conversational French*.

EXAMPLE 4

> In this chapter we'll analyze both types of questions, <u>suggest useful techniques for tackling them, providing some sample items for you to try</u>.

(A) suggest useful techniques for tackling them, providing some sample items for you to try
(B) suggest useful techniques for tackling them, providing some sample items which you can try
(C) suggest useful tactics for tackling them, and provide some sample items for you to try
(D) and suggest useful techniques for tackling them by providing some sample items for you to try
(E) having suggested useful techniques for tackling them and provided some sample items for you to try

To answer questions like this correctly, you must pay particular attention to what the sentence means. You must first decide whether *analyzing, suggesting,* and *providing* are logically equal in importance here. Since they are—all are activities that "we" will do—they should be given equal emphasis. Only Choice C provides the proper parallel structure.

5. Pay particular attention to the shorter answer choices. (This tactic also applies to certain paragraph correction questions.) Good prose is economical. Often the correct answer choice will be the shortest, most direct way of making a point. If you spot no grammatical errors or errors in logic in a concise answer choice, it may well be right.

EXAMPLE 5

> The turning point in the battle of Waterloo probably was <u>Blucher, who was arriving</u> in time to save the day.

(A) Blucher, who was arriving
(B) Blucher, in that he arrived
(C) Blucher's arrival
(D) when Blucher was arriving
(E) that Blucher had arrived

Which answer choice uses the fewest words? Choice C, *Blucher's arrival.* It also happens to be the right answer.

Choice C is both concise in style and correct in grammar. Look back at the original sentence. Strip it of its modifiers, and what is left? "The turning point . . . was Blucher." A turning point is not a person; it is a *thing.* The turning point in the battle was not Blucher, but Blucher's *action,* the thing he did. The correct answer is Choice C, *Blucher's arrival.* Pay particular attention to such concise answer choices. If a concise choice sounds natural when you substitute it for the original underlined phrase, it's a reasonable guess.

IDENTIFYING SENTENCE ERRORS

There are three different kinds of questions on the writing skills section of the PSAT: identifying sentence errors, improving sentences, and improving paragraphs. More than a third of them, fourteen of the thirty-nine, to be exact, are identifying sentence errors questions in which you have to find an error in the underlined section of a sentence. You do *not* have to correct the sentence or explain what is wrong. Here are the directions.

The sentences in this section may contain errors in grammar, usage, choice of words, or idioms. There is either just one error per sentence or the sentence is correct. Some words or phrases are underlined and lettered; everything else in the sentence is correct.

If an underlined word or phrase is incorrect, choose that letter; if the sentence is correct, select No error. Then blacken the appropriate space on your Answer Sheet.

EXAMPLE:

The fields have soil so rich that corn
                    A

                                 Ⓐ Ⓑ ● Ⓓ Ⓔ

growing here commonly had stood more
   B   C

than six feet tall. No error
         D   E

Tips For Handling Identifying Sentence Error Questions

6. Remember that the error, if there is one, must be in an underlined part of the sentence. You don't have to worry about improvements that could be made in the rest of the sentence. For example, if you have a sentence in which the subject is plural and the verb is singular, you could call either one the error. But if only the verb is underlined, the error for that sentence is the verb.

EXAMPLE 6

See how the sixth tip works in dealing with the following sentence:

If one follows the discipline of Hatha Yoga, you know the critical
                    A   B

importance of physical purification to render the body fit for the
                                    C   D

practice of higher meditation. No error
                              E

What's wrong with the sentence above? The writer makes an abrupt, unnecessary shift in person, switching from the pronoun one ("one follows") to the pronoun you ("you know"). There are two ways to fix this sentence. You can rewrite it like this:

> If you follow the discipline of Hatha Yoga, you know the critical importance of physical purification to render the body fit for the practice of higher meditation.

You can also rewrite it like this:

> If one follows the discipline of Hatha Yoga, one knows the critical importance of physical purification to render the body fit for the practice of higher meditation.

However, your job is not to rewrite the sentence. Your job is simply to spot the error, and that error *must be in an underlined part*. In answering error identification questions, focus on the underlined portions of the sentence. Don't waste your time thinking of other ways to make the sentence work.

7. Use your ear for the language. Remember, you don't have to name the error, or be able to explain why it is wrong. All you have to do is recognize that something *is* wrong. On the early, easy questions in the set, if a word or phrase sounds wrong to you, it probably is, even if you don't know why.

EXAMPLE 7

In my history class I learned why the American colonies opposed the British, how
    A   B   C
they organized the militia, and the accomplishments of the Continental Congress.
                                  D
No error
E

The last part of this sentence probably sounds funny to you—awkward, strange, wooden. You may not know exactly what it is, but something sounds wrong here. If you followed your instincts and chose Choice D as the error, you would be right. The error is a lack of parallel structure. The sentence is listing three things you learned, and they should all be in the same form. Your ear expects the pattern to be the same. Since the first two items listed are clauses, the third should be too: "In my history class I learned why the American colonies opposed the British, how they organized the militia, and what the Continental Congress accomplished."

8. Look first for the most common errors. Most of the sentences will have errors. If you are having trouble finding mistakes, check for some of the more common ones: subject-verb agreement, pronoun-antecedent problems, misuse of adjectives and adverbs, dangling modifiers. But look for errors only in the underlined parts of the sentence.

EXAMPLE 8

Marilyn and I ran as fast as we could, but we missed our train, which made us late
     A   B   C   D
for work. No error
      E

Imagine that you have this sentence, and you can't see what is wrong with it. Start at the beginning and check each answer choice. *I* is part of the subject, so it is the right case: after all, you wouldn't say "Me ran fast." *Fast* can be an adverb, so it is being used correctly here. *Which* is a pronoun, and needs a noun for its antecedent. The only available noun is *train*, but that doesn't make sense (the train didn't make us late—*missing* the train made us late). So there is your error, Choice C.

9. Remember that not every sentence contains an error. Ten to twenty percent of the time, the sentence is correct as it stands. Do not get so caught up in hunting for errors that you start seeing errors that aren't there. If no obvious errors strike your eye and the sentence sounds natural to your ear, go with Choice E: No error.

IMPROVING PARAGRAPHS

In the improving paragraph questions, you will confront a flawed student essay followed by five questions. In some cases, you must select the answer choice that best rewrites and combines portions of two separate sentences. In others, you must decide where in the essay a sentence best fits. In still others, you must choose what sort of additional information would most strengthen the writer's argument. Here are the directions.

The passage below is the unedited draft of a student's essay. Some of the essay needs to be rewritten to make the meaning clearer and more precise. Read the essay carefully.

The essay is followed by five questions about changes that might improve all or part of its organization, development, sentence structure, use of language, appropriateness to the audience, or its use of standard written English. Choose the answer that most clearly and effectively expresses the student's intended meaning. Indicate your choice by filling in the corresponding space on the answer sheet.

Tips For Handling Improving Paragraph Questions

10. First read the passage; then read the questions. Whether you choose to skim the student essay quickly or to read it closely, you need to have a reasonable idea of what the student author is trying to say before you set out to correct this rough first draft.

11. First tackle the questions that ask you to improve individual sentences; then tackle the ones that ask you to strengthen the passage as a whole. In the sentence correction questions, you've just been weeding out ineffective sentences and selecting effective ones. Here you're doing more of the same. It generally takes less time to spot an effective sentence than it does to figure out a way to strengthen an argument or link up two paragraphs.

12. Consider whether the addition of signal words or phrases— transitions—would strengthen the passage or particular sentences within it. If the essay is trying to contrast two ideas, it might benefit from the addition of a contrast signal.

Contrast Signals: *although, despite, however, in contrast, nevertheless, on the contrary, on the other hand.*

If one portion of the essay is trying to support or continue a thought developed elsewhere in the passage, it might benefit from the addition of a support signal.

Support Signals: *additionally, furthermore, in addition, likewise, moreover.*

If the essay is trying to indicate that one thing causes another, it might benefit from the addition of a cause and effect signal.

Cause and Effect Signals: *accordingly, as a result of, because, consequently, hence, therefore, thus.*

Pay particular attention to answer choices that contain such signal words.

13. When you tackle the questions, go back to the passage to verify each answer choice. See whether your revised version of a particular sentence sounds right in its context. Ask yourself whether your choice follows naturally from the sentence before.

COMMON GRAMMAR AND USAGE ERRORS

Some errors are more common than others in this section. Here are a dozen that appear frequently on the examination. Watch out for them when you do the practice exercises and when you take the PSAT.

The Run-On Sentence

Mary's party was very exciting, it lasted until 2 A.M.
It is raining today, I need a raincoat.

You may also have heard this error called a comma splice. It can be corrected by making two sentences instead of one:

Mary's party was very exciting. It lasted until 2 A.M.

or by using a semicolon in place of the comma:

Mary's party was very exciting; it lasted until 2 A.M.

or by proper compounding:

Mary's party was very exciting and lasted until 2 A.M.

You can also correct this error with proper subordination. The second example above could be corrected:

Since it is raining today, I need a raincoat.
It is raining today, so I need a raincoat.

The Sentence Fragment

Since John was talking during the entire class, making it impossible for anyone to concentrate.

This is the opposite of the first error. Instead of too much in one sentence, here you have too little. Do not be misled by the length of the fragment. It must have a main clause before it can be a complete sentence. All you have in this example is the cause. You still need a result. For example, the sentence could be corrected:

Since John was talking during the entire class, making it impossible for anyone to concentrate, the teacher made him stay after school.

Error in the Case of a Noun or Pronoun

Between you and I, this test is not really very difficult.

Case problems usually involve personal pronouns, which are in the nominative case (*I, he, she, we, they, who*) when they are used as subjects or predicate nominatives, and in the objective case (*me, him, her, us, them, whom*) when they are used as direct objects, indirect objects, and objects of prepositions. In this example, if you realize that *between* is a preposition, you know that *I* should be changed to the objective *me* because it is the object of a preposition.

Error in Subject-Verb Agreement

Harvard College, along with several other Ivy League schools, are sending students to the conference.

Phrases starting with *along with* or *as well as* or *in addition to* that are placed in between the subject and the verb do not affect the verb. The subject of this sentence is *Harvard College*, so the verb should be *is sending*.

There is three bears living in that house.

Sentences that begin with *there* have the subject after the verb. The subject of this sentence is *bears,* so the verb should be *are.*

Error in Pronoun-Number Agreement

Every one of the girls on the team is trying to do their best.

Every pronoun must have a specific noun or noun substitute for an antecedent, and it must agree with that antecedent in number (singular or plural). In this example, *their* refers to *one* and must be singular:

Every one of the girls on the team is trying to do her best.

Error in the Tense or Form of a Verb

After the sun set behind the mountain, a cool breeze
sprang up and brought relief from the heat.

Make sure the verbs in a sentence appear in the proper sequence of tenses, so that it is clear what happened when. Since, according to the sentence, the breeze did not appear until after the sun had finished setting, the setting belongs in the past perfect tense:

After the sun had set behind the mountain, a cool breeze
sprang up and brought relief from the heat.

Error in Logical Comparison

I can go to California or Florida. I wonder which is best.

When you are comparing only two things, you should use the comparative form of the adjective, not the superlative:

I wonder which is better.

Comparisons must also be complete and logical.

The rooms on the second floor are larger than the first floor.

It would be a strange building that had rooms larger than an entire floor. Logically, this sentence should be corrected to:

The rooms on the second floor are larger than those on the first floor.

Adjective and Adverb Confusion

She did good on the test.

They felt badly about leaving their friends.

These are the two most common ways that adjectives and adverbs are misused. In the first example, when you are talking about how someone did, you want the adverb *well,* not the adjective *good:*

She did well on the test.

In the second example, after a linking verb like *feel* you want a predicate adjective to describe the subject:

They felt bad about leaving their friends.

Error in Modification and Word Order
Reaching for the book, the ladder slipped out from under him.

A participial phrase at the beginning of the sentence should describe the subject of the sentence. Since it doesn't make sense to think of a ladder reaching for a book, this participle is left dangling with nothing to modify. The sentence needs some rewriting:

When he reached for the book, the ladder slipped out from under him.

Error in Parallelism
In his book on winter sports, the author discusses ice-skating, skiing, hockey, and how to fish in an ice-covered lake.

Logically, equal and similar ideas belong in similar form. This shows that they are equal. In this sentence, the author discusses four sports, and all four should be presented the same way:

In his book on winter sports, the author discusses ice-skating, skiing, hockey, and fishing in an ice-covered lake.

Error in Diction or Idiom
The affects of the storm could be seen everywhere.

Your ear for the language will help you handle these errors, especially if you are accustomed to reading standard English. These questions test you on words that are frequently misused, on levels of usage (informal versus formal), and on standard English idioms. In this example, the verb *affect,* meaning "to influence," has been confused with the noun *effect,* meaning "result."

The effects of the storm could be seen everywhere.

The exercises that follow will give you practice in answering the three types of questions you'll find on the Identifying Sentence Errors questions, Improving Sentence questions, and Improving Paragraph questions. When you have completed each exercise, check your answers against the answer key. Then, read the answer explanations for any questions you either answered incorrectly or omitted.

Answers given on pages 150–153.

Practice Exercises

The sentences in this section may contain errors in grammar, usage, choice of words, or idioms. There is either just one error per sentence or the sentence is correct. Some words or phrases are underlined and lettered; everything else in the sentence is correct.

If an underlined word or phrase is incorrect, choose that letter; if the sentence is correct, select No error. Then blacken the appropriate space on your Answer Sheet.

EXAMPLE:

These fields have soil so rich that corn
A
growing here commonly had stood more
B C
than six feet tall. No error
D E

Ⓐ Ⓑ ● Ⓓ Ⓔ

1. We were already to leave for the amusement park when John's car broke down;
A B C
we were forced to postpone our outing. No error
D E

2. By order of the Student Council, the wearing of slacks by we girls in school
A B C
has been permitted. No error
D E

3. Each one of the dogs in the show require a special kind of diet. No error
A B C D E

4. The major difficulty confronting the authorities was the reluctance of the people
A B
to talk; they had been warned not to say nothing to the police. No error
C D E

5. If I were you, I would never permit him to take part in such an
A B C
exhausting and painful activity. No error
D E

6. Stanford White, <u>who</u> is one of America's <u>most notable</u> architects,
                A   B
   <u>have designed</u> many famous buildings, <u>among them</u> the original Madison
       C   D
   Square Garden. <u>No error</u>
                 E

7. The notion <u>of allowing</u> the <u>institution of</u> slavery <u>to continue to</u> exist in a
               A   B   C
   democratic society had no appeal to either the violent followers of John Brown

   <u>nor</u> the peaceful disciples of Sojourner Truth. <u>No error</u>
   D   E

8. Some students <u>prefer</u> watching filmstrips to <u>textbooks</u> because they feel
                A   B
   <u>uncomfortable with</u> the presentation <u>of</u> information in a nonoral form. <u>No error</u>
       C   D   E

9. <u>There</u> was so much conversation <u>in back of</u> me <u>that</u> I <u>couldn't</u> hear the actors
     A   B   C   D
   on the stage. <u>No error</u>
            E

10. This book is <u>too</u> elementary; it can <u>help</u> neither you <u>nor</u> <u>I</u>. <u>No error</u>
              A   B   C D   E

11. In a way <u>we</u> may say <u>that</u> we <u>have reached</u> the <u>end of</u> the Industrial Revolution.
            A   B   C   D
    <u>No error</u>
     E

12. <u>Although</u> the books are <u>altogether</u> on the shelf, <u>they</u> are not arranged in
       A   B   C
    any <u>kind of</u> order. <u>No error</u>
       D   E

13. The <u>reason</u> for my <u>prolonged</u> absence from class <u>was</u> <u>because</u> I was ill for
          A   B   C   D
    three weeks. <u>No error</u>
            E

14. According to researchers, the weapons and work implements used by
    A   B
Cro-Magnon hunters appear being actually quite "modern." No error
                         C   D   E

15. Since we were caught completely unawares, the affect of Ms. Rivera's remarks
                              A   B
was startling; some were shocked, but others were angry. No error
 C   D   E

16. The committee had intended both you and I to speak at the assembly; however,
               A   B   C
only one of us will be able to talk. No error
 D   E

17. The existence of rundown "welfare hotels" in which homeless families reside
                             A   B
at enormous cost to the taxpayer provides a shameful commentary of
       C   D
America's commitment to house the poor. No error
                  E

18. We have heard that the principal has decided whom the prize winners will be
                 A   B   C
and will announce the names in the assembly today. No error
 D   E

19. As soon as the sun had rose over the mountains, the valley became
   A   B   C
unbearably hot and stifling. No error
  D   E

20. They are both excellent books, but this one is best. No error
  A   B   C D   E

21. Although the news had come as a surprise to all in the room, both Jane and
             A   B
Oprah tried to do her work as though nothing had happened. No error
       C   D   E

22. Even well-known fashion designers have difficulty staying on top
$\overline{}$
A

from one season to another because of changeable moods and needs in
$\overline{}$ $\overline{}$ $\overline{}$
        B   C   D

the marketplace. No error
$\overline{}$
           E

23. Arms control has been under discussion for decades with the former Soviet
$\overline{}$
                      A

Union, but solutions are still alluding the major powers. No error
$\overline{}$ $\overline{}$ $\overline{}$ $\overline{}$
     B   C   D   E

24. Perhaps sports enthusiasts are realizing that jogging is not easy on joints and
$\overline{}$ $\overline{}$
                             A   B

tendons, for the latest fad is being walking. No error
$\overline{}$ $\overline{}$ $\overline{}$
         C   D   E

25. Technological advances can cause factual data to become obsolete within
$\overline{}$
                    A

a short time; yet, students should concentrate on reasoning skills, not facts.
$\overline{}$ $\overline{}$ $\overline{}$
    B   C   D

No error
$\overline{}$
  E

26. If anyone cares to join me in this campaign, either now or in the near future,
  $\overline{}$ $\overline{}$ $\overline{}$
A   B   C

they will be welcomed gratefully. No error
$\overline{}$ $\overline{}$
 D   E

27. The poems with which he occasionally desired to regale the fashionable world
     $\overline{}$ $\overline{}$
         A   B

were invariably bad—stereotyped, bombastic, and even ludicrous. No error
   $\overline{}$ $\overline{}$
      C   D   E

28. Ever since the quality of teacher education came under public scrutiny,
$\overline{}$ $\overline{}$
    A   B

suggestions for upgrading the profession are abounding. No error
$\overline{}$ $\overline{}$
        C   D   E

29. Because the door was locked and bolted, the police were forced to break into
$\overline{}$ $\overline{}$ $\overline{}$
    A   B   C

the apartment through the bedroom window. No error
$\overline{}$
        D   E

30. I will always remember you standing by me offering me encouragement.
      A   B   C   D

No error
E

31. With special training, capuchin monkeys can enable quadriplegics as well as
                                            A   B

other handicapped individuals to become increasingly independent. No error
                           C   D   E

32. Contrary to what had previously been reported, the conditions governing the
      A   B

truce between Libya and Chad arranged by the United Nations has not yet
                                   C   D

been revealed. No error
                  E

33. Avid readers generally either admire or dislike Ernest Hemingway's journalistic
                                         A

style of writing; few have no opinion of him. No error
    B   C   D   E

34. In 1986, the nuclear disaster at Chernobyl has aroused intense speculation
                                        A

about the long-term effects of radiation that continued for the better part of
    B   C   D

a year. No error
         E

35. Howard Hughes, who became the subject of bizarre rumors as a result of his
                A   B   C

extreme reclusiveness, was well-known as an aviator, industrialist, and

in producing motion pictures. No error
               D   E

Some or all parts of the following sentences are underlined. The first answer choice, (A), simply repeats the underlined part of the sentence. The other four choices present four alternate ways to phrase the underlined part. Select the answer that produces the most effective sentence, one that is clear and exact, and blacken the appropriate space on your answer sheet. In selecting your choice, be sure that it is standard written English, and that it expresses the meaning of the original sentence.

EXAMPLE:

The first biography of author Eudora Welty came out in 1998 and she was eighty-nine years old at the time.

(A) and she was eighty-nine years old at the time
(B) at the time when she was eighty-nine
(C) upon becoming an eighty-nine year old
(D) when she was eighty-nine
(E) at the age of eighty-nine years old

36. The child is neither encouraged to be critical or to examine all the evidence before forming an opinion.

    (A) neither encouraged to be critical or to examine
    (B) neither encouraged to be critical nor to examine
    (C) either encouraged to be critical or to examine
    (D) encouraged either to be critical nor to examine
    (E) not encouraged either to be critical or to examine

37. The process by which the community influence the actions of its members is known as social control.

    (A) influence the actions of its members
    (B) influences the actions of its members
    (C) had influenced the actions of its members
    (D) influences the actions of their members
    (E) will influence the actions of its members

38. Play being recognized as an important factor improving mental and physical health and thereby reducing human misery and poverty.

    (A) Play being recognized as
    (B) By recognizing play as
    (C) Their recognizing play as
    (D) Recognition of it being
    (E) Play is recognized as

39. To be sure, there would be scarcely any time left over for other things if school children would have been expected to have considered all sides of every matter, on which they hold opinions.

    (A) would have been expected to have considered
    (B) should have been expected to have considered
    (C) were expected to consider
    (D) will be expected to have considered
    (E) were expected to be considered

40. Using it wisely, leisure promotes health, efficiency and happiness.

    (A) Using it wisely
    (B) If it is used wisely
    (C) Having used it wisely
    (D) Because of its wise use
    (E) Because of usefulness

41. In giving expression to the play instincts of the human race, new vigor and effectiveness are afforded by recreation to the body and to the mind.

    (A) new vigor and effectiveness are afforded by recreation to the body and to the mind
    (B) recreation affords new vigor and effectiveness to the body and to the mind
    (C) there are afforded new vigor and effectiveness to the body and to the mind
    (D) by recreation the body and the mind are afforded new vigor and effectiveness
    (E) to the body and to the mind afford new vigor and effectiveness to themselves by recreation

42. Depending on skillful suggestion, argument is seldom used in advertising.

    (A) Depending on skillful suggestion, argument is seldom used in advertising.

    (B) Argument is seldom used in advertising, which depends instead on skillful suggestion.

    (C) Skillful suggestion is depended on by advertisers instead of argument.

    (D) Suggestion, which is more skillful, is used in place of argument by advertisers.

    (E) Instead of suggestion, depending on argument is used by skillful advertisers.

43. When this war is over, no nation will either be isolated in war or peace.

    (A) either be isolated in war or peace

    (B) be either isolated in war or peace

    (C) be isolated in neither war nor peace

    (D) be isolated either in war or in peace

    (E) be isolated neither in war or peace

44. Thanks to the prevailing westerly winds, dust blowing east from the drought-stricken plains travels halfway across the continent to fall on the cities of the East Coast.

    (A) blowing east from the drought-stricken plains

    (B) that, blowing east from the drought-stricken plains,

    (C) from the drought-stricken plains and blows east

    (D) that is from the drought-stricken plains blowing east

    (E) blowing east that is from the plains that are drought-stricken

45. Americans are learning that their concept of a research worker toiling alone in a laboratory and who discovers miraculous cures has been highly idealized and glamorized.

    (A) toiling alone in a laboratory and who discovers miraculous cures

    (B) toiling alone in a laboratory and discovers miraculous cures

    (C) toiling alone in a laboratory to discover miraculous cures

    (D) who toil alone in the laboratory and discover miraculous cures

    (E) has toiled alone hoping to discover miraculous cures

46. However many mistakes have been made in our past, the tradition of America, not only the champion of freedom but also fair play, still lives among millions who can see light and hope scarcely anywhere else.

    (A) not only the champion of freedom but also fair play

    (B) the champion of not only freedom but also of fair play

    (C) the champion not only of freedom but also of fair play

    (D) not only the champion but also freedom and fair play

    (E) not the champion of freedom only, but also fair play

47. <u>Examining the principal movements sweeping through the world, it can be seen</u> that they are being accelerated by the war.

(A) Examining the principal movements sweeping through the world, it can be seen

(B) Having examined the principal movements sweeping through the world, it can be seen

(C) Examining the principal movements sweeping through the world can be seen

(D) Examining the principal movements sweeping through the world, we can see

(E) It can be seen examining the principal movements sweeping through the world

48. <u>The FCC is broadening its view on what constitutes indecent programming,</u> radio stations are taking a closer look at their broadcasters' materials.

(A) The FCC is broadening its view on what constitutes indecent programming

(B) The FCC, broadening its view on what constitutes indecent programming, has caused

(C) The FCC is broadening its view on what constitutes indecent programming, as a result

(D) Since the FCC is broadening its view on what constitutes indecent programming

(E) The FCC, having broadened its view on what constitutes indecent programming

49. As district attorney, Elizabeth Holtzman not only had the responsibility of supervising a staff of dedicated young lawyers <u>but she had the task of maintaining good relations with the police also.</u>

(A) but she had the task of maintaining good relations with the police also

(B) but she also had the task of maintaining good relations with the police

(C) but also had the task of maintaining good relations with the police

(D) but she had the task to maintain good relations with the police also

(E) but also she had the task to maintain good relations with the police

50. Many politicians are now trying to take uncontroversial positions on <u>issues; the purpose being to allow them to appeal</u> to as wide a segment of the voting population as possible.

(A) issues; the purpose being to allow them to appeal

(B) issues in order to appeal

(C) issues, the purpose is to allow them to appeal

(D) issues and the purpose is to allow them to appeal

(E) issues; that was allowing them to appeal

The passage below is the unedited draft of a student's essay. Some of the essay needs to be rewritten to make the meaning clearer and more precise. Read the essay carefully.

The essay is followed by five questions about changes that might improve all or part of its organization, development, sentence structure, use of language, appropriateness to the audience, or use of standard written English. Choose the answer that most clearly and effectively expresses the student's intended meaning. Indicate your choice by filling in the corresponding space on the answer sheet.

[1] Throughout history, people have speculated about the future. [2] Will it be a utopia? they wondered. [3] Will injustice and poverty be eliminated? [4] Will people accept ethnic diversity, learning to live in peace? [5] Will the world be clean and unpolluted? [6] Or will technology aid us in creating a trap for ourselves we cannot escape, for example such as the world in 1984? [7] With the turn of the millennium just around the corner these questions are in the back of our minds.

[8] Science fiction often portrays the future as a technological Garden of Eden. [9] With interactive computers, TVs and robots at our command, we barely need to lift a finger to go to school, to work, to go shopping, and education is also easy and convenient. [10] Yet, the problems of the real twentieth century seem to point in another direction. [11] The environment, far from improving, keeps deteriorating. [12] Wars and other civil conflicts breakout regularly. [13] The world's population is growing out of control. [14] The majority of people on earth live in poverty. [15] Many of them are starving. [16] Illiteracy is a problem in most poor countries. [17] Diseases and malnourishment is very common. [18] Rich countries like the U.S.A. don't have the resources to help the "have-not" countries.

[19] Instead, think instead of all the silly inventions such as tablets you put in your toilet tank to make the water blue, or electric toothbrushes. [20] More money is spent on space and defense than on education and health care. [21] Advancements in agriculture can produce enough food to feed the whole country, yet people in the U.S. are starving.

[22] Although the USSR is gone, the nuclear threat continues from small countries like Iran. [23] Until the world puts its priorities straight, we can't look for a bright future in the twenty-first century, despite the rosy picture painted for us by the science fiction writers.

51. Considering the context of paragraph 1, which of the following is the best revision of sentence 6?

(A) Or will technology create a trap for ourselves from which we cannot escape, for example the world in *1984*?

(B) Or will technology aid people in creating a trap for themselves that they cannot escape; for example, the world in *1984*?

(C) Or will technology create a trap from which there is no escape, as it did in the world in *1984*?

(D) Or will technology trap us in an inescapable world, for example, it did so in the world of *1984*?

(E) Perhaps technology will aid people in creating a trap for themselves from which they cannot escape, just as they did it in the world of *1984*.

52. With regard to the essay as a whole, which of the following best describes the writer's intention in paragraph 1?

(A) To announce the purpose of the essay

(B) To compare two ideas discussed later in the essay

(C) To take a position on the essay's main issue

(D) To reveal the organization of the essay

(E) To raise questions that will be answered in the essay

53. Which of the following is the best revision of the underlined segment of sentence 9 below?

[9] With interactive computers, TVs and robots at our command, we barely need to lift a finger to go to school, to work, to go shopping, and education is also easy and convenient.

(A) and to go shopping, while education is also easy and convenient

(B) to go shopping, and getting an education is also easy and convenient

(C) to go shopping as well as educating ourselves are all easy and convenient

(D) to shop, and an easy and convenient education

(E) to shop, and to get an easy and convenient education

54. Which of the following is the most effective way to combine sentences 14, 15, 16, and 17?

(A) The majority of people on earth are living in poverty and are starving, with illiteracy, and disease and being malnourished are also a common problems.

(B) Common problems for the majority of people on earth are poverty, illiteracy, diseases, malnourishment, and many are illiterate.

(C) The majority of people on earth are poor, starving, sick, malnourished and illiterate.

(D) Common among the poor majority on earth is poverty, starvation, disease, malnourishment, and illiteracy.

(E) The majority of the earth's people living in poverty with starvation, disease, malnourishment and illiteracy a constant threat.

55. Which of the following revisions would most improve the overall coherence of the essay?

(A) Move sentence 7 to paragraph 2

(B) Move sentence 10 to paragraph 1

(C) Move sentence 22 to paragraph 2

(D) Delete sentence 8

(E) Delete sentence 23

Answer Key

1. **A**	11. **E**	21. **C**	31. **E**	41. **B**	51. **C**
2. **C**	12. **B**	22. **E**	32. **D**	42. **B**	52. **E**
3. **B**	13. **D**	23. **D**	33. **D**	43. **D**	53. **E**
4. **D**	14. **C**	24. **D**	34. **A**	44. **A**	54. **C**
5. **E**	15. **B**	25. **C**	35. **D**	45. **C**	55. **C**
6. **C**	16. **B**	26. **D**	36. **E**	46. **C**	
7. **D**	17. **D**	27. **E**	37. **B**	47. **D**	
8. **B**	18. **B**	28. **D**	38. **E**	48. **D**	
9. **B**	19. **B**	29. **E**	39. **C**	49. **C**	
10. **D**	20. **D**	30. **C**	40. **B**	50. **B**	

Answer Explanations

1. **(A)** Error in diction. Should be *all ready*. *All ready* means the group is ready; *already* means prior to a given time, previously.

2. **(C)** Error in pronoun case. Should be *us*. The expression *us girls* is the object of the preposition *by*.

3. **(B)** Error in subject-verb agreement. Should be *requires*. Verb should agree with the subject (*each one*).

4. **(D)** Should be *to say anything*. *Not to say nothing* is a double negative.

5. **(E)** Sentence is correct.

6. **(C)** Error in subject-verb agreement. Since the subject is Stanford White (singular), change *have designed* to *has designed*.

7. **(D)** Error in use of correlatives. Change *nor* to *or*. The correct form of the correlative pairs *either* with *or*.

8. **(B)** Error in parallel structure. Change *textbooks* to *reading textbooks*. To have parallel structure, the linked sentence elements must share the same grammatical form.

9. **(B)** Error in diction. Change *in back of* to *behind*.

10. **(D)** Error in pronoun case. Should be *me*. Pronoun is the object of the verb *can help*.

11. **(E)** Sentence is correct.

12. **(B)** Error in diction. Should be *all together*. *All together* means in a group; *altogether* means entirely.

13. **(D)** Improper use of *because*. Change to *that* (*The reason . . . was that . . . .*).

14. **(C)** Incorrect verbal. Change the participle *being* to the infinitive *to be*.

15. **(B)** Error in diction. Change *affect* (a verb meaning to influence or pretend) to *effect* (a noun meaning result).

16. **(B)** Error in pronoun case. Should be *me*. Subjects of infinitives are in the objective case.

17. **(D)** Error in idiom. Change *commentary of* to *commentary on.*
18. **(B)** Error in pronoun case. Should be *who.* The pronoun is the predicate complement of *will be* and is in the nominative case.
19. **(B)** Should be *had risen.* The past participle of the verb *to rise* is *risen.*
20. **(D)** Error in comparison of modifiers. Should be *better.* Do not use the superlative when comparing two things.
21. **(C)** Error in pronoun-number agreement. Should be *her* instead of *their.* The antecedent of the pronoun is *Jane and Oprah* (plural).
22. **(E)** Sentence is correct.
23. **(D)** Error in diction. Change *alluding* (meaning to refer indirectly) to *eluding* (meaning to evade).
24. **(D)** Confusion of verb and gerund (verbal noun). Change *is being walking* to *is walking.*
25. **(C)** Error in coordination and subordination. Change *yet* to *therefore* or another similar connector to clarify the connection between the clauses.
26. **(D)** Error in pronoun-number agreement. Should be *he or she.* The antecedent of the pronoun is *anyone* (singular).
27. **(E)** Sentence is correct.
28. **(D)** Error in sequence of tenses. Change *are abounding* to *have abounded.* The present perfect tense talks about an action that occurs at one time, but is seen in relation to another time.
29. **(E)** Sentence is correct.
30. **(C)** Error in pronoun case. Should be *your.* The pronoun modifying a gerund (verbal noun) should be in the possessive case.
31. **(E)** Sentence is correct.
32. **(D)** Error in subject-verb agreement. Since the subject is *conditions* (plural), change *has* to *have.*
33. **(D)** Error in pronoun. Since the sentence speaks about Hemingway's style rather than about Hemingway, the phrase should read *of it,* not *of him.*
34. **(A)** Error in sequence of tenses. Change *has aroused* to *aroused.* The present perfect tense (*has aroused*) is used for indefinite time. In this sentence, the time is defined as *the better part of a year.*
35. **(D)** Lack of parallel structure. Change *in producing motion pictures* to *motion picture producer.*
36. **(E)** This question involves two aspects of correct English. *Neither* should be followed by *nor; either* by *or.* Choices A and D are, therefore, incorrect. The words *neither . . . nor* and *either . . . or* should be placed before the two items being discussed—*to be critical* and *to examine.* Choice E meets both requirements.
37. **(B)** This question tests agreement. Errors in subject-verb agreement and pronoun-number agreement are both involved. *Community* (singular) needs a

singular verb, *influences*. Also, the pronoun that refers to *community* should be singular *(its)*.

38. (E) Error in following conventions. This is an incomplete sentence or fragment. The sentence needs a verb to establish a principal clause. Choice E provides the verb (*is recognized*) and presents the only complete sentence in the group.

39. (C) *Would have been expected* is incorrect as a verb in a clause introduced by the conjunction *if*. *Had been expected* or *were expected* is preferable. *To have considered* does not follow correct sequence of tense and should be changed to *to consider*.

40. (B) Error in modification and word order. One way of correcting a dangling participle is to change the participial phrase to a clause. Choices B and D substitute clauses for the phrase. However, Choice D changes the meaning of the sentence. Choice B is correct.

41. (B) Error in modification and word order. As it stands, the sentence contains a dangling modifier. This is corrected by making *recreation* the subject of the sentence, in the process switching from the passive to the active voice. Choice E also provides a subject for the sentence; however, the meaning of the sentence is changed in Choice E.

42. (B) Error in modification and word order. As presented, the sentence contains a dangling participle, *depending*. Choice B corrects this error. The other choices change the emphasis presented by the author.

43. (D) Error in word order. *Either . . . or* should precede the two choices offered (*in war* and *in peace*).

44. (A) Sentence is correct.

45. (C) Error in parallelism. In the underlined phrase, you will find two modifiers of *worker-toiling* and *who discovers*. The first is a participial phrase and the second a clause. This results in an error in parallel structure. Choice B also has an error in parallel structure. Choice C corrects this by eliminating one of the modifiers of *worker*. Choice D corrects the error in parallel structure but introduces an error in agreement between subject and verb—*who* (singular) and *toil* (plural). Choice E changes the tense and also the meaning of the original sentence.

46. (C) Error in parallelism. Parallel structure requires that *not only* and *but also* immediately precede the words they limit.

47. (D) Error in modification and word order. Choices A, B, and E are incorrect because of the dangling participle. Choice C is incoherent. Choice D correctly eliminates the dangling participle by introducing the subject *we*.

48. (D) Error in comma splice. The punctuation in Choices A and C creates a run-on sentence. Choices B and E are both ungrammatical. Choice D corrects the run-on sentence by changing the beginning clause into the adverb clause that starts with the subordinating conjunction *since*.

49. (C) Error in parallelism. Since the words *not only* immediately precede the verb in the first half of the sentence, the words *but also* should immediately precede the verb in the second half. This error in parallel structure is corrected in Choice C.

50. (B) Error in coordination and subordination. The punctuation in Choices A, C, D, and E creates an incomplete sentence or fragment. Choice B corrects the error by linking the elements with *in order to.*

51. (C) Choice A is awkward and shifts the pronoun usage in the paragraph from third to first person. Choice B is awkward and contains a semicolon error. A semicolon is used to separate two independent clauses. The material after the semicolon is a sentence fragment. Choice C is succinctly and accurately expressed. It is the best answer. Choice D contains a comma splice between *world* and *for.* A comma may not be used to join two independent clauses. Choice E is awkwardly expressed and contains the pronoun *it,* which lacks a clear referent.

52. (E) Choice A indirectly describes the purpose of paragraph 1 but does not identify the writer's main intention. Choices B, C, and D fail to describe the writer's main intention. Choice E accurately describes the writer's main intention. It is the best answer.

53. (E) Choice A is grammatically correct but cumbersome. Choice B contains an error in parallel construction. The clause that begins *and getting* is not grammatically parallel to the previous items on the list. Choice C contains a mixed construction. The first and last parts of the sentence are grammatically unrelated. Choice D contains faulty parallel structure. Choice E is correct and accurately expressed. It is the best answer.

54. (C) Choice A is wordy and awkwardly expressed. Choice B contains an error in parallel structure. The clause *and many are illiterate* is not grammatically parallel to the previous items on the list of problems. Choice C is concise and accurately expressed. It is the best answer. Choice D is concise, but it contains an error in subject-verb agreement. The subject is *poverty, starvation . . . etc.,* which requires a plural verb; the verb *is* is singular. Choice E is a sentence fragment; it has no main verb.

55. (C) Choice A should stay put because it provides a transition between the questions in paragraph 1 and the beginning of paragraph 2. Choice B is a pivotal sentence in paragraph 2 and should not be moved. Choice C fits the topics of paragraph 2; therefore, sentence 22 should be moved to paragraph 2. Choice C is the best answer. Choice D is needed as an introductory sentence in paragraph 2. It should not be deleted. Choice E provides the essay with a meaningful conclusion and should not be deleted.

7 Two Practice Tests

A two-hour and ten-minute test can be exhausting. Here are some tips that will help you cope on the day of the test:

- Build up your stamina. You have to get used to answering tough questions for more than two hours straight. Take these two practice tests under timed conditions. Try to stay focused the entire time. This practice will pay off when you take the actual test.
- Be well rested on the day of the test. Last-minute cramming will only tire you out. Try to organize your study plan so that you can quit prepping a few days before you take the test. Above all, get a good night's sleep the night before the test.
- As you take the test, use the short breaks to stretch and get out the kinks. Breathe in deeply, and let go of the tension as you breathe out. You've done a good job preparing, so think positive, and relax.

ANSWER SHEET—PRACTICE TEST 1

Section 1
Critical Reading
25 minutes

1 Ⓐ Ⓑ Ⓒ Ⓓ Ⓔ
2 Ⓐ Ⓑ Ⓒ Ⓓ Ⓔ
3 Ⓐ Ⓑ Ⓒ Ⓓ Ⓔ
4 Ⓐ Ⓑ Ⓒ Ⓓ Ⓔ
5 Ⓐ Ⓑ Ⓒ Ⓓ Ⓔ
6 Ⓐ Ⓑ Ⓒ Ⓓ Ⓔ
7 Ⓐ Ⓑ Ⓒ Ⓓ Ⓔ
8 Ⓐ Ⓑ Ⓒ Ⓓ Ⓔ
9 Ⓐ Ⓑ Ⓒ Ⓓ Ⓔ
10 Ⓐ Ⓑ Ⓒ Ⓓ Ⓔ
11 Ⓐ Ⓑ Ⓒ Ⓓ Ⓔ
12 Ⓐ Ⓑ Ⓒ Ⓓ Ⓔ
13 Ⓐ Ⓑ Ⓒ Ⓓ Ⓔ
14 Ⓐ Ⓑ Ⓒ Ⓓ Ⓔ
15 Ⓐ Ⓑ Ⓒ Ⓓ Ⓔ
16 Ⓐ Ⓑ Ⓒ Ⓓ Ⓔ
17 Ⓐ Ⓑ Ⓒ Ⓓ Ⓔ
18 Ⓐ Ⓑ Ⓒ Ⓓ Ⓔ
19 Ⓐ Ⓑ Ⓒ Ⓓ Ⓔ
20 Ⓐ Ⓑ Ⓒ Ⓓ Ⓔ
21 Ⓐ Ⓑ Ⓒ Ⓓ Ⓔ
22 Ⓐ Ⓑ Ⓒ Ⓓ Ⓔ
23 Ⓐ Ⓑ Ⓒ Ⓓ Ⓔ
24 Ⓐ Ⓑ Ⓒ Ⓓ Ⓔ

Section 2
Math
25 minutes

1 Ⓐ Ⓑ Ⓒ Ⓓ Ⓔ
2 Ⓐ Ⓑ Ⓒ Ⓓ Ⓔ
3 Ⓐ Ⓑ Ⓒ Ⓓ Ⓔ
4 Ⓐ Ⓑ Ⓒ Ⓓ Ⓔ
5 Ⓐ Ⓑ Ⓒ Ⓓ Ⓔ
6 Ⓐ Ⓑ Ⓒ Ⓓ Ⓔ
7 Ⓐ Ⓑ Ⓒ Ⓓ Ⓔ
8 Ⓐ Ⓑ Ⓒ Ⓓ Ⓔ
9 Ⓐ Ⓑ Ⓒ Ⓓ Ⓔ
10 Ⓐ Ⓑ Ⓒ Ⓓ Ⓔ
11 Ⓐ Ⓑ Ⓒ Ⓓ Ⓔ
12 Ⓐ Ⓑ Ⓒ Ⓓ Ⓔ
13 Ⓐ Ⓑ Ⓒ Ⓓ Ⓔ
14 Ⓐ Ⓑ Ⓒ Ⓓ Ⓔ
15 Ⓐ Ⓑ Ⓒ Ⓓ Ⓔ
16 Ⓐ Ⓑ Ⓒ Ⓓ Ⓔ
17 Ⓐ Ⓑ Ⓒ Ⓓ Ⓔ
18 Ⓐ Ⓑ Ⓒ Ⓓ Ⓔ
19 Ⓐ Ⓑ Ⓒ Ⓓ Ⓔ
20 Ⓐ Ⓑ Ⓒ Ⓓ Ⓔ

Section 3
Critical Reading
25 minutes

25 Ⓐ Ⓑ Ⓒ Ⓓ Ⓔ
26 Ⓐ Ⓑ Ⓒ Ⓓ Ⓔ
27 Ⓐ Ⓑ Ⓒ Ⓓ Ⓔ
28 Ⓐ Ⓑ Ⓒ Ⓓ Ⓔ
29 Ⓐ Ⓑ Ⓒ Ⓓ Ⓔ
30 Ⓐ Ⓑ Ⓒ Ⓓ Ⓔ
31 Ⓐ Ⓑ Ⓒ Ⓓ Ⓔ
32 Ⓐ Ⓑ Ⓒ Ⓓ Ⓔ
33 Ⓐ Ⓑ Ⓒ Ⓓ Ⓔ
34 Ⓐ Ⓑ Ⓒ Ⓓ Ⓔ
35 Ⓐ Ⓑ Ⓒ Ⓓ Ⓔ
36 Ⓐ Ⓑ Ⓒ Ⓓ Ⓔ

37 Ⓐ Ⓑ Ⓒ Ⓓ Ⓔ
38 Ⓐ Ⓑ Ⓒ Ⓓ Ⓔ
39 Ⓐ Ⓑ Ⓒ Ⓓ Ⓔ
40 Ⓐ Ⓑ Ⓒ Ⓓ Ⓔ
41 Ⓐ Ⓑ Ⓒ Ⓓ Ⓔ
42 Ⓐ Ⓑ Ⓒ Ⓓ Ⓔ
43 Ⓐ Ⓑ Ⓒ Ⓓ Ⓔ
44 Ⓐ Ⓑ Ⓒ Ⓓ Ⓔ
45 Ⓐ Ⓑ Ⓒ Ⓓ Ⓔ
46 Ⓐ Ⓑ Ⓒ Ⓓ Ⓔ
47 Ⓐ Ⓑ Ⓒ Ⓓ Ⓔ
48 Ⓐ Ⓑ Ⓒ Ⓓ Ⓔ

Section 4
Math
25 minutes

21 Ⓐ Ⓑ Ⓒ Ⓓ Ⓔ
22 Ⓐ Ⓑ Ⓒ Ⓓ Ⓔ
23 Ⓐ Ⓑ Ⓒ Ⓓ Ⓔ
24 Ⓐ Ⓑ Ⓒ Ⓓ Ⓔ
25 Ⓐ Ⓑ Ⓒ Ⓓ Ⓔ
26 Ⓐ Ⓑ Ⓒ Ⓓ Ⓔ
27 Ⓐ Ⓑ Ⓒ Ⓓ Ⓔ
28 Ⓐ Ⓑ Ⓒ Ⓓ Ⓔ

29

30

Section 5
Writing
30 minutes

1 Ⓐ Ⓑ Ⓒ Ⓓ Ⓔ
2 Ⓐ Ⓑ Ⓒ Ⓓ Ⓔ
3 Ⓐ Ⓑ Ⓒ Ⓓ Ⓔ
4 Ⓐ Ⓑ Ⓒ Ⓓ Ⓔ
5 Ⓐ Ⓑ Ⓒ Ⓓ Ⓔ
6 Ⓐ Ⓑ Ⓒ Ⓓ Ⓔ
7 Ⓐ Ⓑ Ⓒ Ⓓ Ⓔ
8 Ⓐ Ⓑ Ⓒ Ⓓ Ⓔ
9 Ⓐ Ⓑ Ⓒ Ⓓ Ⓔ
10 Ⓐ Ⓑ Ⓒ Ⓓ Ⓔ
11 Ⓐ Ⓑ Ⓒ Ⓓ Ⓔ
12 Ⓐ Ⓑ Ⓒ Ⓓ Ⓔ
13 Ⓐ Ⓑ Ⓒ Ⓓ Ⓔ
14 Ⓐ Ⓑ Ⓒ Ⓓ Ⓔ
15 Ⓐ Ⓑ Ⓒ Ⓓ Ⓔ
16 Ⓐ Ⓑ Ⓒ Ⓓ Ⓔ
17 Ⓐ Ⓑ Ⓒ Ⓓ Ⓔ
18 Ⓐ Ⓑ Ⓒ Ⓓ Ⓔ
19 Ⓐ Ⓑ Ⓒ Ⓓ Ⓔ
20 Ⓐ Ⓑ Ⓒ Ⓓ Ⓔ

21 Ⓐ Ⓑ Ⓒ Ⓓ Ⓔ
22 Ⓐ Ⓑ Ⓒ Ⓓ Ⓔ
23 Ⓐ Ⓑ Ⓒ Ⓓ Ⓔ
24 Ⓐ Ⓑ Ⓒ Ⓓ Ⓔ
25 Ⓐ Ⓑ Ⓒ Ⓓ Ⓔ
26 Ⓐ Ⓑ Ⓒ Ⓓ Ⓔ
27 Ⓐ Ⓑ Ⓒ Ⓓ Ⓔ
28 Ⓐ Ⓑ Ⓒ Ⓓ Ⓔ
29 Ⓐ Ⓑ Ⓒ Ⓓ Ⓔ
30 Ⓐ Ⓑ Ⓒ Ⓓ Ⓔ
31 Ⓐ Ⓑ Ⓒ Ⓓ Ⓔ
32 Ⓐ Ⓑ Ⓒ Ⓓ Ⓔ
33 Ⓐ Ⓑ Ⓒ Ⓓ Ⓔ
34 Ⓐ Ⓑ Ⓒ Ⓓ Ⓔ
35 Ⓐ Ⓑ Ⓒ Ⓓ Ⓔ
36 Ⓐ Ⓑ Ⓒ Ⓓ Ⓔ
37 Ⓐ Ⓑ Ⓒ Ⓓ Ⓔ
38 Ⓐ Ⓑ Ⓒ Ⓓ Ⓔ
39 Ⓐ Ⓑ Ⓒ Ⓓ Ⓔ

PRACTICE TEST 1

SECTION 1/CRITICAL READING
Time—25 minutes   24 questions (1–24)

> For each question in this section, select the best answer from among the choices given and fill in the corresponding circle on the answer sheet.

Each sentence below has one or two blanks, each blank indicating that something has been omitted. Beneath the sentence are five words or sets of words labeled A through E. Choose the word or set of words that, when inserted in the sentence, best fits the meaning of the sentence as a whole.

EXAMPLE:

Medieval kingdoms did not become constitutional republics overnight; on the contrary, the change was ----.

(A) unpopular   (B) unexpected
(C) advantageous   (D) sufficient   (E) gradual

---

1. Unhappily, the psychology experiment was ---- by the subjects' awareness of the presence of observers in their midst.
   (A) muted   (B) palliated   (C) marred
   (D) clarified   (E) concluded

2. Until James learned to be more ---- about writing down his homework assignments, he seldom knew when any assignment was due.

   (A) obstinate   (B) contrary   (C) opportunistic   (D) methodical
   (E) literate

3. Despite all the advertisements singing the ---- of the new product, she remained ---- its merits, wanting to see what *Consumer Reports* had to say about its claims.

   (A) virtues..an optimist about
   (B) praises..a skeptic about
   (C) joys..a convert to
   (D) defects..a cynic about
   (E) advantages..a believer in

4. After working on the project night and day for two full months, Sandy felt that she had earned a ----.

(A) penalty   (B) scolding   (C) degree
(D) chore   (E) respite

5. Even though the basic organization of the brain does not change after birth, details of its structure and function remain ---- for some time, particularly in the cerebral cortex.

(A) plastic   (B) immutable   (C) essential
(D) unknown   (E) static

The passages below are followed by questions on their content; questions following a pair of related passages may also be based on the relationship between the paired passages. Answer the questions on the basis of what is stated or implied in the passages and in any introductory material that may be provided.

Questions 6–9 are based on the following passages.

Passage 1

Spiders, and in particular hairy spiders, possess a highly developed sense of touch. Tarantulas, for example, perceive three distinct types of touch: a light whisper that flutters the sensitive leg hairs; a smooth
Line rubbing of the body hair; a steady pressure against the body wall. Press
(5) a pencil against the tarantula's body wall and it will back away cautiously without reacting defensively. However, if the tarantula sees the pencil approaching from above, the motion will excite a defensive reaction: it will rear up, lifting its front legs and baring its fangs, maintaining this attack stance until the pencil stops moving.

Passage 2

(10) "The eensy-weensy spider climbed up the waterspout..."
Tarantulas are the world's largest spiders. The very largest live in the jungles of South America, and, in the days when bananas were transported as large bunches on stalks, tarantulas often were accidentally imported with the fruit. Stout-bodied and hairy, tarantulas can create
(15) great panic among arachnophobes (people who fear spiders). Actually, these large spiders are gentle giants, whose temperaments do not match their intimidating appearance. Docile and non-aggressive, tarantulas do not bite unless they are severely provoked. Even if they do bite, their bites are not particularly dangerous; they are about as painful as bee
(20) stings, and should be treated similarly.

6. In Passage 1, the author's attitude toward tarantulas can best be described as

   (A) apprehensive   (B) sentimental
   (C) approving   (D) objective   (E) defensive

7. The word "excite" in line 7 most nearly means

   (A) irritate   (B) delight   (C) stimulate
   (D) exhilarate   (E) discompose

8. Which statement best expresses the relationship between the two passages?

   (A) Passage 1 describes its subject by supplying details with which the author of Passage 2 would disagree.
   (B) Passage 1 provides scientific observations of the subject, while Passage 2 offers a popular introduction to the subject.
   (C) Passage 1 presents its subject in highly figurative terms, while Passage 2 is more technical in nature.
   (D) Both Passage 1 and Passage 2 assume readers will have an automatically negative response to the subject under discussion.
   (E) Passage 2 is objective in its presentation, while Passage 1 is more personal in tone.

9. Which generalization about tarantulas is supported by both passages?

   (A) They have a marked degree of intelligence.
   (B) Their gentleness belies their frightening looks.
   (C) They have been unfairly maligned by arachnophobes.
   (D) They are capable of acting to defend themselves.
   (E) They are easily intimidated by others.

Each passage below is followed by questions based on its content. Answer the questions following each passage on the basis of what is stated or implied in that passage and in any introductory material that may be provided.

Questions 10–15 are based on the following passage.

The following passage is from a book written by the naturalist Konrad Lorenz and published in 1952.

In the chimney the autumn wind sings the song of the elements, and the old firs before my study window wave excitedly with their arms and sing so loudly in chorus that I can hear their sighing melody through the double panes. Suddenly, from above, a dozen black, streamlined projectiles shoot across the piece of clouded sky for which my window forms a frame. Heavily as stones they fall, fall to the tops of the firs where they

Line

(5)

suddenly sprout wings, become birds and then light feather rags that the storm seizes and whirls out of my line of vision, more rapidly than they were borne into it.

(10)   I walk to the window to watch this extraordinary game that the jackdaws are playing with the wind. A game? Yes, indeed, it is a game, in the most literal sense of the word: practiced movements, indulged in and enjoyed for their own sake and not for the achievement of a special object. And rest assured, these are not merely inborn, purely instinctive *(15)* actions, but movements that have been carefully learned. All these feats that the birds are performing, their wonderful exploitation of the wind, their amazingly exact assessment of distances and, above all, their understanding of local wind conditions, their knowledge of all the up-currents, air pockets and eddies—all this proficiency is no inheritance, *(20)* but, for each bird, an individually acquired accomplishment.

    And look what they do with the wind! At first sight, you, poor human being, think that the storm is playing with the birds, like a cat with a mouse, but soon you see, with astonishment, that it is the fury of the elements that here plays the role of the mouse and that the jackdaws are *(25)* treating the storm exactly as the cat its unfortunate victim. Nearly, but only nearly, do they give the storm its head, let it throw them high, high into the heavens, till they seem to fall upwards, then, with a casual flap of a wing, they turn themselves over, open their pinions for a fraction of a second from below against the wind, and dive—with an acceleration *(30)* far greater than that of a falling stone—into the depths below. Another tiny jerk of the wing and they return to their normal position and, on close-reefed sails, shoot away with breathless speed into the teeth of the gale, hundreds of yards to the west: this all playfully and without effort, just to spite the stupid wind that tries to drive them towards the *(35)* east. The sightless monster itself must perform the work of propelling the birds through the air at a rate of well over 80 miles an hour; the jackdaws do nothing to help beyond a few lazy adjustments of their black wings. Sovereign control over the power of the elements, intoxicating triumph of the living organism over the pitiless strength of the inorganic!

10. The "arms" mentioned in line 2 are

  (A) wings .(B) storm winds   (C) heraldic emblems
  (D) branches   (E) missiles

11. According to the passage, the bird's skill in adapting to wind conditions is

  (A) genetically determined   (B) limited   (C) undependable
  (D) dependent on the elements   (E) gained through practice

12. The phrase "rest assured" in line 14 most likely means

    (A) sleep securely

    (B) others are certain

    (C) be confident

    (D) remain poised

    (E) in their sure leisure

13. The "sightless monster" mentioned in line 35 is

    (A) an unobservant watcher

    (B) a falling stone

    (C) an airplane

    (D) the powerful windstorm

    (E) a blind predator

14. Throughout the passage, the author is most impressed by

    (A) the direction-finding skills of the birds

    (B) the jackdaws' superhuman strength

    (C) his inability to join the jackdaws in their game

    (D) the fleeting nature of his encounter with the birds

    (E) the jackdaws' mastery of the forces of nature

15. The author does all of the following EXCEPT

    (A) use a metaphor

    (B) argue a cause

    (C) clarify a term

    (D) describe a behavior

    (E) dismiss a notion

Questions 16–24 are based on the following passage.

The passage below, taken from a museum bulletin, discusses tapestry making as an art form.

        Tapestries are made on looms. Their distinctive weave is basically simple: the colored weft threads interface regularly with the mono-chrome warps, as in darning or plain cloth, but as they do so, they form
Line a design by reversing their direction when a change of color is needed.
(5) The wefts are beaten down to cover the warps completely. The result is a design or picture that is the fabric itself, not one laid upon a ground like an embroidery, a print, or brocading. The back and front of a tapestry show the same design. The weaver always follows a preexisting model, generally a drawing or painting, known as the cartoon, which in most
(10) cases he reproduces as exactly as he can. Long training is needed to

become a professional tapestry weaver. It can take as much as a year to produce a yard of very finely woven tapestry.

Tapestry-woven fabrics have been made from China to Peru and from very early times to the present day, but large wall hangings in this tech-

(15) nique, mainly of wool, are typically Northern European. Few examples predating the late fourteenth century have survived, but from about 1400 tapestries were an essential part of aristocratic life. The prince or great nobleman sent his plate and his tapestries ahead of him to furnish his castles before his arrival as he traveled through his domains; both had

(20) the same function, to display his wealth and social position. It has frequently been suggested that tapestries helped to heat stone-walled rooms, but this is a modern idea; comfort was of minor importance in the Middle Ages. Tapestries were portable grandeur, instant splendor, taking the place, north of the Alps, of painted frescoes further south.

(25) They were hung without gaps between them, covering entire walls and often doors as well. Only very occasionally were they made as individual works of art such as altar frontals. They were usually commissioned or bought as sets, or "chambers," and constituted the most important furnishings of any grand room, except for the display of plate, throughout

(30) the Middle Ages and the sixteenth century. Later, woven silks, ornamental wood carving, stucco decoration, and painted leather gradually replaced tapestry as expensive wall coverings, until at last wallpaper was introduced in the late eighteenth century and eventually swept away almost everything else.

(35) By the end of the eighteenth century, the "tapestry-room" [a room with every available wall surface covered with wall hangings] was no longer fashionable: paper had replaced wall coverings of wool and silk. Tapestries, of course, were still made, but in the nineteenth century they often seem to have been produced mainly as individual works of art that

(40) astonish by their resemblance to oil paintings, tours de force woven with a remarkably large number of wefts per inch. In England during the second half of the century, William Morris attempted to reverse this trend and to bring tapestry weaving back to its true principles, those he considered to have governed it in the Middle Ages. He imitated medieval

(45) tapestries in both style and technique, using few warps to the inch, but he did not make sets; the original function for which tapestry is so admirably suited—completely covering the walls of a room and providing sumptuous surroundings for a life of pomp and splendor—could not be revived. Morris's example has been followed, though with less imita-

(50) tion of medieval style, by many weavers of the present century, whose coarsely woven cloths hang like single pictures and can be admired as examples of contemporary art.

16. Tapestry weaving may be characterized as which of the following?

   I. Time-consuming
   II. Spontaneous in concept
   III. Faithful to an original

   (A) I only   (B) III only   (C) I and II only
   (D) I and III only   (E) II and III only

17. The word "distinctive" in line 1 means

   (A) characteristic
   (B) stylish
   (C) discriminatory
   (D) eminent
   (E) articulate

18. Renaissance nobles carried tapestries with them to demonstrate their

   (A) piety
   (B) consequence
   (C) aesthetic judgment
   (D) need for privacy
   (E) dislike for cold

19. The word "ground" in line 6 means

   (A) terrain   (B) dust   (C) thread   (D) base   (E) pigment

20. The statement in line 22 ("but this . . , idea") is best described as an example of

   (A) a definition of a central concept
   (B) an acknowledgment of a principle
   (C) a dismissal of a common view
   (D) an emotional refutation
   (E) a moral proclamation

21. In line 28, the quotation marks around the work "chambers" serves to

   (A) emphasize the inadequacy of the particular choice of words
   (B) point out the triteness of the term
   (C) indicate the use of a colloquialism
   (D) illustrate the need for the word to be stressed when spoken aloud
   (E) indicate the word is being used in a special sense

22. The author regards William Morris (lines 42–44) as

   (A) a bold innovator
   (B) an uninspired hack
   (C) a medieval nobleman
   (D) a cartoonist
   (E) a traditionalist

23. In contrast to nineteenth-century tapestries, contemporary tapestries

    (A) are displayed in sets of panels
    (B) echo medieval themes
    (C) faithfully copy oil paintings
    (D) have a less fine weave
    (E) indicate the owner's social position

24. The primary purpose of the passage is to

    (A) explain the process of tapestry making
    (B) contrast Eastern and Western schools of tapestry
    (C) analyze the reasons for the decline in popularity of tapestries
    (D) provide a historical perspective on tapestry making
    (E) advocate a return to a more colorful way of life

IF YOU FINISH IN LESS THAN 25 MINUTES,
YOU MAY CHECK YOUR WORK ON THIS **S T O P**
SECTION ONLY. DO NOT TURN TO ANY
OTHER SECTION IN THE TEST.

SECTION 2/MATHEMATICAL REASONING
Time—25 minutes   20 questions (1–20)

For each question in this section, determine which of the five choices is correct and blacken that choice on your answer sheet. You may use any blank space on the page for your work.

Notes:

- You may use a calculator whenever you believe it will be helpful.
- Use the diagrams provided to help you solve the problems. Unless you see the phrase "<u>Note</u>: Figure not drawn to scale" under a diagram, it has been drawn as accurately as possible. Unless it is stated that a figure is three-dimensional, you may assume that it lies in a plane.

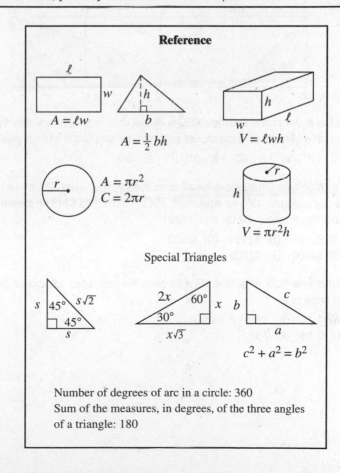

Reference

$A = \ell w$

$A = \frac{1}{2} bh$

$V = \ell wh$

$A = \pi r^2$
$C = 2\pi r$

$V = \pi r^2 h$

Special Triangles

$c^2 + a^2 = b^2$

Number of degrees of arc in a circle: 360
Sum of the measures, in degrees, of the three angles of a triangle: 180

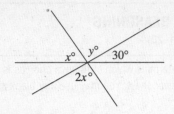

1. In the figure above, what is the value of y?

   (A) 50   (B) 70   (C) 90   (D) 100   (E) 140

2. If $(a + 12) - 12 = 12$, then $a =$

   (A) -12 (B) 0   (C) 12   (D) 24   (E) 36

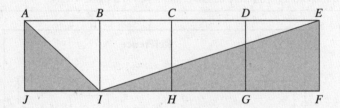

3. In the figure above, rectangle *AEFJ* is divided into four equal squares. What is the ratio of the area of the shaded region to the area of the white region?

   (A) 1:2   (B) 3:5   (C) 5:8   (D) 1:1   (E) 5:3

4. The Albertville Little League raised some money. They used 72% of the money to buy uniforms, 19% for equipment, and the remaining $243 for a team party. How much money did the team raise?

   (A) $2400   (B) $2450   (C) $2500
   (D) $2600   (E) $2700

5. If it is now 1:30, what time will it be when the hour hand has moved through an angle of 20°?

   (A) 1:45   (B) 1:50   (C) 2:00
   (D) 2:10   (E) 2:15

6. In the figure above, lines k and ℓ are parallel, and line k passes through C, one of the vertices of equilateral triangle ABC. What is the value of a?

(A) 40   (B) 50   (C) 60   (D) 80   (E) 90

7. If the difference of two numbers is less than the sum of the numbers, which of the following must be true?

(A) Neither number is positive.
(B) At least one of the numbers is positive.
(C) Exactly one of the numbers is positive.
(D) Both numbers are positive.
(E) None of these statements must be true.

8. 20 is what percent of C?

(A) $20C\%$ (B) $\dfrac{1}{20C}\%$ (C) $\dfrac{20}{C}\%$

(D) $\dfrac{200}{C}\%$ (E) $\dfrac{2000}{C}\%$

9. Two sides of a right triangle are 5 and 9. Which of the following could be the length of the third side?

I. $\sqrt{56}$

II. $\sqrt{76}$

III. $\sqrt{106}$

(A) I only   (B) III only   (C) I and II only
(D) I and III only   (E) I, II, and III

10. Which of the following is an equation of a line that is parallel to the line whose equation is $y = 2x - 3$?

(A) $y = 2x + 3$ (B) $y = -2x - 3$

(C) $y = \dfrac{1}{2}x - 3$ (D) $y = -\dfrac{1}{2}x + 3$

(E) $y = -\dfrac{1}{2}x - 3$

11. If n is an integer and n, $n + 1$, and $n + 2$ are the lengths of the sides of a triangle, which of the following could be the value of n?

   I. 1
   II. 3
   III. 13

   (A) I only   (B) II only   (C) III only
   (D) II and III only   (E) I, II, and III

12. A bank raised the minimum payment on its charge accounts from $10 to $20 per month. What was the percent increase in the minimum monthly payment?

   (A) 10%   (B) 20%   (C) 50%
   (D) 100%   (E) 200%

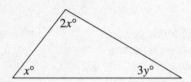

13. For the figure above, which of the following is an expression for y in terms of x?

   (A) x (B) $60 - x$ (C) $x - 60$
   (D) $180 - 3x$ (E) $90 - x$

Questions 14–15 refer to the following definition.

For any number x, $\|x\| = \dfrac{2}{3}x^2$.

14. What is the value of $\|16^2\|$?
   (A) 16   (B) 24   (C) 144   (D) 576   (E) 864

15. If $y = \dfrac{2}{3}x$, which of the following is an expression for $\|y\|$ in terms of x?

   (A) $\dfrac{2}{3}x^3$ (B) $\dfrac{4}{9}x^2$ (C) $\dfrac{4}{9}x^3$ (D) $\dfrac{8}{27}x^2$ (E) $\dfrac{8}{27}x^3$

16. If $f(x) = 9x + 9^x$, what is the value of $f\left(\dfrac{1}{2}\right)$?
   (A) 3   (B) 6   (C) 7.5   (D) 9   (E) 9.9

17. The road from Jack's house to Jill's is exactly 10 kilometers. At different times, Jack and Jill each left home and walked toward the other's house. They walked at the same rate and they met at noon, 4 kilometers from Jill's house. If Jack left at 10:00, at what time did Jill leave?

(A) 9:40   (B) 10:00   (C) 10:40
(D) 11:00   (E) 11:20

18. The Northport High School French Club has twice as many female members as male members. One day, the percentage of female members attending a meeting of the club was twice the percentage of male members. What percent of those attending the meeting were males?

(A) 20%   (B) 25%   (C) $33\frac{1}{3}$%   (D) 50%

(E) It cannot be determined from the information given.

19. If a and b are the lengths of the legs of a right triangle whose hypotenuse is 10 and whose area is 20, what is the value of $(a + b)^2$?

(A) 100   (B) 120   (C) 140   (D) 180   (E) 200

20. A lottery prize worth d dollars was to be divided equally among 4 winners. It was subsequently discovered that there were 2 additional winners, and the prize would now be divided equally among all the winners. How much more money, in dollars, would each original winner have received if the additional winners were not discovered?

(A) $\frac{d}{12}$ (B) $\frac{d}{6}$ (C) $\frac{d}{4}$ (D) $\frac{12}{d}$ (E) $\frac{6}{d}$

IF YOU FINISH IN LESS THAN 25 MINUTES, YOU MAY CHECK YOUR WORK ON THIS SECTION ONLY. DO NOT TURN TO ANY OTHER SECTION IN THE TEST.   **STOP**

SECTION 3/CRITICAL READING
Time—25 minutes   24 questions (25–48)

> For each question in this section, select the best answer from among the choices given and fill in the corresponding oval on the answer sheet.

Each sentence below has one or two blanks, each blank indicating that something has been omitted. Beneath the sentence are five words or sets of words labeled A through E. Choose the word or set of words that, when inserted in the sentence, best fits the meaning of the sentence as a whole.

EXAMPLE:

Medieval kingdoms did not become constitutional republics overnight; on the contrary, the change was ----.

(A) unpopular   (B) unexpected
(C) advantageous   (D) sufficient   (E) gradual

Ⓐ Ⓑ Ⓒ Ⓓ ●

---

25. Nothing anyone could say was able to alter North's ---- that his attempt to lie to Congress was justified.

(A) demand   (B) conviction   (C) maxim   (D) fear   (E) ambivalence

26. Excessive use of coal and oil eventually may ---- the earth's supply of fossil fuels, leaving us in need of a new source of energy.

(A) replenish   (B) magnify   (C) merge   (D) deplete   (E) redirect

27. Contemporary authorities have come to ---- the use of "healthy" in place of "healthful"; however, they still reject the use of "disinterested" in place of "uninterested."

(A) condone   (B) evaluate   (C) imitate   (D) disdain   (E) repudiate

28. Michael's severe bout of the flu ---- him so much that he was too tired to go to work for a week.

(A) recuperated   (B) diagnosed   (C) incarcerated
(D) captivated   (E) debilitated

29. Though Alec Guinness was determined to make a name for himself on the stage, when he considered the uncertainties of an actor's life, his ---- wavered.

(A) resolution   (B) reverence   (C) affectation   (D) theatricality
(E) skepticism

30. In *Gulliver's Travels*, Swift's intent is ----; he exposes the follies of English society by ridiculing the follies of the Lilliputians.

(A) elegiac   (B) prophetic   (C) satirical
(D) questionable   (E) derivative

31. Even the threat of sudden death could not ---- the intrepid pilot and explorer Beryl Markham; a true ----, she risked her life countless times to set records for flying small planes.

(A) intimidate..patrician
(B) divert..renegade
(C) interest..dilettante
(D) daunt..daredevil
(E) survive..firebrand

32. As an indefatigable consumer advocate, Ralph Nader is constantly engaged in ---- the claims of unscrupulous merchandisers and cautioning the public to exercise a healthy ----.

(A) asserting..autonomy
(B) deflating..prodigality
(C) debunking..skepticism
(D) affirming..indifference
(E) exaggerating..optimism

Each of the passages below precedes two questions based on its content. Answer the questions following each passage on the basis of what is stated or implied in that passsage.

Questions 33 and 34 are based on the following passage.

Can prison reform people, positively transforming their lives? Some who answer yes to this question point to the example of Malcolm Little, later known as Malcolm X. *The Autobiography of Malcolm X* describes
Line how Malcolm, a high school dropout, in prison set himself the task of
(5) reading straight through the dictionary; to him, reading was purposeful, not aimless, and he plowed his way through its hundreds of pages, from A for *aardvark* to Z for *zymurgy*.

33. The author's attitude toward Malcolm's activities in prison can best be described as

(A) nostalgic   (B) pessimistic   (C) condescending
(D) approving   (E) apologetic

34. In line 6, "plowed" most nearly means

(A) harrowed   (B) cultivated   (C) plunged recklessly
(D) prepared hastily   (E) proceeded steadily

Questions 35 and 36 are based on the following passage.

Many primates live together in an organized troop or social group
that includes members of all ages and both sexes. Such troops always
move compactly together in a stable social unit. A typical primate troop
Line characteristically exhibits a ranking hierarchy among the males in the
(5)   troop. This ranking hierarchy serves to alleviate conflict within the troop.
The highest-ranking male or males defend, control, and lead the troop;
the strong social bond among members and their safety is maintained.

35. According to the passage, primate societies are

(A) generally unstable
(B) hierarchically flexible
(C) extremely competitive
(D) dominated by adult males
(E) frequently in conflict with each other

36. According to the passage, the hierarchic structure within a troop serves to

(A) protect the members of the troop
(B) facilitate food-gathering
(C) establish friendships within the group
(D) keep members of other troops from joining
(E) teach the youngest members how to survive

The passages below are followed by questions on their content; questions following a pair of related passages may also be based on the relationship between the paired passages. Answer the questions on the basis of what is stated or implied in the passages and in any introductory material that may be provided.

Questions 37–48 are based on the following passages.

The following passages present two portraits of grandmothers. In Passage 1 Mary McCarthy shares her memories of her Catholic grandmother, who raised McCarthy and her brother after their parents' death. In Passage 2 Caroline Heilbrun tells of her Jewish grandmother, who died when Heilbrun was 10.

Passage 1

Luckily, I am writing a memoir and not a work of fiction, and therefore I do not have to account for my grandmother's unpleasing character and look for the Oedipal fixation or the traumatic experience which
Line would give her that clinical authenticity that is nowadays so desirable in
(5) portraiture. I do not know how my grandmother got the way she was; I assume, from family photographs and from the inflexibility of her habits, that she was always the same, and it seems as idle to inquire into her childhood as to ask what was ailing Iago or look for the error in toilet-training that was responsible for Lady Macbeth. My grandmother's sex-
(10) ual history, bristling with infant mortality in the usual style of her period, was robust and decisive: three tall, handsome sons grew up, and one attentive daughter. Her husband treated her kindly. She had money, many grandchildren, and religion to sustain her. White hair, glasses, soft skin, wrinkles, needlework—all the paraphernalia of motherliness were
(15) hers; yet it was a cold, grudging, disputatious old woman who sat all day in her sunroom making tapestries from a pattern, scanning religious periodicals, and setting her iron jaw against any infraction of her ways.
Combativeness was, I suppose, the dominant trait in my grand-mother's nature. An aggressive churchgoer, she was quite without
(20) Christian feeling; the mercy of the Lord Jesus had never entered her heart. Her piety was an act of war against the Protestant ascendancy. The religious magazines on her table furnished her not with food for meditation but with fresh pretexts for anger; articles attacking birth control, divorce, mixed marriages, Darwin, and secular education were her
(25) favorite reading. The teachings of the Church did not interest her, except as they were a rebuke to others; "Honor thy father and thy mother," a commandment she was no longer called upon to practice, was the one most frequently on her lips. The extermination of Protestantism, rather than spiritual perfection, was the boon she prayed for. Her mind was

(30)   preoccupied with conversion; the capture of a soul for God much
diverted her fancy—it made one less Protestant in the world. Foreign
missions, with their overtones of good will and social service, appealed
to her less strongly; it was not a *harvest* of souls that my grandmother
had in mind.

(35)   This pugnacity of my grandmother's did not confine itself to sectarian
enthusiasm. There was the defense of her furniture and her house
against the imagined encroachments of visitors. With her, this was not
the gentle and tremulous protectiveness endemic in old ladies, who fear
for the safety of their possessions with a truly touching anxiety, inferring

(40)   the fragility of all things from the brittleness of their old bones and hear-
ing the crash of mortality in the perilous tinkling of a tea-cup. My grandmother's sentiment was more autocratic: she hated having her chairs sat
in or her lawns stepped on or the water turned on in her basins, for no
reason at all except pure officiousness; she even grudged the mailman

(45)   his daily promenade up her sidewalk. Her home was a center of power,
and she would not allow it to be derogated by easy or democratic usage.
Under her jealous eye, its social properties had atrophied, and it func-
tioned in the family structure simply as a political headquarters. The
family had no friends, and entertaining was held to be a foolish and

(50)   unnecessary courtesy as between blood relations. Holiday dinners fell,
as a duty, on the lesser members of the organization: the daughters and
daughters-in-law (converts from the false religion) offered up Baked
Alaska on a platter like the head of John the Baptist, while the old people
sat enthroned at the table, and only their digestive processes acknowl-

(55)   edged, with rumbling, enigmatic salvos, the festal day.

Passage 2

          My grandmother, one of Howe's sustaining women, not only ruled
the household with an arm of iron, but kept a store to support them all,
her blond, blue-eyed husband enjoying life rather than struggling
through it. My grandmother was one of those powerful women who

(60)   know that they stand between their families and an outside world filled
with temptations to failure and shame. I remember her as thoroughly
loving. But there can be no question that she impaired her six daughters
for autonomy as thoroughly as if she had crippled them—more so. The
way to security was marriage; the dread that stood in the way of this

(65)   was sexual dalliance, above all pregnancy. The horror of pregnancy in an
unmarried girl is difficult, perhaps, to recapture now. For a Jewish girl
not to be a virgin on marriage was failure. The male's rights were
embodied in her lack of sexual experience, in the knowledge that he was
the first, the owner.

(70)   All attempts at autonomy had to be frustrated. And of course, my grandmother's greatest weapon was her own vulnerability. She had worked hard, only her daughters knew how hard. She could not be comforted or repaid—as *my* mother would feel repaid—by a daughter's accomplishments, only by her marriage.

37. McCarthy's attitude toward her grandmother is best described as

(A) tolerant   (B) appreciative   (C) indifferent
(D) nostalgic   (E) sardonic

38. The word "idle" in line 7 means

(A) slothful   (B) passive   (C) fallow
(D) useless   (E) unoccupied

39. According to McCarthy, a portrait of a character in a work of modern fiction must have

(A) photographic realism
(B) psychological validity
(C) sympathetic attitudes
(D) religious qualities
(E) historical accuracy

40. McCarthy's primary point in describing her grandmother's physical appearance (lines 13–17) is best summarized by which of the following axioms?

(A) Familiarity breeds contempt.
(B) You can't judge a book by its cover.
(C) One picture is worth more than ten thousand words.
(D) There's no smoke without fire.
(E) Blood is thicker than water.

41. By describing (in lines 37–41) the typical old woman's fear for the safety of her possessions, McCarthy emphasizes that

(A) her grandmother feared the approach of death
(B) old women have dangerously brittle bones
(C) her grandmother possessed considerable wealth
(D) her grandmother had different reasons for her actions
(E) visitors were unwelcome in her grandmother's home

42. The word "properties" in line 47 means

(A) belongings   (B) aspects   (C) holdings   (D) titles   (E) acreage

43. Heilbrun is critical of her grandmother primarily because

   (A) she would not allow her husband to enjoy himself
   (B) she could not accept her own vulnerability
   (C) she fostered a sense of sexual inadequacy
   (D) she discouraged her daughters' independence
   (E) she physically injured her children

44. By describing the extent of the feeling against pregnancy in unmarried girls (lines 65–69), Heilbrun helps the reader understand

   (A) her fear of being scorned as an unwed mother
   (B) why her grandmother strove to limit her daughters' autonomy
   (C) her disapproval of contemporary sexual practices
   (D) her awareness of her mother's desire for happiness
   (E) how unforgiving her grandmother was

45. In stating that her grandmother's greatest weapon was her own vulnerability (lines 70–71), Heilbrun implies that her grandmother got her way by exploiting her children's

   (A) sense of guilt
   (B) innocence of evil
   (C) feeling of indifference
   (D) abdication of responsibility
   (E) lack of experience

46. Both passages mention which of the following as being important to the writer's grandmother?

   (A) Governing the actions of others
   (B) Contributing to religious organizations
   (C) Protecting her children's virtue
   (D) Marrying off her daughters
   (E) Being surrounded by a circle of friends

47. Which technique is used in Passage 1 but not in Passage 2?

   (A) relating the author's own experience
   (B) stating an opinion
   (C) making an assertion
   (D) drawing a contrast
   (E) making literary references

48. McCarthy would most likely react to the characterization of her grandmother, like Heilbrun's grandmother, as one of the "sustaining women" (line 56) by pointing out that

(A) this characterization is not in good taste

(B) the characterization fails to account for her grandmother's piety

(C) the details of the family's social life support this characterization

(D) her grandmother's actual conduct is not in keeping with this characterization

(E) this characterization slightly exaggerates her grandmother's chief virtue

IF YOU FINISH IN LESS THAN 25 MINUTES, YOU MAY CHECK YOUR WORK ON THIS SECTION ONLY. DO NOT TURN TO ANY OTHER SECTION IN THE TEST.

S T O P

SECTION 4/MATHEMATICAL REASONING
Time—25 minutes   18 questions (21–38)

For questions 21–28, determine which of the five choices is correct, and blacken that choice on your answer sheet. You may use any blank space on the page for your work.

Notes:

- You may use a calculator whenever you believe it will be helpful.
- Use the diagrams provided to help you solve the problems. Unless you see the phrase "<u>Note</u>: Figure not drawn to scale" under a diagram, it has been drawn as accurately as possible. Unless it is stated that a figure is three-dimensional, you may assume that it lies in a plane.

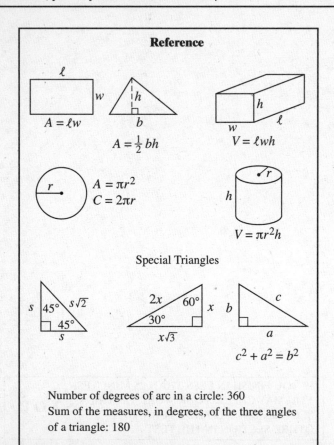

Reference

$A = \ell w$

$A = \frac{1}{2} bh$

$V = \ell wh$

$A = \pi r^2$
$C = 2\pi r$

$V = \pi r^2 h$

Special Triangles

$c^2 + a^2 = b^2$

Number of degrees of arc in a circle: 360
Sum of the measures, in degrees, of the three angles
of a triangle: 180

21. If the ratio of the number of boys to girls in a club is 2:3, what percent of the club members are girls?

    (A) $33\frac{1}{3}$%   (B) 40%   (C) 50%

    (D) 60%   (E) $66\frac{2}{3}$%

22. The Salem Soccer League is divided into d divisions. Each division has t teams, and each team has p players. How many players are there in the entire league?

    (A) $\frac{pt}{d}$ (B) $\frac{dt}{p}$ (C) $\frac{d}{pt}$ (D) $d + t + p$ (E) dtp

23. Which of the following is *NOT* a solution of $3x^2 + 2y = 5$?

    (A) $x = 1$ and $y = 1$
    (B) $x = -1$ and $y = 1$
    (C) $x = 1$ and $y = -1$
    (D) $x = 3$ and $y = -11$
    (E) $x = -3$ and $y = -11$

24. Sally wrote the number 1 on 1 slip of paper, the number 2 on 2 slips of paper, the number 3 on 3 slips of paper, the number 4 on 4 slips of paper, the number 5 on 5 slips of paper, and the number 6 on 6 slips of paper. All the slips of paper were placed in a bag, and Lana drew one slip at random. What is the probability that the number on the slip Lana drew was odd?

    (A) $\frac{1}{9}$ (B) $\frac{1}{7}$ (C) $\frac{3}{7}$ (D) $\frac{1}{2}$ (E) $\frac{4}{7}$

25. If $|x| = |y|$, which of the following must be true?

    I. $-x = -y$
    II. $x^2 = y^2$
    III. $x^3 = y^3$

    (A) I only   (B) II only   (C) I and II only
    (D) II and III only   (E) I, II, and III

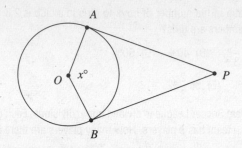

26. In the figure above, $\overline{PA}$ and $\overline{PB}$ are tangent to circle O. If $m\angle P = 50°$, what is the value of x?

(A) 50   (B) 90   (C) 120   (D) 130   (E) 150

27. Which of the following expressions is equal to $2^{3x} + 2^{3x} + 2^{3x} + 2^{3x}$?

(A) 2^{3x+2} (B) 2^{3x+4} (C) 2^{6x}
(D) 2^{12x} (E) 2^{9x^2}

28. The circumference of circle II is 4 feet longer than the circumference of circle I. How many feet longer is the radius of circle II than the radius of circle I?

(A) $\dfrac{1}{4\pi}$ (B) $\dfrac{2}{\pi}$ (C) $\dfrac{1}{\pi}$ (D) 2

(E) It cannot be determined from the information given.

Directions for Student-Produced Response Questions (Grid-ins)

In questions 29–38, first solve the problem, and then enter your answer on the grid provided on the answer sheet. The instructions for entering your answers follow.

- First, write your answer in the boxes at the top of the grid.
- Second, grid your answer in the columns below the boxes.
- Use the fraction bar in the first row or the decimal point in the second row to enter fractions and decimals.

Answer: $\frac{8}{15}$ Answer: 1.75

Write your answer
in the boxes

Grid in your answer

Answer: 100

Either position is acceptable

- Grid only one space in each column.
- Entering the answer in the boxes is recommended as an aid in gridding, but is not required.
- The machine scoring your exam can read only what you grid, so you **must grid in your answers correctly to get credit.**
- If a question has more than one correct answer, grid in only one of them.
- The grid does not have a minus sign, so no answer can be negative.
- A mixed number *must* be converted to an improper fraction or a decimal before it is gridded. Enter $1\frac{1}{4}$ as $\frac{5}{4}$ or 1.25; the machine will interpret 1 1/4 as $\frac{11}{4}$ and mark it wrong.

- **All decimals must be entered as accurately as possible.** Here are the three acceptable ways of gridding
$$\frac{3}{11} = 0.272727...$$

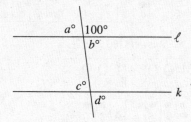

- Note that rounding to .273 is acceptable, because you are using the full grid, but you would receive **no credit** for .3 or .27, because they are less accurate.

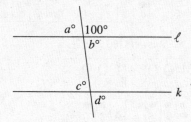

Lines ℓ and k are parallel.

29. In the figure above, what is the value of $a + b + c + d$?

30. If $a = 6$ and $b = -6$, what is the value of $2a - 3b$?

31. If A is the median of {1, 2, 3, 4, 5, 6} and B is the median of {1, 2, 3, 4, 5, 6, 7}, what is the average (arithmetic mean) of A and B?

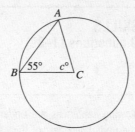

32. In the figure above, *C* is the center of the circle. What is the value of *c*?

33. If Elaine drove 190 kilometers between 12:00 noon and 3:20 P.M., what was her average speed, in kilometers per hour?

34. From 1990 until 1998 the value of an investment increased by 10% every year. The value of that investment on January 1, 1996 was how many times greater than the value on January 1, 1994?

35. How many two-digit numbers do not contain the digit 9?

36. If the average (arithmetic mean) of five numbers is 95, and the average of three of them is 100, what is the average of the other two?

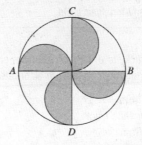

37. In the circle above, diameters *AB* and *CD* are perpendicular, and each of the four shaded regions is a semicircle. The shaded area is how many times the white area?

38. When a group of people were tested for a rare disease, 99.6% of them were found not to have the disease. If 10 people did have the disease, how many people were tested?

IF YOU FINISH IN LESS THAN 25 MINUTES, YOU MAY CHECK YOUR WORK ON THIS SECTION ONLY. DO NOT TURN TO ANY OTHER SECTION IN THE TEST.

S T O P

SECTION 5/WRITING SKILLS
Time—30 minutes   39 questions (1–39)

Some or all parts of the following sentences are underlined. The first answer choice, (A), simply repeats the underlined part of the sentence. The other four choices present four alternative ways to phrase the underlined part. Select the answer that produces the most effective sentence, one that is clear and exact, and blacken the appropriate space on your answer sheet. In selecting your choice, be sure that it is standard written English and that it expresses the meaning of the original sentence.

EXAMPLE:

The first biography of author Eudora Welty came out in 1998, and she was eighty-nine years old at the time.

(A) and she was eighty-nine years old at the time
(B) at the time when she was eighty-nine
(C) upon becoming an eighty-nine year old
(D) when she was eighty-nine
(E) at the age of eighty-nine years old

1. Although serfs were lucky to drink their ale from cracked wooden bowls, nobles customarily drunk their wine from elaborately chased drinking horns.

(A) drunk their wine from
(B) have drinked their wine from
(C) drank their wine from
(D) had drunken their wine from
(E) drinking their wine from

2. Before the search party reached the scene of the accident, the rain began to fall, making rescue efforts more difficult.

(A) the rain began to fall
(B) the rain had began to fall
(C) it began to rain
(D) the rain had begun to fall
(E) it started to rain

3. For many students, <u>keeping a journal during college seems satisfying their</u> <u>need</u> for self-expression.

   (A) keeping a journal during college seems satisfying their need
   (B) keeping a journal during college seems to satisfy their need
   (C) keeping a journal during college seeming satisfying their need
   (D) to keep a journal during college seems satisfying their need
   (E) the keeping of a journal during college seems to satisfy their need

4. Peter Martins began to develop his own choreographic <u>style, but he was able</u> to free himself from the influence of Balanchine.

   (A) style, but he was able to
   (B) style; but he was able to
   (O) style only when he was able to
   (D) style only when he is able to
   (E) style: only when he was able to

5. <u>Irregardless of the outcome</u> of this dispute, our two nations will remain staunch allies.

   (A) Irregardless of the outcome
   (B) Regardless of how the outcome
   (C) With regard to the outcome
   (D) Regardless of the outcome
   (E) Disregarding the outcome

6. With the onset of winter, <u>the snows began to fall, we were soon forced to</u> <u>remain indoors</u> most of the time.

   (A) the snows began to fall, we were soon forced to remain indoors
   (B) the snows began to fall; we were soon forced to remain indoors
   (C) the snows began to fall: we were soon forced to remain indoors
   (D) the snows began to fall, having forced us to remain indoors
   (E) the snows had begun to fall; we were soon forced to remain indoors

7. "Araby," along with several other stories from Joyce's *Dubliners*, <u>are going to</u> <u>be read at</u> Town Hall by the noted Irish actor Brendan Coyle.

   (A) are going to be read
   (B) were going to be read
   (C) are gone to be read
   (D) is going to be read
   (E) is gone to be read

8. In 1980 the Democrats <u>lost not only the executive branch, but also their majority</u> in the United States Senate.

   (A) lost not only the executive branch but also their majority
   (B) lost not only the executive branch but also its majority
   (C) not only lost the executive branch but also their majority
   (D) lost the executive branch but also their majority
   (E) lost not only the executive branch but their majority also

9. <u>Before considering an applicant for this job, he must have</u> a degree in electrical engineering as well as three years in the field.

   (A) Before considering an applicant for this job, he must have
   (B) Before considering an applicant for this job, he should have
   (C) We will not consider an applicant for this job without
   (D) To consider an applicant for this job, he must have
   (E) We will not consider an applicant for this job if he does not have

10. <u>To invest intelligently for the future, mutual funds</u> provide an excellent opportunity for the average investor.

   (A) To invest intelligently for the future, mutual funds
   (B) As an intelligent investment for the future, mutual funds
   (C) Investing intelligently for the future, mutual funds
   (D) To invest with intelligence, mutual funds
   (E) Having invested intelligently, you must determine that mutual funds

11. She was told to give the award <u>to whomever she thought</u> had contributed most to the welfare of the student body.

   (A) to whomever she thought
   (B) to whoever she thought
   (C) to the senior whom she thought
   (D) to whomever
   (E) to him whom she thought

12. <u>Since he is lying the book on the table where it does not belong.</u>

   (A) Since he is lying the book on the table where it does not belong.
   (B) He is lying the book on the table where it does not belong.
   (C) Because he is laying the book on the table where it does not belong.
   (D) Since he is laying the book on the table where it does not belong.
   (E) He is laying the book on the table where it does not belong.

13. Mary is <u>as fast as, if not faster than, anyone</u> in her class and should be on the team.

    (A) as fast as, if not faster than, anyone
    (B) as fast, if not faster than, anyone else
    (C) as fast as, if not more fast than, anyone
    (D) as fast as, if not faster than, anyone else
    (E) as swift as, if not faster than, anyone

14. Senator Schumer is <u>one of the legislators who are going</u> to discuss the budget with the president.

    (A) one of the legislators who are going
    (B) one of the legislators who is going
    (C) one of the legislators who has gone
    (D) the legislators who is going
    (E) the legislators who has gone

15. New research studies show that alcohol and tobacco <u>are as harmful to elderly women as elderly men.</u>

    (A) are as harmful to elderly women as elderly men
    (B) are so harmful to elderly women as elderly men
    (C) being as harmful to elderly women as elderly men
    (D) are as harmful to elderly women as to elderly men
    (E) are as harmful to elderly women as to men being elderly

16. Chronic fatigue syndrome is not a normal <u>condition; rather, it is an abnormal response to stress factors such as anxiety or infection.</u>

    (A) condition; rather, it is an abnormal response to stress factors such as
    (B) condition, it is a rather abnormal response to stress factors such as
    (C) condition; but it is an abnormal response to stress factors such as
    (D) condition rather, it is an abnormal response to stress factors like
    (E) condition, rather it is a way of responding abnormally to such stress factors as

17. A cynic is when someone has a tendency to disbelieve that any actions can have wholly unselfish motivations.

    (A) A cynic is when someone has a tendency to disbelieve that any actions can have wholly unselfish motivations.

    (B) Someone who has a tendency to disbelieve that any actions can have wholly unselfish motivations, and he is a cynic.

    (C) A cynic is when someone tends not to believe that any actions might have had wholly unselfish motivations.

    (D) A cynic is someone which has a tendency to disbelieve that any actions can be wholly unselfishly motivated.

    (E) A cynic is someone who tends to disbelieve that any actions can have wholly unselfish motivations.

18. When NASA has been informed of the dangerous weather conditions, the head of the space agency decided to postpone the shuttle launch.

    (A) When NASA has been informed of the dangerous weather conditions

    (B) Because NASA having been informed of the dangerous weather conditions

    (C) Although NASA was informed with the dangerous weather conditions

    (D) When NASA was informed of the dangerous weather conditions

    (E) When NASA has been informed with the dangerous weather conditions

19. Henry James wrote the play *Guy Domville* primarily because he hoped revitalizing of his waning literary career.

    (A) he hoped revitalizing of his waning literary career

    (B) he hoped revitalizing of his literary career that was waning

    (C) his hoping was the revitalizing of his waning literary career

    (D) he hoped to revitalize his waning literary career

    (E) he hoped revitalizing of his literary career that had waned

20. While strolling in Golden Gate Park one day, seeing the carousel with its elegantly carved horses delighted the young couple.

    (A) seeing the carousel with its elegantly carved horses delighted the young couple

    (B) the sight of the carousel with its elegantly carved horses delighted the young couple

    (C) the young couple was delighted by the sight of the carousel with its elegantly carved horses

    (D) the carousel delighted the young couple with its elegantly carved horses when they saw it

    (E) to have seen the carousel's elegantly carved horses delighted the young couple

---

The sentences in this section may contain errors in grammar, usage, choice of words, or idioms. There is either just one error per sentence, or the sentence is correct. Some words or phrases are underlined and lettered; everything else in the sentence is correct.

If an underlined word or phrase is incorrect, choose that letter; if the sentence is correct, select <u>No error</u>. Then blacken the appropriate space on your Answer Sheet.

EXAMPLE:

The region has a climate so <u>severe that</u> plants
$\qquad\qquad\qquad\quad$ A
<u>growing there</u> rarely <u>had been</u> more than twelve
$\qquad$ B $\qquad\qquad\qquad$ C
inches <u>high</u>. <u>No error</u>
$\qquad$ D $\quad$ E

$\qquad\qquad\qquad\qquad\qquad\qquad$ Ⓐ Ⓑ ● Ⓓ Ⓔ

---

21. <u>Being that</u> my car is getting <u>its</u> annual tune-up, I <u>will not be</u> able <u>to pick you up</u>
$\qquad$ A $\qquad\qquad\qquad\qquad$ B $\qquad\qquad$ C $\qquad\qquad$ D
tomorrow morning. <u>No error</u>
$\qquad\qquad\qquad$ E

22. The average taxpayer <u>can't hardly</u> believe that income tax fraud is
$\qquad\qquad\qquad\qquad$ A
<u>so widespread as</u> <u>to justify</u> such precautions as the authorities <u>have taken</u>.
$\qquad$ B $\qquad\qquad$ C $\qquad\qquad\qquad\qquad\qquad\qquad$ D
<u>No error</u>
$\quad$ E

23. No one <u>but</u> <u>he</u> knew <u>which</u> questions <u>were going</u> to be asked on this test.
$\qquad\quad$ A $\quad$ B $\qquad$ C $\qquad\qquad$ D
<u>No error</u>
$\quad$ E

24. You are being <u>quite</u> cynical when you say <u>that the reason</u> we have <u>such a large</u>
$\qquad\qquad\qquad$ A $\qquad\qquad\qquad\qquad$ B $\qquad\qquad$ C
turnout <u>is because</u> we are serving refreshments. <u>No error</u>
$\qquad$ D $\qquad\qquad\qquad\qquad\qquad\qquad$ E

25. Although I am playing golf for more than three years, I cannot manage
         A   B   C
to break 90. No error
   D   E

26. Studies have found that a mild salt solution is more affective than the
              A   B   C
commercial preparations available in drug stores in the treatment of this
                                                   D
ailment. No error
       E

27. If I have to make a choice between John, Henry and her, I think I'll select
A   B   C
Henry because of his self-control during moments of stress. No error
                           D   E

28. In order to raise public consciousness concerning environmental problems,
   A
you should distribute leaflets, write to your representative in Congress,
  B   C
as well as signing the necessary petitions. No error
     D   E

29. Members of a scientific expedition discovered the *Titanic*, which sank after it
                                                   A   B
struck an iceberg, furthermore it was not possible for them to raise it. No error
               C   D   E

30. Scientists show that change, whether good or bad, leads to stress and that the
       A   B   C
accumulation from stress-related changes can cause major illness. No error
       D   E

31. We have spent all together too much money on this project; we have exceeded
                A   B   C
our budget and can expect no additional funds until the beginning of the new
              D
year. No error
    E

32. Between thirty and forty students seem willing to volunteer; the rest are not
               A   B   C
planning to participate in the program. No error
   D   E

33. The horse that won the trophies differed with the other horses in
         A   B   C

overall appearance as well as ability. No error
         D   E

34. The business executive, planning to attend the conference in New Orleans,
                                  A

could not decide whether to travel on or remaining at the hotel was the better
          B   C   D

choice. No error
        E

The passage below is the unedited draft of a student's essay. Some of the essay needs to be rewritten to make the meaning clearer and more precise. Read the essay carefully.

The essay is followed by five questions about changes that might improve all or part of its organization, development, sentence structure, use of language, appropriateness to the audience, or its use of standard written English. Choose the answer that most clearly and effectively expresses the student's intended meaning. Indicate your choice by filling in the corresponding space on the answer sheet.

---

[1] In the twentieth century, women have held a major part in influencing social change and social status. [2] In such developing countries as Saudi Arabia, restrictions on women are gradually being lifted, and they have gained the right to be in public without your head covered.

[3] In the area of social status, women have fought for better treatment and more respect. [4] An example of this is the fight for women in the workplace. [5] Not long ago most women stayed at home and took care of their families, while their husbands worked at white collar and blue collar jobs. [6] But now many women work as doctors, lawyers, and other established positions. [7] Women are finally out in the work force competing with men for the same jobs.

[8] In the area of politics and government, many women have attained high positions. [9] Hillary Rodham Clinton became a role model for many young women in this country. [10] Two women are now members of the U.S. Supreme Court.

[11] Several women also are governors, senators and representatives. [12] There will never again be an all-male cabinet. [13] Ever since women's suffrage, women have won the rights reserved for men. [14] The result was that women now have a voice in the actions of our country.

[15] In the areas of health, medicine, sciences, and the military, women have also come into their own. [16] Although the world still has a long way to go before women achieve total equality with men, the twentieth century may long be remembered as the time when the first steps were taken.

35. Considering the essay as a whole, which revision of sentence 1 would serve best as the essay's opening sentence?

   (A) The social status of women has undergone a major change during the twentieth century.
   (B) Twentieth century women will have a major influence in changing their social status.
   (C) As a major influence in the twentieth century, women have had their social status changed.
   (D) Under the influence of twentieth century women, their status has changed.
   (E) Being influenced by social change in the twentieth century, the status of women has changed.

36. Which is the most effective revision of the underlined segment of sentence 2 below?

   In such developing countries as Saudi Arabia, restrictions on women are gradually being lifted, and they have gained the right to be in public without your head covered.

   (A) for example, women are gaining rights like the one to be in public bareheaded
   (B) which means that they have gained the right to be in public with their heads uncovered
   (C) and they have the right, for example, for you to go bareheaded in public
   (D) and women now have gained the right to be bareheaded in public
   (E) to the extent that women can exercise the right of going into public with their head uncovered

37. Which revision of sentence 8 provides the best transition between the second and the third paragraphs?

(A) The competition has extended into politics and government, where many women have replaced men in high positions.

(B) Irregardless, in the field of politics and government many women have attained high positions.

(C) High positions in government and politics have been attained by women.

(D) Among the jobs that women have attained are in politics and government.

(E) The world of politics and government has changed because women have attained high positions.

38. Sentence 8 is the topic sentence of the third paragraph. Which of the following is the best revision of sentence 9?

(A) The wife of the President, Hillary Rodham Clinton, made herself a role model for many young American women.

(B) In the 1992 national election, Hillary Rodham Clinton helped her husband win the Presidency of the United States.

(C) After seven years as Prime Minister of England, Margaret Thatcher was finally defeated by a male, John Major.

(D) While she was the leader of India, Indira Ghandi was assassinated.

(E) In recent years both Margaret Thatcher of England and Indira Ghandi of India, for example, served as leaders of their countries.

39. Which sentence in the third paragraph should be revised or deleted because it contributes least to the development of the main idea of the paragraph?

(A) Sentence 10   (B) Sentence 11   (C) Sentence 12
(D) Sentence 13   (E) Sentence 14

IF YOU FINISH IN LESS THAN 30 MINUTES, YOU MAY CHECK YOUR WORK ON THIS SECTION ONLY. DO NOT TURN TO ANY OTHER SECTION IN THE TEST.

S T O P

Answer Key

Section 1 Critical Reading

1. C	9. D	17. A
2. D	10. D	18. B
3. B	11. E	19. D
4. E	12. C	20. C
5. A	13. D	21. E
6. D	14. E	22. E
7. C	15. B	23. D
8. B	16. D	24. D

Section 2 Mathematical Reasoning

1. D	8. E	15. D
2. C	9. D	16. C
3. D	10. A	17. C
4. E	11. D	18. A
5. D	12. D	19. D
6. D	13. B	20. A
7. B	14. E	

Section 3 Critical Reading

25. B	33. D	41. D
26. D	34. E	42. B
27. A	35. D	43. D
28. E	36. A	44. B
29. A	37. E	45. A
30. C	38. D	46. A
31. D	39. B	47. E
32. C	40. B	48. D

Section 4 Mathematical Reasoning

21. D	24. C	27. A
22. E	25. B	28. B
23. C	26. D	

29. $3\ 2\ 0$

30. $3\ 0$

31. $3\ .\ 7\ 5$

or 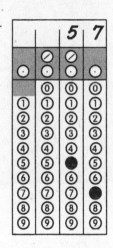 $1\ 5\ /\ 4$

32. $7\ 0$

33. $5\ 7$

34. $1\ .\ 2\ 1$

35.

		7	2
	⊘	⊘	
⊙	⊙	⊙	⊙
	⓪	⓪	⓪
①	①	①	①
②	②	②	●
③	③	③	③
④	④	④	④
⑤	⑤	⑤	⑤
⑥	⑥	⑥	⑥
⑦	⑦	●	⑦
⑧	⑧	⑧	⑧
⑨	⑨	⑨	⑨

36.

8	7	.	5
	⊘	⊘	
⊙	⊙	●	⊙
	⓪	⓪	⓪
①	①	①	①
②	②	②	②
③	③	③	③
④	④	④	④
⑤	⑤	⑤	●
⑥	⑥	⑥	⑥
⑦	●	⑦	⑦
●	⑧	⑧	⑧
⑨	⑨	⑨	⑨

37.

			1
	⊘	⊘	
⊙	⊙	⊙	⊙
	⓪	⓪	⓪
①	①	①	●
②	②	②	②
③	③	③	③
④	④	④	④
⑤	⑤	⑤	⑤
⑥	⑥	⑥	⑥
⑦	⑦	⑦	⑦
⑧	⑧	⑧	⑧
⑨	⑨	⑨	⑨

38.

2	5	0	0
	⊘	⊘	
⊙	⊙	⊙	⊙
	⓪	●	●
①	①	①	①
●	②	②	②
③	③	③	③
④	④	④	④
⑤	●	⑤	⑤
⑥	⑥	⑥	⑥
⑦	⑦	⑦	⑦
⑧	⑧	⑧	⑧
⑨	⑨	⑨	⑨

Section 5 Writing Skills

1. **C**	11. **B**	21. **A**	31. **A**
2. **D**	12. **E**	22. **A**	32. **E**
3. **B**	13. **D**	23. **B**	33. **B**
4. **C**	14. **A**	24. **D**	34. **C**
5. **D**	15. **D**	25. **B**	35. **A**
6. **B**	16. **A**	26. **B**	36. **D**
7. **D**	17. **E**	27. **B**	37. **A**
8. **A**	18. **D**	28. **D**	38. **E**
9. **E**	19. **D**	29. **C**	39. **E**
10. **B**	20. **C**	30. **D**	

Answer Explanations

Section 1 Critical Reading

1. **(C)** The use of "Unhappily" tells us that the experiment was somehow damaged or *marred* by the presence of observers.

2. **(D)** James didn't know when assignments were due because there was something wrong with the way he wrote them down. He was not orderly or *methodical* about it.

3. **(B)** The word "despite" signals a contrast. Despite the advertised *praises*, she had doubts—she remained *a skeptic* about the product. Note also that "singing the praises of" is a cliché, a customary phrase.

4. **(E)** Again, think of your own answer before looking at the choices. What would you need after two full months of solid work? A rest, or *respite*.

5. **(A)** The phrase "even though" tells us that there will be a contrast. This requires a word that is opposite in meaning to "does not change." *Plastic* can mean adaptable or pliable when used as an adjective, as it is here.

6. **(D)** The author's presentation of factual information about tarantulas is scientifically *objective* (impartial).

7. **(C)** To excite a defensive response is to *stimulate* or arouse that reaction.

8. **(B)** Passage 1 describes what you would see if you subjected a tarantula to various forms of stimuli (pressing a pencil against its body-wall, holding a pencil above it, etc.). In other words, it *provides scientific observations of the subject* (the tarantula). Passage 2, in contrast, offers highly general, chatty information about tarantulas, providing *a popular introduction to the subject*.

9. **(D)** You can answer this question by using the process of elimination.
    Do both passages indicate that tarantulas have a marked degree of intelligence? Nothing in either passage suggests this. You can eliminate Choice A.
    Do both passages indicate that the tarantulas' gentleness belies (contradicts) their frightening looks? No. Although Passage 2 states that tarantulas are gentler creatures than their appearance suggests, Passage 1 says nothing about their being gentle. You can eliminate Choice B.
    Do both passages indicate that tarantulas have been maligned (slandered; bad-mouthed) by arachnophobes? No. Passage 1 says nothing at all about arachnophobes. You can eliminate Choice C.
    Do both passages indicate that tarantulas are capable of acting to defend themselves? Yes. Passage 1 portrays a tarantula's defensive reaction to a perceived threat: the spider immediately goes into its attack stance. Passage 2 indicates that tarantulas will bite if they are severely provoked; thus, they *are capable of acting to defend themselves*. The correct answer is most likely Choice D.

Confirm your answer choice by checking Choice E. Do both passages indicate that tarantulas are easily intimidated (frightened) by others? No. Nothing in either passage indicates this. You can eliminate Choice E. Only Choice D is left. It is the correct answer.

10. **(D)** Blown about by the storm, the *branches* of the fir trees move from side to side: "the old firs ... wave excitedly with their arms."

11. **(E)** The author states that the jackdaw's proficiency is not inherited or innate, but "an individually acquired accomplishment." In other words, it has been *gained through practice.*

12. **(C)** The author is stressing that you can *be* sure or *confident* of the truth of what he says.

13. **(D)** The "sightless monster" is the "stupid wind" that tries to dive the jackdaws toward the east. Note how the author personifies the wind, writing as if the wind had some degree of human intelligence and responsiveness.

14. **(E)** The concluding sentence of the passage celebrates the birds' "Sovereign control over the power of the elements," in other words, their *mastery of the forces of nature*. Though Choice B may seem tempting, you can rule it out: Lorenz emphasizes the storm's strength ("the pitiless strength of the inorganic"), not the strength of the birds. Choices A, C, and D are unsupported by the passage.

15. **(B)** The author uses several metaphors ("close-reefed sails," "the teeth of the gale," etc.) and clarifies what he means by the term *game*. He describes the jackdaws' behavior in detail and dismisses the notion that their behavior is purely instinctive. However, he never *argues a cause*.

16. **(D)** Tapestry weaving is time-consuming, taking "as much as a year to produce a yard." In addition, it is faithful to the original ("The weaver always follows a preexisting model"). It is not, however, spontaneous in concept.

17. **(A)** The author mentions tapestry's distinctive or *characteristic* weave as something that distinguishes tapestry-woven materials from other fabrics (prints, brocades, etc.).

18. **(B)** By using tapestries "to display his wealth and social position," the nobleman is using them to demonstrate his *consequence* or importance.

19. **(D)** The "ground" upon which embroidery is laid is the cloth *base* upon which the embroiderer stitches a design.

20. **(C)** The author refers to the suggestion that tapestries served primarily as a source of warmth only to *dismiss* or reject the idea. To prove his point he asserts that comfort had little importance in medieval times.

21. **(E)** Here the word "chambers" *is being used in a special sense* to mean a set of wall hangings made to fit a specific room.

22. (E) In describing Morris as someone who attempted to bring back tapestry making to its true, medieval principles, the author depicts him as a *traditionalist*, someone who attempts to preserve or restore ancient cultural practices or beliefs.

23. (D) In comparison to the tightly-woven tapestries of the nineteenth-century, present-day wall hangings are described as "coarsely woven cloths." Thus, they *have a less fine weave* than their predecessors.

24. (D) Although the passage explains the process of tapestry making and mentions that large wall hangings are Western rather than Eastern in origin, Choices A and B do not reflect the passage's primary purpose. This purpose is to *provide a historical perspective on tapestry making.*

Section 2   Mathematical Reasoning

In each mathematics section, for some problems, an alternative solution, indicated by two asterisks (**), follows the first solution. When this occurs, usually one of the solutions is the direct mathematical one and the other is based on one of the tactics discussed in Chapter 5.

1. (D) Since $x + y + 30 = 180$ and $y = 2x$, we get
$$x + 2x + 30 = 180 \Rightarrow 3x = 150 \Rightarrow$$
$$x = 50 \Rightarrow y = 2x = 100.$$

2. (C) The left hand side of $(a + 12) - 12 = 12$ is just a. So, $a = 12$.

   Of course, you can use **TACTIC 1: backsolve, starting (and ending) with C.

3. (D) Let each side of the small squares be 1. Then each square has area 1, and the area of rectangle *AEFJ* is 4. The shaded area consists of $\triangle AJI$ and $\triangle EFI$. The white region is $\triangle AEI$, whose area is $\frac{1}{2}(4)(1) = 2$. The area of the shaded region is $4 - 2 = 2$, and so the ratio of the areas is $2:2 = 1:1$.

   **Just look at the diagram. Exactly half of square *ABIJ* and exactly half of rectangle *BEFI* are shaded. The areas of the shaded and white regions are equal.

4. (E) Since $72\% + 19\% = 91\%$, the $243 spent on the party represents the other 9% of the money raised. Then $.09m = 243 \Rightarrow m = 243 \div .09 = 2700$.

5. (D) Every hour the hour hand moves through $30°$ ($\frac{1}{12}$ of $360°$). So it will move through $20°$ in $\frac{2}{3}$ of an hour or 40 minutes; 40 minutes after 1:30 is 2:10.

6. (D) Since *ABC* is an equilateral triangle, $x = 60$. So, $60 + 40 + y = 180 \Rightarrow y = 80$. Then by **FACT 40** (when parallel lines are cut by a transversal, the four acute angles have the same measure), $y = a$. So, $a = 80$.

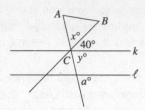

Use TACTIC 6 (trust the diagram)—*a* appears to be slightly less than a 90° angle.

7. **(B)** Let *x* and *y* be the two numbers:

$x - y < x + y \Rightarrow -y < y \Rightarrow 0 < 2y \Rightarrow y$ is positive. Therefore, at least one of the numbers is positive. (Note that there are no restrictions on *x*.)

8. **(E)** Solve the equation, $20 = \frac{x}{100}C$:

$2000 = xC \Rightarrow x = \frac{2000}{C}\%$.

Use TACTIC 3: substitute an easy-to-use number: 20 is 100% of 20. Which of the choices is equal to 100% when $C = 20$? Only $\frac{2000}{C}\%$.

9. **(D)** Whenever we know two of the three sides of a right triangle, we can find the third side by using the Pythagorean theorem. First, assume that the two given sides are both legs, and let *x* represent the hypotenuse. Then

$$x^2 = 5^2 + 9^2 = 25 + 81 = 106 \Rightarrow x = \sqrt{106}$$

and III is true. Now assume that one side is a leg, the longer side is the hypotenuse, and let *y* represent the other leg. Then

$$5^2 + y^2 = 9^2 \Rightarrow 25 + y^2 = 81 \Rightarrow$$
$$y^2 = 56 \Rightarrow y = \sqrt{56}$$

and I is true. Therefore, I and III only are true.

10. **(A)** The slope of the line $y = 2x - 3$ is 2, and parallel lines have equal slopes. Only choice A, $y = 2x + 3$, also has a slope equal to 2.

11. **(D)** Just check each choice. Is there a triangle whose sides are 1, 2, 3? No, the sum of any two sides of a triangle must be *greater* than the third side (**FACT 48**). (I is false.) Are there triangles whose sides are 3, 4, 5 and 13, 14, 15? Yes. (II and III are true.) Statements II and III only are true.

12. **(D)** By **FACT 26**, the percent increase in the bank's charge is $\frac{\text{the actual increase}}{\text{the original amount}} \times 100\%$. The charge was originally \$10 and the actual increase was \$10. So, the percent increase is $\frac{10}{10} \times 100 = 100\%$.

13. **(B)** Since the sum of the three measures is $180°$:

$$180 = x + 2x + 3y = 3x + 3y = 3(x + y) \Rightarrow$$
$$x + y = 60 \Rightarrow y = 60 - x.$$

Use **TACTIC 3: pick an easy-to-use value for x. Note that in the diagram x appears to be about 50, but you can pick any value: say 10. Then

$$10 + 20 + 3y = 180 \Rightarrow 3y = 150 \Rightarrow y = 50.$$

Which of the choices equals 10 when y is 50? Only $60 - x$.

14. **(E)** $\|16^2\| = \frac{2}{3}(6^2)^2 = \frac{2}{3}(36)^2 = \frac{2}{3}(1296) = 864.$

15. **(D)** $\|y\| = \|\frac{2}{3}x\| = \frac{2}{3}(\frac{2}{3}x)^2 = \frac{2}{3}(\frac{4}{9}x^2) = \frac{8}{27}x^2.$

Use **TACTIC 2: replace the variables with numbers. Let $x = 3$. Then $y = \frac{2}{3}(3) = 2$, and $\|2\| = \frac{2}{3}(2)^2 = \frac{2}{3}(4) = \frac{8}{3}$. Which of the choices is equal to $\frac{8}{3}$ when $x = 3$? Only $\frac{8}{27}x^2$.

16. **(C)** $f(\frac{1}{2}) = 9(\frac{1}{2}) + 9^{\frac{1}{2}} = 4.5 + \sqrt{9} = 4.5 + 3 = 7.5.$

17. **(C)** Jill walked 4 kilometers and Jack walked 6 kilometers; so Jill walked $\frac{4}{6} = \frac{2}{3}$ the distance that Jack walked. Since their rates were the same, she did it in $\frac{2}{3}$ the time: $\frac{2}{3}$ of 2 hours is $\frac{4}{3}$ of an hour or 1 hour and 20 minutes. She left at 10:40.

**Jack walked 6 kilometers in exactly 2 hours; so, he was walking at a rate of 3 kilometers per hour. Jill walked 4 kilometers, also at 3 kilometers per hour, so her walking time was $4 \div 3$ or $1\frac{1}{3}$ hours ($t = d \div r$. See Fact 34). Therefore, Jill left $1\frac{1}{3}$ hours, or 1 hour and 20 minutes, before noon—at 10:40.

18. **(A)** Even if you can do the algebra, this type of problem is easier by using **TACTIC 3**: choose easy-to-use numbers. Assume that there are 100 females and 50 males in the club, and that 20% of the females and 10% of the males attended the meeting. Then, 20 females and 5 males were there, and 5 is 20% of 25, the total number attending.

19. **(D)** $(a + b)^2 = a^2 + 2ab + b^2 = (a^2 + b^2) + 2ab$. By the Pythagorean Theorem, $a^2 + b^2 = 10^2 = 100$; and since the area is 20, $\frac{1}{2}ab = 20 \Rightarrow ab = 40$, and $2ab = 80$. Then $(a^2 + b^2) + 2ab = 100 + 80 = 180$.

20. **(A)** Originally the fund of d dollars was to be divided among 4 winners, in which case each of them would have received $\frac{d}{4}$ dollars. Instead, the fund was divided among 6 winners, and each received $\frac{d}{6}$ dollars. This represents a loss to each of the original winners of $\frac{d}{4} - \frac{d}{6} = \frac{3d}{12} - \frac{2d}{12} = \frac{d}{12}$ dollars.

**Unless you are comfortable with the algebra, plug in a number for d; say $d = 24$. Then the 4 winners would have received $24 \div 4 = 6$ dollars each. Now the 6 winners will receive $24 \div 6 = 4$ dollars each, a difference of \$2. Which of the choices is equal to 2 when $d = 24$? Only $\frac{d}{12}$.

Section 3 Critical Reading

25. **(B)** Remember to think of your own answer before looking at the choices. North clearly had a strong belief; no one's words could convince him otherwise. This would guide you to choose *conviction*, one meaning of which is belief.

26. **(D)** If we are likely to be in need of a new source of energy, we must be about to run out of the old source of fuel. This would happen if we *deplete* or exhaust our supply. The phrase "Excessive use" is also a clue that we may be running out, through using too much.

27. **(A)** The word "however" signals a contrast. The sentence says the authorities reject the use of "disinterested." Therefore, *in contrast*, they accept or *condone* the use of "healthy."

28. **(E)** The flu weakened or *debilitated* Michael, leaving him too tired to return to work.

29. **(A)** The word "though" also signals a contrast. Although Alec Guinness had his mind set on becoming an actor, his determination or *resolution* wavered. Note that *resolution* is not just a statement of intent; it can mean firmness of intent as well.

30. **(C)** The key word here is "ridiculing," meaning making fun of or mocking. It complements *satirical* or sarcastic and cutting.

31. **(D)** Someone who risks his or her life frequently is a *daredevil*. Since the threat of death does not keep Markham from such activities, the first missing word must be *daunt*, meaning to frighten or lessen one's courage.

32. **(C)** "Unscrupulous merchandisers" make false claims. *Debunking* means exposing falseness in something. Nader, who is an advocate or protector of the consumer, teaches people to be suspicious and to exercise *skepticism*. Note that "exercising skepticism" is a cliché, a very commonly used phrase.

33. **(D)** The author's attitude is clearly *approving*: she notes that some commentators cite Malcolm's change in prison as an example of positive transformation; she also uses words with positive connotations ("purposeful") to describe Malcolm's method of tackling his task.

34. **(E)** In plowing his way through the dictionary, Malcolm *proceeded steadily* and purposefully from the beginning to the end.

35. **(D)** Line 6 of the passage says that in primate troops, males "defend, control and lead the troop." Therefore, the troops are *dominated by adult males*.

36. **(A)** The passage says that the ranking hierarchy lessens conflict within the troop. Therefore, it is meant to *protect the members of the troop* from internal strife.

37. **(E)** In candidly exposing her grandmother's flaws, the author exhibits a *sardonic* or scornful and sarcastic attitude.

38. **(D)** McCarthy sees as little point in speculating about her grandmother's childhood as she does in wondering about the toilet training of a fictional character like Lady Macbeth. Such speculations are, to McCarthy's mind, idle or *useless*.

39. **(B)** The author states (somewhat ironically) that modern fictional characters must have "clinical authenticity." In other words, they must appear to be genuine or *valid* in *psychological* terms.

40. **(B)** Although the grandmother's outward appearance was soft and motherly, her essential nature was hard as nails. Clearly, you cannot judge a book (person) by its cover (outward appearance).

41. **(D)** McCarthy is building up a portrait of her grandmother as a pugnacious, autocratic person. She describes the fear old ladies have for their belongings as a very human (and understandable) reaction: aware of their own increasing fragility (and eventual death), the old ladies identify with their fragile possessions and are protective of them. McCarthy's grandmother was also protective of her belongings, but she was not the typical "gentle and tremulous" elderly woman. She was a petty tyrant and had decidedly *different reasons for her actions*.

42. **(B)** Because her grandmother was more interested in maintaining her power than in being hospitable, the social properties or *aspects* of the family home had withered and decayed till no real sociability existed.

43. **(D)** Heilbrun's central criticism is that her grandmother "impaired her six daughters for autonomy" or independence. In other words, *she discouraged her daughters' independence*.

44. **(B)** Heilbrun realizes that people nowadays may have difficulty understanding what motivated her grandmother to control her daughters' lives and restrict their autonomy so thoroughly. By describing how great the horror of pregnancy in an unmarried girl was, she helps the reader understand *why her grandmother* acted as she did.

45. **(A)** By dwelling on how hard she had worked to support her daughters and how much she would be hurt if they failed to pay her back by making good marriages, Heilbrun's grandmother exploited their *sense of guilt*.

46. **(A)** The common factor in both grandmothers' lives is their need to govern the *actions of others*. McCarthy's grandmother tyrannized everyone from the mailman to her daughters and daughters-in-law; Heilbrun's grandmother "ruled the household with an arm of iron," governing her daughters' lives.

47. **(E)** McCarthy refers casually to Iago and Lady Macbeth, key figures in Shakespeare's tragedies. Heilbrun makes no such *literary references*.

48. **(D)** While Heilbrun's grandmother was a "sustaining woman" who provided for her family, McCarthy's grandmother was a grudging woman, not a sustaining one. Thus, McCarthy would most likely point out that *her grandmother's actual conduct is not in keeping with this characterization*.

Section 4 Mathematical Reasoning

21. **(D)** Since the ratio of the number of boys to girls is $2:3$, the number of boys is $2x$, the number of girls is $3x$, and the total number of members is $2x + 3x = 5x$. So the girls make up $\frac{3x}{5x} = \frac{3}{5} = 60\%$ of the members.

22. **(E)** Since d divisions each have t teams, multiply to get dt teams, and since each team has p players, multiply the number of teams (dt) by p to get the total number of players: *dtp*.

    Use TACTIC 2. Choose easy-to-use numbers for t, d, and p. For example, assume that there are 2 divisions, each with 4 teams So, there are $2 \times 4 = 8$ teams. Then assume that each of the teams has 10 players, for a total of $8 \times 10 = 80$ players. Now check the five choices. Which one is equal to 80 when $d = 2$, $t = 4$, and $p = 10$? Only *dtp*.

23. **(C)** Test each set of values to see which one does not work. Only Choice C, $x = 1$ and $y = -1$ does not work: $3(1)^2 + 2(-1) = 3 - 2 = 1$, not 5. The other choices all work.

24. **(C)** There is a total of $1 + 2 + 3 + 4 + 5 + 6 = 21$ slips of paper. Since odd numbers are written on $1 + 3 + 5 = 9$ of them, the probability of drawing an odd number is $\frac{9}{21} = \frac{3}{7}$.

25. **(B)** If $|x| = |y|$, then $x = y$ or $x = -y$. So $x^2 = y^2$ or $x^2 = (-y)^2 = y^2$. (II is true.) If $x = 1$ and $y = -1$, then both I and III are false. Only statement II is true.

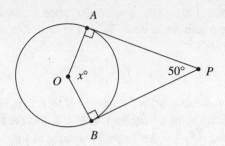

26. **(D)** Since $\overline{OA}$ and $\overline{OB}$ are radii drawn to the points of contact of two tangents, $\overline{OA}\perp\overline{PA}$ and $\overline{OB}\perp\overline{PB}$. So angles A and B are right angles. Finally, by **FACT 51**, the sum of the measures of the four angles in any quadrilateral is 360, so $90 + 90 + 50 + x = 360 \Rightarrow 230 + x = 360 \Rightarrow x = 130$.

27. **(A)** $2^{3x} + 2^{3x} + 2^{3x} + 2^{3x} = 4(2^{3x}) = 2^2(2^{3x}) = 2^{3x+2}$.

    **Let $x = 1$; then $2^{3x} = 2^3 = 8$, and
    $$2^{3x} + 2^{3x} + 2^{3x} + 2^{3x} = 8 + 8 + 8 + 8 = 32.$$
    Which of the choices equals 32 when $x = 1$? Only $2^{3x+2}(2^5 = 32)$.

28. **(B)** Let r and R be the radii of circle I and circle II, respectively. Since the circumference of circle I is $2\pi r$, the circumference of circle II is $2\pi r + 4 = 2(\pi r + 2)$. But, of course, the circumference of circle II is also $2\pi R$. Therefore,
    $$2\pi R = 2(\pi r + 2) \Rightarrow \pi R = \pi r + 2 \Rightarrow$$
    $$R = r + \frac{2}{\pi}.$$

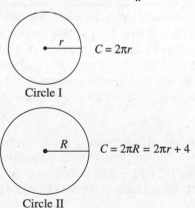

Circle I $C = 2\pi r$

Circle II $C = 2\pi R = 2\pi r + 4$

29. **(320)** Since $a + 100 = 180$, $a = 80$. But since ℓ and k are parallel, the four acute angles are all equal: $80 = a = b = c = d$, so their sum is $4 \times 80 = 320$.

30. **(30)** Evaluate: $2(6) - 3(-6) = 12 + 18 = 30$.

31. $\left(\mathbf{3.75}\ \textbf{or}\ \frac{\mathbf{15}}{\mathbf{4}}\right)$ The median of the 7 numbers 1, 2, 3, 4, 5, 6, 7 is the middle one: 4. The median of the 6 numbers 1, 2, 3, 4, 5, 6 is the average of the two middle ones: $\frac{3+4}{2} = 3.5$. Finally, the average of 4 and 3.5 is 3.75 or $\frac{15}{4}$.

32. **(70)** Since all of the radii of a circle have the same length, $CA = CB$. Therefore,
$$m\angle A = m\angle B = 55°, \text{ and}$$
$$c = 180 - (55 + 55) = 180 - 110 = 70.$$

33. **(57)** To find Elaine's average speed in kilometers per hour, divide the distance she went, in kilometers (190), by the time it took, in hours. Elaine drove for 3 hours and 20 minutes, which is $3\frac{1}{3}$ hours (20 minutes $= \frac{20}{60}$ hour $= \frac{1}{3}$ hour). Elaine's average speed is $190 \div 3\frac{1}{3} = 190 \div \frac{10}{3} = 190 \times \frac{3}{10} = 57$.

34. **(1.21)** Since this is a percent problem, assume the value of the investment on January 1, 1994 was $100. Since 10% of 100 is 10, one year later the value of the investment had increased by $10 to $110. Now, 10% of 110 is 11, so in the next year the value increased by $11 to $121. Finally, 121 is 1.21×100.

35. **(72)** There are 90 two-digit numbers (the integers from 10 to 99 inclusive). To find out how many of them do not contain the digit 9, calculate how many of them *do* contain the digit 9, and subtract that number from 90. There are a total of 18 two-digit numbers that contain the digit 9—the 10 numbers from 90 to 99 plus the 8 other numbers that end in 9: 19, 29, . . . , 89. Finally, there are $90 - 18 = 72$ two-digit numbers that do not contain the digit 9.

36. **(87.5)** If the average of 5 numbers is 95, the sum of those numbers is $5 \times 95 = 475$. Similarly, the sum of the 3 numbers whose average is 100 is 300, leaving 175 ($475 - 300$) as the sum of the 2 remaining numbers. The average of these 2 numbers is their sum divided by 2: $175 \div 2 = 87.5$.

37. **(1)** Assume that the radius of the large circle is 2. Then the area of the circle is 4π. The radius of each semicircle is 1, and since the area of a circle of radius 1 is π, the area of each semicircle is $\frac{1}{2}\pi$, and the total shaded area is $4\left(\frac{1}{2}\pi\right) = 2\pi$. Since the shaded area is exactly one-half of the circle, the white area is also one-half of the circle. The areas are equal, and so the shaded area is 1 times the white area.

38. **(2500)** If 99.6% of the people tested did not have the disease, then 0.4% of them did have the disease. If $x =$ the number of people tested, then $10 = 0.004x \Rightarrow x = 10 \div .004 = 2500$.

Section 5 Writing Skills

1. **(C)** Choice C uses *drank*, the correct form of the irregular verb *drink*.

2. **(D)** Error in tense. Change *began* to *had begun*.

3. **(D)** Error in idiom. *Seems satisfying their need* is unidiomatic. *Seems to satisfy their need* is correct.

4. **(C)** Error in coordination and subordination. Choice C corrects the error in conjunction use.

5. **(D)** Error in following conventions. *Irregardless* is a nonstandard use of *regardless*.

6. **(B)** Comma splice. The run-on sentence is corrected in Choice B.

7. **(D)** Errors in subject-verb agreement. The phrase *along with several other stories* is not part of the subject of the sentence. The subject is *"Araby"* (singular); the verb should be *is going to be read* (singular).

8. **(A)** Sentence is correct. Choice B introduces an error in agreement. Choices C, D, and E misuse the *not only . . . but also* construction.

9. **(E)** Error in modification and word order. The dangling modifier is corrected in Choice E.

10. **(B)** Error in modification and word order. The dangling construction is corrected in Choices B and E. However, only Choice B retains the meaning of the original sentence.

11. **(B)** The error in case is corrected in Choice B. *Whoever* is the subject of the verb *had contributed*.

12. **(E)** In this question we find two errors. Both the sentence fragment and the misuse of the intransitive verb *lie* are corrected in Choice E.

13. **(D)** Error in logical comparison. The faulty comparison is corrected in Choice D.

14. **(A)** The original sentence is correct. The subject of *are going* is *legislators* (plural). Therefore, Choices B and C are incorrect. Choices D and E change the meaning of the original sentence.

15. **(D)** Incomplete comparison. They are as harmful *to* women as they are *to* men.

16. **(A)** Sentence is correct.

17. **(E)** Error in usage. Do not use *when* or *where* after *is* in making a definition.

18. **(D)** Error in sequence of tenses. The present perfect tense ("has been informed") indicates some vague time before now, or a time that lasts up to the present. NASA, however, was told about the dangerous weather conditions at a definite time in the past. Therefore, you should use either the simple past tense ("was informed") or the past perfect tense ("had been informed") here.

19. **(D)** Error in idiom. Either James hoped *for* the revitalization of his career, or he hoped *to* revitalize it. In this case, the verbal *to revitalize* is correct.

20. **(C)** Dangling modifier. Ask yourself who are strolling in the park. Choice C rearranges the words in the sentence to make "While strolling in Golden Gate Park one day" clearly refer to "the young couple."

21. **(A)** Error in diction. Change *Being that* to *Since*.

22. **(A)** Error in following conventions. Double negative. Change *can't* to *can*.

23. **(B)** Error in pronoun case. *But*, as used in this sentence, is a preposition meaning *except*. Change *he* to *him*.

24. **(D)** Error in following conventions. Change *reason . . . is because* to *reason . . . is that*.

25. **(B)** Error in tense. Change *am playing* to *have been playing*.

26. **(B)** Error in diction. Change *affective* to *effective*.

27. **(B)** Error in diction. *Among* should be used when three or more items are being considered.

28. **(D)** Error in parallelism. Change *as well as signing* to *and sign* in order to match the other items in the list.

29. **(C)** Error in coordination and subordination. Incorrect sentence connector. Change *furthermore* to the coordinating conjunction *but* to clarify the relationship between the clauses.

30. **(D)** Error in idiom. Change *accumulation from* to *accumulation of*.

31. **(A)** Error in diction. *Altogether* is correct.

32. **(E)** Sentence is correct.

33. **(B)** Error in idiom. Change *differ with* (which relates to difference of opinion) to *differ from* (which relates to difference in appearance).

34. **(C)** Error in parallelism. Change *remaining at* to the infinitive *to remain at* in order to match *to travel on*.

35. **(A)** Choice A accurately describes the content of the essay. The original introductory sentence is misleading. The essay is about changes in the status

of women, not about the role women played in causing the changes. It is the best answer.

Choice B is a variation of the original introductory sentence but the use of the future verb tense fails to convey the actual content of the essay.

Choice C is a confusing sentence consisting of two illogically unrelated clauses.

Choice D fails to convey the contents of the essay. It also contains the pronoun *their*, which does not have a clear antecedent.

Choice E is virtually meaningless. It also contains a dangling participle. The phrase that begins *Being influenced . . .* should modify *women*, not *status*.

36. (D) Choice A inserts a comma splice between *lifted* and *for example*. Two independent clauses should be separated by a period or semicolon.

Choice B contains the pronoun *they*, which lacks a specific reference.

Choice C improperly shifts pronouns from third person to second person.

Choice D is effectively expressed. It is the best answer.

Choice E is cumbersome and awkwardly worded.

The phrase *the right of going into public* contains an idiom error. The correct phrase is *right to go into public*.

37. (A) Choice A provides a smooth transition by alluding to the discussion of competition in the second paragraph and introducing the main topic of the third. A is the best answer.

Choice B uses a nonstandard transitional word *irregardless*, which in the context makes no sense.

Choice C contains no specifically transitional material.

Choice D would be a decent transition were it not for its mixed construction. The first half of the sentence doesn't fit grammatically with the second half.

Choice E introduces a new idea that is unrelated to the content of the third paragraph.

38. (E) Choice A is illogical; becoming a role model is not an example of attaining a high position in politics and government.

Choice B is not a good example of attaining a high position in politics.

Choice C is irrelevant. Margaret Thatcher's defeat is not an example of an achievement in politics and government.

Choice D is slightly off the mark. The sentence emphasizes Indira Ghandi's assassination instead of her leadership.

Choice E gives two examples of women who have attained a high position in politics and government. It is the best answer.

39. (E) All the sentences except sentence 14 support the idea stated in the topic sentence, that women have made gains in politics and government. Therefore, Choice E is the best answer.

ANSWER SHEET—PRACTICE TEST 2

Section 1
Critical Reading
25 minutes

1 Ⓐ Ⓑ Ⓒ Ⓓ Ⓔ
2 Ⓐ Ⓑ Ⓒ Ⓓ Ⓔ
3 Ⓐ Ⓑ Ⓒ Ⓓ Ⓔ
4 Ⓐ Ⓑ Ⓒ Ⓓ Ⓔ
5 Ⓐ Ⓑ Ⓒ Ⓓ Ⓔ
6 Ⓐ Ⓑ Ⓒ Ⓓ Ⓔ
7 Ⓐ Ⓑ Ⓒ Ⓓ Ⓔ
8 Ⓐ Ⓑ Ⓒ Ⓓ Ⓔ
9 Ⓐ Ⓑ Ⓒ Ⓓ Ⓔ
10 Ⓐ Ⓑ Ⓒ Ⓓ Ⓔ
11 Ⓐ Ⓑ Ⓒ Ⓓ Ⓔ
12 Ⓐ Ⓑ Ⓒ Ⓓ Ⓔ
13 Ⓐ Ⓑ Ⓒ Ⓓ Ⓔ
14 Ⓐ Ⓑ Ⓒ Ⓓ Ⓔ
15 Ⓐ Ⓑ Ⓒ Ⓓ Ⓔ
16 Ⓐ Ⓑ Ⓒ Ⓓ Ⓔ
17 Ⓐ Ⓑ Ⓒ Ⓓ Ⓔ
18 Ⓐ Ⓑ Ⓒ Ⓓ Ⓔ
19 Ⓐ Ⓑ Ⓒ Ⓓ Ⓔ
20 Ⓐ Ⓑ Ⓒ Ⓓ Ⓔ
21 Ⓐ Ⓑ Ⓒ Ⓓ Ⓔ
22 Ⓐ Ⓑ Ⓒ Ⓓ Ⓔ
23 Ⓐ Ⓑ Ⓒ Ⓓ Ⓔ
24 Ⓐ Ⓑ Ⓒ Ⓓ Ⓔ

Section 2
Math
25 minutes

1 Ⓐ Ⓑ Ⓒ Ⓓ Ⓔ
2 Ⓐ Ⓑ Ⓒ Ⓓ Ⓔ
3 Ⓐ Ⓑ Ⓒ Ⓓ Ⓔ
4 Ⓐ Ⓑ Ⓒ Ⓓ Ⓔ
5 Ⓐ Ⓑ Ⓒ Ⓓ Ⓔ
6 Ⓐ Ⓑ Ⓒ Ⓓ Ⓔ
7 Ⓐ Ⓑ Ⓒ Ⓓ Ⓔ
8 Ⓐ Ⓑ Ⓒ Ⓓ Ⓔ
9 Ⓐ Ⓑ Ⓒ Ⓓ Ⓔ
10 Ⓐ Ⓑ Ⓒ Ⓓ Ⓔ
11 Ⓐ Ⓑ Ⓒ Ⓓ Ⓔ
12 Ⓐ Ⓑ Ⓒ Ⓓ Ⓔ
13 Ⓐ Ⓑ Ⓒ Ⓓ Ⓔ
14 Ⓐ Ⓑ Ⓒ Ⓓ Ⓔ
15 Ⓐ Ⓑ Ⓒ Ⓓ Ⓔ
16 Ⓐ Ⓑ Ⓒ Ⓓ Ⓔ
17 Ⓐ Ⓑ Ⓒ Ⓓ Ⓔ
18 Ⓐ Ⓑ Ⓒ Ⓓ Ⓔ
19 Ⓐ Ⓑ Ⓒ Ⓓ Ⓔ
20 Ⓐ Ⓑ Ⓒ Ⓓ Ⓔ

Section 3
Critical Reading
25 minutes

25	Ⓐ Ⓑ Ⓒ Ⓓ Ⓔ			37	Ⓐ Ⓑ Ⓒ Ⓓ Ⓔ
26	Ⓐ Ⓑ Ⓒ Ⓓ Ⓔ			38	Ⓐ Ⓑ Ⓒ Ⓓ Ⓔ
27	Ⓐ Ⓑ Ⓒ Ⓓ Ⓔ			39	Ⓐ Ⓑ Ⓒ Ⓓ Ⓔ
28	Ⓐ Ⓑ Ⓒ Ⓓ Ⓔ			40	Ⓐ Ⓑ Ⓒ Ⓓ Ⓔ
29	Ⓐ Ⓑ Ⓒ Ⓓ Ⓔ			41	Ⓐ Ⓑ Ⓒ Ⓓ Ⓔ
30	Ⓐ Ⓑ Ⓒ Ⓓ Ⓔ			42	Ⓐ Ⓑ Ⓒ Ⓓ Ⓔ
31	Ⓐ Ⓑ Ⓒ Ⓓ Ⓔ			43	Ⓐ Ⓑ Ⓒ Ⓓ Ⓔ
32	Ⓐ Ⓑ Ⓒ Ⓓ Ⓔ			44	Ⓐ Ⓑ Ⓒ Ⓓ Ⓔ
33	Ⓐ Ⓑ Ⓒ Ⓓ Ⓔ			45	Ⓐ Ⓑ Ⓒ Ⓓ Ⓔ
34	Ⓐ Ⓑ Ⓒ Ⓓ Ⓔ			46	Ⓐ Ⓑ Ⓒ Ⓓ Ⓔ
35	Ⓐ Ⓑ Ⓒ Ⓓ Ⓔ			47	Ⓐ Ⓑ Ⓒ Ⓓ Ⓔ
36	Ⓐ Ⓑ Ⓒ Ⓓ Ⓔ			48	Ⓐ Ⓑ Ⓒ Ⓓ Ⓔ

Section 4
Math
25 minutes

21	Ⓐ Ⓑ Ⓒ Ⓓ Ⓔ
22	Ⓐ Ⓑ Ⓒ Ⓓ Ⓔ
23	Ⓐ Ⓑ Ⓒ Ⓓ Ⓔ
24	Ⓐ Ⓑ Ⓒ Ⓓ Ⓔ
25	Ⓐ Ⓑ Ⓒ Ⓓ Ⓔ
26	Ⓐ Ⓑ Ⓒ Ⓓ Ⓔ
27	Ⓐ Ⓑ Ⓒ Ⓓ Ⓔ
28	Ⓐ Ⓑ Ⓒ Ⓓ Ⓔ

29

30

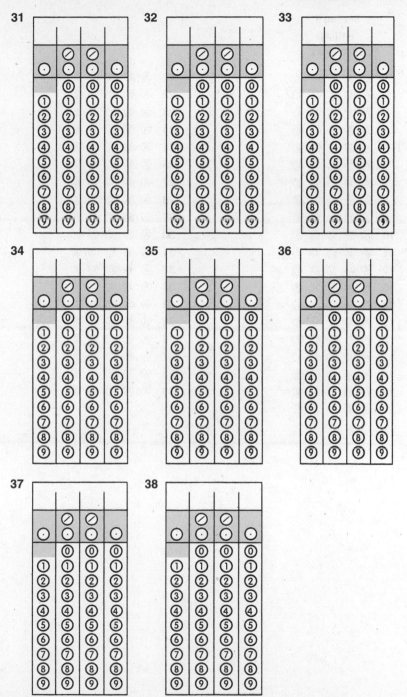

Section 5
Writing
30 minutes

1 Ⓐ Ⓑ Ⓒ Ⓓ Ⓔ
2 Ⓐ Ⓑ Ⓒ Ⓓ Ⓔ
3 Ⓐ Ⓑ Ⓒ Ⓓ Ⓔ
4 Ⓐ Ⓑ Ⓒ Ⓓ Ⓔ
5 Ⓐ Ⓑ Ⓒ Ⓓ Ⓔ
6 Ⓐ Ⓑ Ⓒ Ⓓ Ⓔ
7 Ⓐ Ⓑ Ⓒ Ⓓ Ⓔ
8 Ⓐ Ⓑ Ⓒ Ⓓ Ⓔ
9 Ⓐ Ⓑ Ⓒ Ⓓ Ⓔ
10 Ⓐ Ⓑ Ⓒ Ⓓ Ⓔ
11 Ⓐ Ⓑ Ⓒ Ⓓ Ⓔ
12 Ⓐ Ⓑ Ⓒ Ⓓ Ⓔ
13 Ⓐ Ⓑ Ⓒ Ⓓ Ⓔ
14 Ⓐ Ⓑ Ⓒ Ⓓ Ⓔ
15 Ⓐ Ⓑ Ⓒ Ⓓ Ⓔ
16 Ⓐ Ⓑ Ⓒ Ⓓ Ⓔ
17 Ⓐ Ⓑ Ⓒ Ⓓ Ⓔ
18 Ⓐ Ⓑ Ⓒ Ⓓ Ⓔ
19 Ⓐ Ⓑ Ⓒ Ⓓ Ⓔ
20 Ⓐ Ⓑ Ⓒ Ⓓ Ⓔ

21 Ⓐ Ⓑ Ⓒ Ⓓ Ⓔ
22 Ⓐ Ⓑ Ⓒ Ⓓ Ⓔ
23 Ⓐ Ⓑ Ⓒ Ⓓ Ⓔ
24 Ⓐ Ⓑ Ⓒ Ⓓ Ⓔ
25 Ⓐ Ⓑ Ⓒ Ⓓ Ⓔ
26 Ⓐ Ⓑ Ⓒ Ⓓ Ⓔ
27 Ⓐ Ⓑ Ⓒ Ⓓ Ⓔ
28 Ⓐ Ⓑ Ⓒ Ⓓ Ⓔ
29 Ⓐ Ⓑ Ⓒ Ⓓ Ⓔ
30 Ⓐ Ⓑ Ⓒ Ⓓ Ⓔ
31 Ⓐ Ⓑ Ⓒ Ⓓ Ⓔ
32 Ⓐ Ⓑ Ⓒ Ⓓ Ⓔ
33 Ⓐ Ⓑ Ⓒ Ⓓ Ⓔ
34 Ⓐ Ⓑ Ⓒ Ⓓ Ⓔ
35 Ⓐ Ⓑ Ⓒ Ⓓ Ⓔ
36 Ⓐ Ⓑ Ⓒ Ⓓ Ⓔ
37 Ⓐ Ⓑ Ⓒ Ⓓ Ⓔ
38 Ⓐ Ⓑ Ⓒ Ⓓ Ⓔ
39 Ⓐ Ⓑ Ⓒ Ⓓ Ⓔ

PRACTICE TEST 2

SECTION 1/CRITICAL READING
Time—25 minutes   24 questions (1–24)

For each question in this section, select the best answer from among the choices given and fill in the corresponding circle on the answer sheet.

Each sentence below has one or two blanks, each blank indicating that something has been omitted. Beneath the sentence are five words or sets of words labeled A through E. Choose the word or set of words that, when inserted in the sentence, best fits the meaning of the sentence as a whole.

EXAMPLE:

Medieval kingdoms did not become constitutional republics overnight; on the contrary, the change was ----.

(A) unpopular   (B) unexpected
(C) advantageous   (D) sufficient   (E) gradual

---

1. Impressed by the extraordinary potential of the new superconductor, scientists predict that its use will ---- the computer industry, creating new products overnight.
   (A) justify   (B) alienate   (C) nullify
   (D) revolutionize   (E) overestimate

2. No matter how ---- the revelations of the coming year may be, they will be hard put to match those of the past decade, which have ---- transformed our view of the emergence of Mayan civilization.
   (A) minor..dramatically
   (B) profound..negligibly
   (C) striking..radically
   (D) bizarre..nominally
   (E) questionable..possibly

3. Few other plants can grow beneath the canopy of the sycamore tree, whose leaves and pods produce a natural herbicide that leaches into the soil, ---- other plants that might compete for water and nutrients.

   (A) inhibiting
   (B) distinguishing
   (C) nourishing
   (D) encouraging
   (E) refreshing

4. Black women authors such as Zora Neale Hurston, originally ---- by both white and black literary establishments to obscurity as minor novelists, are being rediscovered by black feminist critics today.

   (A) inclined   (B) relegated   (C) subjected
   (D) diminished   (E) characterized

5. Critics of the movie version of *The Color Purple* ---- its saccharine, overoptimistic mood as out of keeping with the novel's more ---- tone.

   (A) applauded..somber
   (B) condemned..hopeful
   (C) acclaimed..positive
   (D) denounced..sanguine
   (E) decried..acerbic

The passages below are followed by questions on their content; questions following a pair of related passages may also be based on the relationship between the paired passages. Answer the questions on the basis of what is stated or implied in the passages and in any introductory material that may be provided.

Questions 6–9 are based on the following passages.

Passage 1

There was a time when poetry mattered in America—a time when T. S. Eliot could fill a football stadium with poetry fans, when literature enjoyed a central place in our culture, and young men and women
Line dreamed about becoming writers. That time is long gone. Today if
(5) young people dream of writing at all, they dream of writing rap songs or sitcom scripts, pop lit, not enduring works of art.

Passage 2

Recently a children's book about writing poetry came out. It was called *Poetry Matters*. In essence, that's the question poets face today. Does poetry matter? As Billy Collins wrote, "One of the ridiculous
(10) aspects of being a poet is the huge gulf between how seriously we take ourselves and how generally we are ignored by everybody else." We think that what we write matters, but for the most part, in America no one cares. It may be different elsewhere on the globe—Ossip Mandelstam once maintained that only in Russia was poetry respected
(15) because there it got people killed. Here, we don't get killed, but we're dying anyway.

6. In Passage 1, the reference to the football stadium (line 2) serves primarily to

   (A) demonstrate the connection between sports and poetry
   (B) show Eliot's deep appreciation of football
   (C) emphasize the popularity of poetry in the period
   (D) suggest a potential site for poetry readings today
   (E) point out Eliot's enduring vision

7. In Passage 1, the word "enjoyed" (line 3) most nearly means

   (A) fancied
   (B) relished
   (C) possessed
   (D) appreciated
   (E) flourished

8. In Passage 2, the statement "we're dying anyway" (lines 15–16) is an example of

   (A) an apology
   (B) a metaphor
   (C) a euphemism
   (D) a hypothesis
   (E) an understatement

9. The authors of Passage 1 and Passage 2 agree that

   (A) poetry plays a significant role in modern culture
   (B) poets must take themselves seriously if poetry is to survive
   (C) rap songs are a valid form of poetic expression
   (D) poetry is more appealing to children than to adults
   (E) the climate for poetry in America is inauspicious

Each passage below is followed by questions based on its content. Answer the questions following each passage on the basis of what is stated or implied in that passage and in any introductory material that may be provided.

Questions 10–15 are based upon the following passage.

In the following passage from Jane Austen's novel Pride and Prejudice, *the heroine Elizabeth Bennet faces an unexpected encounter with her father's cousin (and prospective heir), the clergyman Mr. Collins.*

It was absolutely necessary to interrupt him now.

"You are too hasty, Sir," she cried. "You forget that I have made no answer. Let me do it without further loss of time. Accept my thanks for
Line   the compliment you are paying me. I am very sensible of the honour of
(5)   your proposals, but it is impossible for me to do otherwise than decline them."

"I am not now to learn," replied Mr. Collins with a formal wave of the hand, "that it is usual with young ladies to reject the addresses of the man whom they secretly mean to accept, when he first applies for their
(10)   favour; and that sometimes the refusal is repeated a second or even a third time. I am therefore by no means discouraged by what you have just said, and shall hope to lead you to the altar ere long."

"Upon my word, Sir," cried Elizabeth, "your hope is rather an extraordinary one after my declaration. I do assure you that I am not one of
(15)   those young ladies (if such young ladies there are) who are so daring as to risk their happiness on the chance of being asked a second time. I am perfectly serious in my refusal. You could not make *me* happy, and I am convinced that I am the last woman in the world who would make *you* so. Nay, were your friend Lady Catherine to know me, I am persuaded
(20)   she would find me in every respect ill qualified for the situation."

"Were it certain that Lady Catherine would think so," said Mr. Collins very gravely—"but I cannot imagine that her ladyship would at all disapprove of you. And you may be certain that when I have the honour of seeing her again I shall speak in the highest terms of your modesty,
(25)   economy, and other amiable qualifications."

"Indeed, Mr. Collins, all praise of me will be unnecessary. You must give me leave to judge for myself, and pay me the compliment of believing what I say. I wish you very happy and very rich, and by refusing your hand, do all in my power to prevent your being otherwise. In making me
(30)   the offer, you must have satisfied the delicacy of your feelings with regard to my family, and may take possession of Longbourn estate

whenever it falls, without any self-reproach. This matter may be considered, therefore, as finally settled." And rising as she thus spoke, she
would have quitted the room, had not Mr. Collins thus addressed her.

(35)   "When I do myself the honour of speaking to you next on this subject
I shall hope to receive a more favourable answer than you have now
given me; though I am far from accusing you of cruelty at present,
because I know it to be the established custom of your sex to reject a
man on the first application, and perhaps you have even now said as

(40) much to encourage my suit as would be consistent with the true delicacy
of the female character."

     "Really, Mr. Collins," cried Elizabeth with some warmth, "you puzzle
me exceedingly. If what I have hitherto said can appear to you in the
form of encouragement, I know not how to express my refusal in such a

(45) way as may convince you of its being one."

10. It can be inferred that in the paragraphs immediately preceding this passage

   (A) Elizabeth and Mr. Collins quarreled
   (B) Elizabeth met Mr. Collins for the first time
   (C) Mr. Collins asked Elizabeth to marry him
   (D) Mr. Collins gravely insulted Elizabeth
   (E) Elizabeth discovered that Mr. Collins was a fraud

11. The word "sensible" in line 4 means

   (A) logical
   (B) perceptible
   (C) sound in judgment
   (D) keenly aware
   (E) appreciable

12. Instead of having the intended effect, Elizabeth's initial refusal of Mr. Collins
(lines 2–6)

   (A) causes her to rethink rejecting him
   (B) makes him less inclined to wed
   (C) gives her the opportunity to consider other options
   (D) persuades him she dislikes him intensely
   (E) fails to put an end to his suit

13. It can be inferred from lines 21–23 that Mr. Collins

    (A) will take Elizabeth's words seriously
    (B) admires Elizabeth's independence
    (C) is very disappointed by her decision
    (D) would accept Lady Catherine's opinion
    (E) means his remarks as a joke

14. The reason Elizabeth insists all praise of her "will be unnecessary" (line 26) is because she

    (A) feels sure Lady Catherine will learn to admire her in time
    (B) is too shy to accept compliments readily
    (C) has no intention of marrying Mr. Collins
    (D) believes a clergyman should be less effusive
    (E) values her own worth excessively

15. On the basis of his behavior in this passage, Mr. Collins may best be described as

    (A) malicious in intent
    (B) both obtuse and obstinate
    (C) unsure of his acceptance
    (D) kindly and understanding
    (E) sensitive to Elizabeth's wishes

Questions 16–24 are based on the following passage.

African elephants now are an endangered species. The following passage, taken from a newspaper article written in 1989, discusses the potential ecological disaster that might occur if the elephant were to become extinct.

        The African elephant—mythic symbol of a continent, keystone of its ecology and the largest land animal remaining on earth—has become the object of one of the biggest, broadest international efforts yet
Line mounted to turn a threatened species off the road to extinction. But it is
(5) not only the elephant's survival that is at stake, conservationists say. Unlike the endangered tiger, unlike even the great whales, the African elephant is in great measure the architect of its environment. As a voracious eater of vegetation, it largely shapes the forest-and-savanna surroundings in which it lives, thereby setting the terms of existence for
(10) millions of other storied animals—from zebras to gazelles to giraffes and wildebeests—that share its habitat. And as the elephant disappears, scientists and conservationists say, many other species will also disappear from vast stretches of forest and savanna, drastically altering and impoverishing whole ecosystems.
(15)   Just as the American buffalo was hunted almost to extinction a cen-

tury ago, so the African elephant is now the victim of an onslaught of
commercial killing, stimulated in this case by soaring global demand for
ivory. Most of the killing is illegal, and conservationists say that although
the pressure of human population and development contributes to the
(20) elephants' decline, poaching is by far the greatest threat. The elephant
may or may not be on the way to becoming a mere zoological curiosity
like the buffalo, but the trend is clear.

In an atmosphere of mounting alarm among conservationists, a new
international coordinating group backed by 21 ivory-producing and
(25) ivory-consuming countries has met and adopted an ambitious plan of
action. Against admittedly long odds, the multinational rescue effort is
aimed both at stopping the slaughter of the elephants in the short term
and at nurturing them as a vital "keystone species" in the long run.

It is the elephant's metabolism and appetite that make it a disturber
(30) of the environment and therefore an important creator of habitat. In a
constant search for the 300 pounds of vegetation it must have every day,
it kills small trees and underbrush and pulls branches off big trees as
high as its trunk will reach. This creates innumerable open spaces in
both deep tropical forests and in the woodlands that cover part of the
(35) African savannas. The resulting patchwork, a mosaic of vegetation in
various stages of regeneration, in turn creates a greater variety of forage
that attracts a greater variety of other vegetation-eaters than would otherwise be the case.

In studies over the last 20 years in southern Kenya near Mount
(40) Kilimanjaro, Dr. David Western has found that when elephants are
allowed to roam the savannas naturally and normally, they spread out at
"intermediate densities." Their foraging creates a mixture of savanna
woodlands (what the Africans call bush) and grassland. The result is a
highly diverse array of other plant-eating species: those like the zebra,
(45) wildebeest and gazelle, that graze; those like the giraffe, bushbuck and
lesser kudu, that browse on tender shoots, buds, twigs and leaves; and
plant-eating primates like the baboon and vervet monkey. These herbi-
vores attract carnivores like the lion and cheetah.

When the elephant population thins out, Dr. Western said, the wood-
(50) lands become denser and the grazers are squeezed out. When pressure
from poachers forces elephants to crowd more densely onto reserva-
tions, the woodlands there are knocked out and the browsers and primates disappear.

Something similar appears to happen in dense tropical rain forests.
(55) In their natural state, because the overhead forest canopy shuts out sunlight and prevents growth on the forest floor, rain forests provide slim
pickings for large, hoofed plant-eaters. By pulling down trees and eating

new growth, elephants enlarge natural openings in the canopy, allowing
plants to regenerate on the forest floor and bringing down vegetation
(60)   from the canopy so that smaller species can get at it.

In such situations, the rain forest becomes hospitable to large plant-
eating mammals such as bongos, bush pigs, duikers, forest hogs,
swamp antelopes, forest buffaloes, okapis, sometimes gorillas and
always a host of smaller animals that thrive on secondary growth. When
(65)   elephants disappear and the forest reverts, the larger animals give way
to smaller, nimbler animals like monkeys, squirrels and rodents.

16. The passage is primarily concerned with

(A) explaining why elephants are facing the threat of extinction
(B) explaining difficulties in providing sufficient forage for plant-eaters
(C) explaining how the elephant's impact on its surroundings affects other
species
(D) distinguishing between savannas and rain forests as habitats for
elephants
(E) contrasting elephants with members of other endangered species

17. The word "mounted" in line 4 means

(A) ascended
(B) increased
(C) launched
(D) attached
(E) exhibited

18. In the opening paragraph, the author mentions tigers and whales in order to
emphasize which point about the elephant?

(A) Like them, it faces the threat of extinction
(B) It is herbivorous rather than carnivorous
(C) It moves more ponderously than either the tiger or the whale
(D) Unlike them, it physically alters its environment
(E) It is the largest extant land mammal

19. A necessary component of the elephant's ability to transform the landscape
is its

(A) massive intelligence
(B) fear of predators
(C) ravenous hunger
(D) lack of grace
(E) ability to regenerate

20. It can be inferred from the passage that

    (A) the lion and the cheetah commonly prey upon elephants

    (B) the elephant is dependent upon the existence of smaller plant-eating mammals for its survival

    (C) elephants have an indirect effect on the hunting patterns of certain carnivores

    (D) the floor of the tropical rain forest is too overgrown to accommodate larger plant-eating species

    (E) the natural tendency of elephants is to crowd together in packs

21. In line 28, the quotation marks around the phrase "keystone species" serve to

    (A) emphasize the triteness of the phrase

    (B) contradict the literal meaning of the term

    (C) indicate the author's desire to write colloquially

    (D) imply the phrase has ironic connotations

    (E) indicate the phrase is being used in a special or technical sense

22. The passage contains information that would answer which of the following questions?

    I. How does the elephant's foraging affect its surroundings?

    II. How do the feeding patterns of gazelles and giraffes differ?

    III. What occurs in the rain forest when the elephant population dwindles?

        (A) I only

        (B) II only

        (C) I and II only

        (D) II and III only

        (E) I, II, and III

23. The word "host" in line 64 means

    (A) food source for parasites

    (B) very large number

    (C) provider of hospitality

    (D) military force

    (E) angelic company

24. Which of the following statements best expresses the author's attitude toward the damage to vegetation caused by foraging elephants?

(A) It is a regrettable by-product of the feeding process.

(B) It is a necessary but undesirable aspect of elephant population growth.

(C) It fortuitously results in creating environments suited to diverse species.

(D) It has the unexpected advantage that it allows scientists access to the rain forest.

(E) It reinforces the impression that elephants are a disruptive force.

IF YOU FINISH IN LESS THAN 25 MINUTES, YOU MAY CHECK YOUR WORK ON THIS SECTION ONLY. DO NOT TURN TO ANY OTHER SECTION IN THE TEST.   **S T O P**

SECTION 2/MATHEMATICAL REASONING
Time—25 minutes   20 questions (1–20)

For each question in this section, determine which of the five choices is correct and blacken that choice on your answer sheet. You may use any blank space on the page for your work.

Notes:

- You may use a calculator whenever you believe it will be helpful.
- Use the diagrams provided to help you solve the problems. Unless you see the phrase "Note: Figure not drawn to scale" under a diagram, it has been drawn as accurately as possible. Unless it is stated that a figure is three-dimensional, you may assume that it lies in a plane.

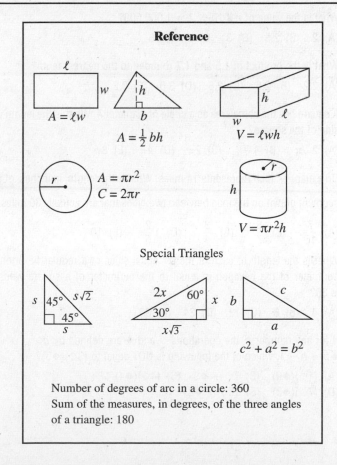

Reference

$A = \ell w$

$A = \frac{1}{2} bh$

$V = \ell wh$

$A = \pi r^2$
$C = 2\pi r$

$V = \pi r^2 h$

Special Triangles

$c^2 + a^2 = b^2$

Number of degrees of arc in a circle: 360
Sum of the measures, in degrees, of the three angles of a triangle: 180

1. If $b - 8 = 0$, what is the value of $b + 8$?

(A) -16 (B) -8 (C) 0   (D) 8   (E) 16

2. Isaac has twice as many toys as Sidney. If Isaac has t toys, how many does Sidney have?

(A) $2t$ (B) t^2 (C) $\frac{t}{2}$ (D) $\frac{2}{t}$ (E) $t + 2$

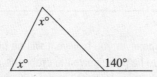

3. In the figure above, what is the value of x?

(A) 40   (B) 60   (C) 70   (D) 80   (E) 140

4. What is the value of n if $10^{2n + 1} = 1{,}000{,}000$?

(A) 2   (B) 2.5   (C) 3   (D) 5   (E) 6

5. What is the product of 1.5 and 1.7 rounded to the nearest tenth?

(A) 2.2   (B) 2.5   (C) 2.6   (D) 3.0   (E) 3.2

6. A square has the same area as a circle of diameter 4. What is the length of each side of the square?

(A) $2\sqrt{\pi}$ (B) $4\sqrt{\pi}$ (C) 2π (D) 4π (E) 8π

7. On a map, $\frac{1}{3}$ inch represents 14 miles. What is the length, in inches, of the line segment drawn on the map between two cities that are actually 30 miles apart?

(A) $\frac{7}{15}$ (B) $\frac{5}{7}$ (C) $\frac{3}{4}$ (D) $1\frac{2}{5}$ (E) 10

8. What is the length of each of the six equal sides of a regular hexagon, if the perimeter of the hexagon is equal to the perimeter of a square whose area is 36?

(A) 4   (B) 6   (C) 12   (D) 24   (E) 36

9. If for any number b, the operations $\diamond$ and $\blacklozenge$ are defined by $b\diamond = b + 1$ and $\blacklozenge b = b - 1$, which of the following is NOT equal to $(3\diamond)(\blacklozenge 5)$?

(A) $(1\diamond)(\blacklozenge 9)$ (B) $7\diamond + \blacklozenge 9$ (C) $(4\diamond)(\blacklozenge 4)$
(D) $(7\diamond)(\blacklozenge 3)$ (E) $15\diamond \div \blacklozenge 2$

10. If $\frac{n+2}{5}$ is an integer, what is the remainder when n is divided by 5?

    (A) 1 (B) 2 (C) 3 (D) 4
    (E) It cannot be determined from the information given.

11. The day of a quiz, only Michelle was absent. The average (arithmetic mean) grade of the other students was 85. When Michelle took a make-up quiz, her grade was 30, which lowered the class's average to 80. How many students are in the class?

    (A) 8 (B) 9 (C) 10 (D) 11 (E) 12

12. At Music Warehouse the regular price for a CD is d dollars. How many CDs can be purchased there for m dollars when the CDs are on sale at 20% off the regular price?

    (A) $\frac{4d}{5m}$ (B) $\frac{4m}{5d}$ (C) $\frac{5d}{4m}$ (D) $\frac{5m}{4d}$ (E) $\frac{md}{20}$

13. In a group of 40 people, 13 own dogs and 18 own cats. If 16 have neither a dog nor a cat, how many people have both?

    (A) 0 (B) 3 (C) 6 (D) 7 (E) 11

14. How many integers are solutions of the inequality $3|x| + 1 < 16$?

    (A) 0 (B) 4 (C) 8 (D) 9 (E) Infinitely many

15. Each of the 15 members of a club owns a certain number of teddy bears. The following chart shows the number of teddy bears owned.

Number of Teddy Bears	Number of Members
6	2
8	5
10	4
13	4

    What is the average (arithmetic mean) of the median and the mode of this set of data?

    (A) 4.5 (B) 8 (C) 8.5 (D) 9 (E) 9.5

16. What is the value of $3^{\frac{1}{2}} \times 3^{\frac{1}{3}} \times 3^{\frac{1}{6}}$?

    (A) $3^{\frac{1}{36}}$ (B) $3^{\frac{1}{11}}$ (C) $27^{\frac{1}{36}}$ (D) $27^{\frac{1}{11}}$ (E) 3

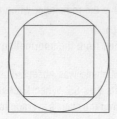

17. In the figure above, the small square is inscribed in the circle, which is inscribed in the large square. What is the ratio of the area of the large square to the area of the small square?

(A) $\sqrt{2}$:1   (B) $\sqrt{3}$:1   (C) 2:1   (D) 2$\sqrt{2}$:1

(E) It cannot be determined from the information given.

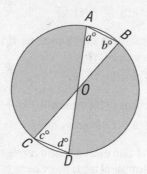

18. In the figure above, O is the center of the circle and $AD = 10$. If the area of the shaded region is 20π, what is the value of $a + b + c + d$?

(A) 144   (B) 216   (C) 240   (D) 270   (E) 288

19. If $r + 2s = a$ and $r - 2s = b$, which of the following is an expression for rs?

(A) ab (B) $\dfrac{a+b}{2}$ (C) $\dfrac{a-b}{2}$

(D) $\dfrac{a^2 - b^2}{4}$ (E) $\dfrac{a^2 - b^2}{8}$

20. If a is increased by 25% and b is decreased by 25%, the resulting numbers will be equal. What is the ratio of a to b?

(A) $\dfrac{3}{5}$ (B) $\dfrac{3}{4}$ (C) $\dfrac{1}{1}$ (D) $\dfrac{4}{3}$ (E) $\dfrac{5}{3}$

IF YOU FINISH IN LESS THAN 25 MINUTES, YOU MAY CHECK YOUR WORK ON THIS SECTION ONLY. DO NOT TURN TO ANY OTHER SECTION IN THE TEST.   **S T O P**

SECTION 3/CRITICAL READING
Time—25 minutes   24 questions (25–48)

For each question in this section, select the best answer from among the choices given and fill in the corresponding circle on the answer sheet.

Each sentence below has one or two blanks, each blank indicating that something has been omitted. Beneath the sentence are five words or sets of words labeled A through E. Choose the word or set of words that, when inserted in the sentence, best fits the meaning of the sentence as a whole.

EXAMPLE:

Medieval kingdoms did not become constitutional republics overnight; on the contrary, the change was ----.

(A) unpopular   (B) unexpected
(C) advantageous   (D) sufficient   (E) gradual

---

25. In order that they may be able to discriminate wisely among the many conflicting arguments put before them, legislators must be trained to ---- the truth.

    (A) confuse   (B) condemn   (C) ignore
    (D) condone   (E) discern

26. In their new collections of lighthearted, provocative dresses, French fashion designers are gambling that even ---- professional women are ready for a bit of ---- in style.

    (A) strict..reticence
    (B) serious..frivolity
    (C) elegant..tradition
    (D) modern..harmony
    (E) unsentimental..propriety

27. The airline customer service representative tried to ---- the ---- passenger by offering her a seat in first class.

    (A) pacify..placid
    (B) thwart..irate
    (C) divert..grateful
    (D) authorize..listless
    (E) mollify..angry

28. People who find themselves unusually ---- and ready to drowse off at unexpected moments may be suffering from a hormonal imbalance.

(A) lethargic   (B) distracted   (C) obdurate   (D) benign   (E) perfunctory

29. The expression "he passed away" is ---- for "he died."

(A) a reminder
(B) a commiseration
(C) a simile
(D) a euphemism
(E) an exaggeration

30. Despite the enormous popularity and influence of his book, *Thunder Out of China,* White's career ----.

(A) soared
(B) endured
(C) accelerated
(D) revived
(E) foundered

31. Written just after King's assassination, Lomax's book has all the virtues of historical ----, but lacks the greater virtue of historical ----, which comes from long and mature reflection upon events.

(A) precision..accuracy
(B) criticism..distance
(C) immediacy..perspective
(D) outlook..realism
(E) currency..testimony

32. Relishing his triumph, Costner especially ---- the chagrin of the critics who had predicted his ----.

(A) regretted..success
(B) acknowledged..comeback
(C) understated..bankruptcy
(D) distorted..mortification
(E) savored..failure

Each of the passages below precedes two questions based on its content. Answer the questions following each passage on the basis of what is stated or implied in that passsage.

Questions 33 and 34 are based on the following passage.

Little vegetation grows in the vast South African tableland known as the Nama Karroo. The open plateau, home to springboks and other members of the antelope family, seems a rocky, inhospitable place. Yet
Line the springboks find sustenance, searching among the rocks and pebbles,
(5) and coming up with mouthfuls of "stones" which they munch content-
edly. These stones are in actuality plants, members of the genus Lithops, some of the strangest succulents in the world. Nature has camouflaged these stone plants so well that even trained botanists have trouble telling them apart from the rocks surrounding them.

33. The quotation marks around the word "stones" (line 5) primarily serve to emphasize that the plants

(A) are extraordinarily hard
(B) are inedible by humans
(C) are not literally stones
(D) can be recognized by antelopes
(E) survive in an arid environment

34. The context suggests that a succulent (line 7) is most likely

(A) a rock form
(B) an antelope
(C) a desert insect
(D) a type of camouflage
(E) a kind of plant

Questions 35 and 36 are based on the following passage.

Echoing leaders in the field such as Noam Chomsky, many linguists argue that the capacity for language is a uniquely human property. They contend that chimpanzees and related primates are incapable of using
Line language because their brains lack the human brain structures that make
(5) language. Other researchers, however, disagree, citing experiments in which apes have been taught to use symbolic communication systems, such as American Sign Language. In one study, for example, Georgia State professor E. Sue Savage-Rambaugh has worked with a "keyboard" consisting of 400 symbols to communicate with bonobos (also known
(10) as pygmy chimpanzees).

35. The word "property" in line 2 most nearly means

(A) trait   (B) wealth   (C) ownership
(D) oddity   (E) affliction

36. Savage-Rambaugh and Chomsky disagree in their evaluations of

(A) primates' value in experimental research
(B) primates' abilities in language acquisition
(C) primates' abilities to manipulate artifacts
(D) researchers' knowledge of American Sign Language
(E) researchers' impartiality in primate studies

The passages below are followed by questions on their content; questions following a pair of related passages may also be based on the relationship between the paired passages. Answer the questions on the basis of what is stated or implied in the passages and in any introductory material that may be provided.

Questions 37–48 are based on the following passages.

The following passages are excerpted from two recent essays that relate writing to sports. The author of Passage 1 deals with having had a novel rejected by his publisher. The author of Passage 2 explores how his involvement in sports affected his writing career.

Passage 1

In consigning this manuscript to a desk drawer, I am comforted by the behavior of baseball players. There are *no* pitchers who do not give up home runs, there are *no* batters who do not strike out. There are *no*
Line major league pitchers or batters who have not somehow learned to .
(5) survive giving up home runs and striking out. That much is obvious.

What seems to me less obvious is how these "failures" must be digested, or put to use, in the overall experience of the player. A jogger once explained to me that the nerves of the ankle are so sensitive and complex that each time a runner sets his foot down, hundreds of mes-
(10) sages are conveyed to the runner's brain about the nature of the terrain and the requirements for weight distribution, balance, and muscle-strength. I'm certain that the ninth-inning home run that Dave Henderson hit off Donny Moore registered complexly and permanently in Moore's mind and body and that the next time Moore faced Henderson, his pitch-
(15) ing was informed by his awful experience of October 1986. Moore's continuing baseball career depended to some extent on his converting that encounter with Henderson into something useful for his pitching. I can

also imagine such an experience destroying an athlete, registering in his mind and body in such a negative way as to produce a debilitating fear.

(20)   Of the many ways in which athletes and artists are similar, one is that, unlike accountants or plumbers or insurance salesmen, to succeed at all they must perform at an extraordinary level of excellence. Another is that they must be willing to extend themselves irrationally in order to achieve that level of performance. A writer doesn't have to write all-out all the

(25)   time, but he or she must be ready to write all-out any time the story requires it. Hold back and you produce what just about any literate citizen can produce, a "pretty good" piece of work. Like the cautious pitcher, the timid writer can spend a lifetime in the minor leagues.

And what more than failure—the strike out, the crucial home run

(30)   given up, the manuscript criticized and rejected—is more likely to produce caution or timidity? An instinctive response to painful experience is to avoid the behavior that produced the pain. To function at the level of excellence required for survival, writers like athletes must go against instinct, must absorb their failures and become stronger, must endlessly

(35)   repeat the behavior that produced the pain.

Passage 2

The athletic advantages of this concentration, particularly for an athlete who was making up for the absence of great natural skill, were considerable. Concentration gave you an edge over many of your opponents, even your betters, who could not isolate themselves to that

(40)   degree. For example, in football if they were ahead (or behind) by several touchdowns, if the game itself seemed to have been settled, they tended to slack off, to ease off a little, certainly to relax their own concentration. It was then that your own unwavering concentration and your own indifference to the larger point of view paid off. At the very least you could

(45)   deal out surprise and discomfort to your opponents.

But it was more than that. Do you see? The ritual of physical concentration, of acute engagement in a small space while disregarding all the clamor and demands of the larger world, was the best possible lesson in precisely the kind of selfish intensity needed to create and to finish a

(50)   poem, a story, or a novel. This alone mattered while all the world going on, with and without you, did not.

I was learning first in muscle, blood, and bone, not from literature and not from teachers of literature or the arts or the natural sciences, but from coaches, in particular this one coach who paid me enough attention

(55)   to influence me to teach some things to myself. I was learning about art and life through the abstraction of athletics in much the same way that a soldier is, to an extent, prepared for war by endless parade ground drill. His body must learn to be a soldier before heart, mind, and spirit can.

Ironically, I tend to dismiss most comparisons of athletics to art and
(60) to "the creative process." But only because, I think, so much that is
claimed for both is untrue. But I have come to believe—indeed I have to
believe it insofar as I believe in the validity and efficacy of art—that what
comes to us first and foremost through the body, as a sensuous affective experience, is taken and transformed by mind and self into a thing of
(65) the spirit. Which is only to say that what the body learns and is taught is
of enormous significance—at least until the last light of the body fails.

37. Why does the author of Passage 1 consign his manuscript to a desk drawer?

  (A) To protect it from the inquisitive eyes of his family
  (B) To prevent its getting lost or disordered
  (C) Because his publisher wishes to take another look at it
  (D) Because he chooses to watch a televised baseball game
  (E) To set it aside as unmarketable in its current state

38. Why is the author of Passage 1 "comforted by the behavior of baseball players" (lines 1–5)?

  (A) He treasures the timeless rituals of America's national pastime.
  (B) He sees he is not alone in having to confront failure and move on.
  (C) He enjoys watching the frustration of the batters who strike out.
  (D) He looks at baseball from the viewpoint of a behavioral psychologist.
  (E) He welcomes any distraction from the task of revising his novel.

39. What function in the passage is served by the discussion of the nerves in the ankle in lines 8–12?

  (A) It provides a momentary digression from the overall narrative flow.
  (B) It emphasizes how strong a mental impact Henderson's home run must have had on Moore.
  (C) It provides scientific confirmation of the neuromuscular abilities of athletes.
  (D) It illustrates that the author's interest in sports is not limited to baseball alone.
  (E) It conveys a sense of how confusing it is for the mind to deal with so many simultaneous messages.

40. The word "registered" in line 13 means

  (A) enrolled formally
  (B) expressed without words
  (C) corresponded exactly
  (D) made an impression
  (E) qualified officially

41. The attitude of the author of Passage 1 to accountants, plumbers, and insurance salesmen (lines 20–24) can best be described as

(A) respectful   (B) cautious   (C) superior
(D) cynical   (E) hypocritical

42. In the concluding paragraphs of Passage 1, the author appears to

(A) romanticize the writer as someone heroic in his or her accomplishments
(B) deprecate athletes for their inability to react to experience instinctively
(C) minimize the travail that artists and athletes endure to do their work
(D) advocate the importance of literacy to the common citizen
(E) suggest a cautious approach would reduce the likelihood of future failure

43. The author of Passage 2 prizes

(A) his innate athletic talent
(B) the respect of his peers
(C) his ability to focus
(D) the gift of relaxation
(E) winning at any cost

44. The word "settled" in line 41 means

(A) judged   (B) decided   (C) reconciled
(D) pacified   (E) inhabited

45. What does the author mean by "indifference to the larger point of view" (lines 43–44)?

(A) Inability to see the greater implications of the activity in which you were involved
(B) Hostility to opponents coming from larger, better trained teams
(C) Reluctance to look beyond your own immediate concerns
(D) Refusing to care how greatly you might be hurt by your opponents
(E) Being more concerned with the task at hand than with whether you win or lose

46. What is the function of the phrase "to an extent" in line 57?

(A) It denies a situation.
(B) It conveys a paradox.
(C) It qualifies a statement.
(D) It represents a metaphor.
(E) It minimizes a liability.

47. The author finds it ironic that he tends to "dismiss most comparisons of athletics to art" (line 59) because

    (A) athletics is the basis for great art
    (B) he finds comparisons generally unhelpful
    (C) he is making such a comparison
    (D) he typically is less cynical
    (E) he rejects the so-called creative process

48. The authors of both passages would agree that

    (A) the lot of the professional writer is more trying than that of the professional athlete
    (B) athletics has little to do with the actual workings of the creative process
    (C) both artists and athletes learn hard lessons in the course of mastering their art
    (D) it is important to concentrate on the things that hurt us in life
    (E) participating in sports provides a distraction from the isolation of a writer's life

IF YOU FINISH IN LESS THAN 25 MINUTES, YOU MAY CHECK YOUR WORK ON THIS SECTION ONLY. DO NOT TURN TO ANY OTHER SECTION IN THE TEST.   **S T O P**

SECTION 4/MATHEMATICAL REASONING
Time—25 minutes   18 questions (21–38)

For questions 21–28, determine which of the five choices is correct. You may use any blank space on the page for your work.

Notes:

- You may use a calculator whenever you believe it will be helpful.
- Use the diagrams provided to help you solve the problems. Unless you see the phrase "<u>Note</u>: Figure not drawn to scale" under a diagram, it has been drawn as accurately as possible. Unless it is stated that a figure is three-dimensional, you may assume that it lies in a plane.

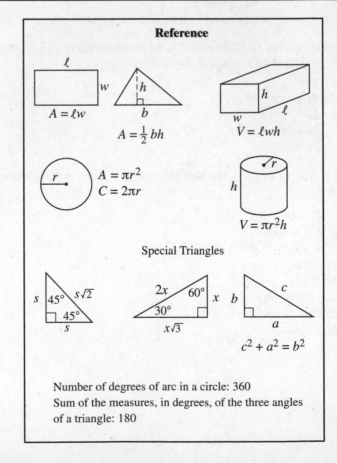

Reference

$A = \ell w$

$A = \frac{1}{2} bh$

$V = \ell w h$

$A = \pi r^2$
$C = 2\pi r$

$V = \pi r^2 h$

Special Triangles

$s\sqrt{2}$ $45°$ $45°$ s

$2x$ $60°$ $30°$ $x\sqrt{3}$ x

c b a

$c^2 + a^2 = b^2$

Number of degrees of arc in a circle: 360
Sum of the measures, in degrees, of the three angles
of a triangle: 180

21. If a basket of fruit contains 5 pounds of apples, 3 pounds of oranges, and 1 pound of pears, by weight, what fraction of the fruit is oranges?

(A) $\frac{1}{9}$ (B) $\frac{1}{5}$ (C) $\frac{1}{3}$ (D) $\frac{3}{8}$ (E) $\frac{1}{2}$

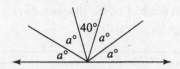

22. In the figure above, what is the value of a?

(A) 30 (B) 35 (C) 36 (D) 45 (E) 80

23. If $\frac{5}{8}$ of the members of the chess club are boys, what is the ratio of girls to boys in the club?

(A) $\frac{4}{8}$ (B) $\frac{3}{5}$ (C) $\frac{5}{3}$ (D) $\frac{8}{5}$

(E) It cannot be determined from the information given.

24. A rectangle has a perimeter equal to the circumference of a circle of radius 3. If the width of the rectangle is 3, what is its length?

(A) $3\pi - 3$
(B) $4.5\pi - 3$
(C) $6\pi - 3$
(D) $9\pi - 3$
(E) $3\pi + 3$

25. If p, q, and r are prime numbers greater than 5, which of the following could be true?

I. $p - q$ is prime
II. $p + q$ is prime
III. $p + q + r$ is prime

(A) I only
(B) II only
(C) I and II only
(D) I and III only
(E) I, II, and III

26. If A (3, -2) and B (7, 2) are the endpoints of a diameter of a circle, what is the area of the circle?

(A) $2\sqrt{2}\,\pi$ (B) $4\sqrt{2}\,\pi$ (C) 8π (D) 16π (E) 32π

27. If $13 - 2\sqrt{x} = 7$, then what is the value of x?

(A) -9 (B) 6   (C) 9   (D) 16   (E) There is no value of x that satisfies the equation

28. The estate of a wealthy man was distributed as follows: 10% to his wife, 5% divided equally among his 3 children, 5% divided equally among his 5 grand-children, and the balance to a charitable trust. If the trust received $1,000,000, how much did each grandchild inherit?

(A) $10,000   (B) $12,500   (C) $20,000
(D) $62,500   (E) $100,000

Directions for Student-Produced Response Questions (Grid-ins)

In questions 29–38, first solve the problem, and then enter your answer on the grid provided on the answer sheet. The instructions for entering your answers follow.

- First, write your answer in the boxes at the top of the grid.
- Second, grid your answer in the columns below the boxes.
- Use the fraction bar in the first row or the decimal point in the second row to enter fractions and decimals.

Answer: $\frac{8}{15}$ Answer: 1.75

Write your answer in the boxes

Grid in your answer

Answer: 100

Either position is acceptable

- Grid only one space in each column.
- Entering the answer in the boxes is recommended as an aid in gridding, but is not required.
- The machine scoring your exam can read only what you grid, so you **must grid in your answers correctly to get credit.**
- If a question has more than one correct answer, grid in only one of them.
- The grid does not have a minus sign, so no answer can be negative.
- A mixed number *must* be converted to an improper fraction or a decimal before it is gridded. Enter $1\frac{1}{4}$ as $\frac{5}{4}$ or 1.25; the machine will interpret 1 1/4 as $\frac{11}{4}$ and mark it wrong.

- **All decimals must be entered as accurately as possible.** Here are the three acceptable ways of gridding
$$\frac{3}{11} = 0.272727...$$

3/11   .272   .273

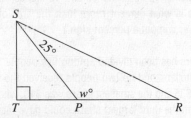

- Note that rounding to .273 is acceptable, because you are using the full grid, but you would receive **no credit** for .3 or .27, because they are less accurate.

29. In the figure above, if *PS* bisects ∠*RST*, what is the value of *w*?

30. There are 150 people in line outside a ballpark. If Peter is the 10th person from the front, and Wendy is the 110th person from the front, how many people are there between Peter and Wendy?

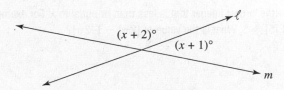

Note: Figure not drawn to scale

31. In the figure above, what is the value of *x*?

32. If *r*, *s*, and *t* are prime numbers less than 15, what is the greatest possible value of $\frac{r-s}{t}$?

33. If $\frac{2}{x} \div \frac{3}{4} = \frac{4}{5}$, then $x =$

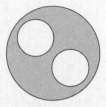

Note: Figure not drawn to scale

34. In the figure above, the radius of the large circle is 3 and the radius of each of the small white circles is 1. If a point, *P*, is chosen at random inside the big circle, what is the probability that *P* lies in the shaded region?

35. Two circles have diameters of 12 inches and 10 inches, respectively. The area of the larger circle is what percent *more* than the area of the smaller circle? (Grid in your answer without a percent sign.)

36. One hundred dollars has been divided among five people. Each one received a whole number of dollars, and no two people received the same amount. If the largest share was $35 and the smallest share was $10, what is the most money that the person with the third largest share could have received?

37. Twenty-five students took a quiz and the grades they earned ranged from 2 to 10. If exactly 22 of them passed, by earning a grade of 7 or higher, what is the highest possible average (arithmetic mean) the class could have earned on the quiz?

38. Let [*x*] = the largest integer that is less than or equal to *x*. For example, [2.66] = 2 and [5] = 5. What is the value of $[2\pi] - [-2\pi]$?

IF YOU FINISH IN LESS THAN 25 MINUTES,
YOU MAY CHECK YOUR WORK ON THIS   **STOP**
SECTION ONLY. DO NOT TURN TO ANY
OTHER SECTION IN THE TEST.

SECTION 5/WRITING SKILLS
Time—30 minutes   39 questions (1–39)

Some or all parts of the following sentences are underlined. The first answer choice, (A), simply repeats the underlined part of the sentence. The other four choices present four alternate ways to phrase the underlined part. Select the answer that produces the most effective sentence, one that is clear and exact, and blacken the appropriate space on your answer sheet. In selecting your choice, be sure that it is standard written English, and that it expresses the meaning of the original sentence.

EXAMPLE:

The first biography of author Eudora Welty came out in 1998
and she was eighty-nine years old at the time.

(A) and she was eighty-nine years old at the time.
(B) at the time when she was eighty-nine.
(C) upon becoming an eighty-nine year old.
(D) when she was eighty-nine.
(E) at the age of eighty-nine years old.

1. Fifty-three thousand shouting enthusiasts filled the stadium, they had come to watch the first game of the season and to cheer the home team.

(A) enthusiasts filled the stadium, they had come
(B) enthusiasts filled the stadium to come
(C) enthusiasts, filling the stadium, had come
(D) enthusiasts filled the stadium; and had come
(E) enthusiasts filling the stadium, who had come

2. During the judging of the animals at the show, the judges could not decide whether Brown's collie or Jones's terrier was the best dog.

(A) whether Brown's collie or Jones's terrier was the best
(B) if Brown's collie or Jones's terrier was the better
(C) whether Brown's collie or Jones's terrier was the better
(D) if Brown's collie or Jones's terrier was the best
(E) whether Brown's collie or Jones's terrier had been the best

3. Finally reviewing the extensive evidence against the defendant, he was found guilty.

   (A) Finally reviewing the extensive evidence against the defendant,
   (B) Reviewing the extensive evidence against the defendant,
   (C) The jury finally reviewed the extensive evidence against the defendant,
   (D) When the jury finally reviewed the extensive evidence against the defendant,
   (E) The jury finally reviewed the evidence against the defendant,

4. Paul Gauguin was married and had family responsibilities and he ran away to the South Seas to paint.

   (A) Paul Gauguin was married and had family responsibilities and he
   (B) Although being married and having family responsibilities, Paul Gauguin
   (C) Although Paul Gauguin was married and had family responsibilities, he
   (D) Being married, and therefore having family responsibilities, Paul Gauguin
   (E) Despite the fact that Paul Gauguin was married and had family responsibilities, he

5. A key difference between mice and voles is tail length, a mouse's tail is twice as long as the tail of a vole.

   (A) length, a mouse's tail is
   (B) length; a mouse's tail is
   (C) length, the tail of a mouse is
   (D) length; a mouse's tail, it is
   (E) length, mice's tails are

6. As a retired executive, he is now busier than ever; he makes his living by speaking before business and philanthropic groups, writing books and articles, and he is a director of three major corporations.

   (A) by speaking before business and philanthropic groups, writing books and articles, and he is a director of
   (B) by speaking before business and philanthropic groups, and he writes books and articles as well as being a director of
   (C) by speaking before business and philanthropic groups, and he writes books and articles, and directs
   (D) by speaking before business and philanthropic groups, writing books and articles, and directing
   (E) by speaking before business and philanthropic groups, in addition to writing books and articles, and he is a director of

7. The president established a special commission for the space program; the purpose being to investigate the causes of the *Challenger* disaster.

   (A) program; the purpose being to
   (B) program; whose purpose being to
   (C) program, the purpose was to
   (D) program to
   (E) program; in order to

8. When Harriet Tubman decided to help runaway slaves escape to the North, she knew that her mission would bring her into danger in both South and North.

   (A) When Harriet Tubman decided to help runaway slaves escape
   (B) When Harriet Tubman decides to help runaway slaves escape
   (C) When Harriet Tubman decided about helping runaway slaves escape
   (D) After the decision by Harriet Tubman to help runaway slaves escape
   (E) After Harriet Tubman's making of the decision to help runaway slaves escape

9. The growing impoverishment of women and children in American society distresses Senator Clinton, and she is also infuriated.

   (A) distresses Senator Clinton, and she is also infuriated
   (B) distresses Senator Clinton, infuriating her
   (C) distresses and infuriates Senator Clinton
   (D) is distressing Senator Clinton, making her infuriated
   (E) is a cause of distress to Senator Clinton, and of a fury

10. Being a successful reporter demands powers of observation, fluency, and persistence.

    (A) Being a successful reporter demands
    (B) Being a successful reporter who demands
    (C) To be a successful reporter who demands
    (D) Being a successful reporter demanding
    (E) To be a successful reporter demanding

11. Had I been at the scene of the accident, I could have administered first aid to the victims.

    (A) Had I been at the scene of the accident
    (B) If I were at the scene of the accident
    (C) If I was at the scene of the accident
    (D) I should have been at the scene of the accident
    (E) I should have been at the scene of the accident, and

12. The Northern Lights, or Aurora Borealis, is so named because it is a light display that takes place in the northern skies.

    (A) because it is a light display that takes place
    (B) as a light display taking place
    (C) because of taking place
    (D) due to the fact that it is a light display
    (E) contrary to the fact of taking place

13. It is not for you to assume responsibility; it is rather me who is the guilty person in this matter.

    (A) me who is
    (B) me who am
    (C) I who is
    (D) I who are
    (E) I who am

14. Brightly colored birds soared to and fro, indifferent with the ships that ploughed the blue Caribbean waters.

    (A) Brightly colored birds soared to and fro, indifferent with the ships that ploughed
    (B) Brightly colored birds soared to and from, indifferent with the ships which ploughed
    (C) Brightly colored birds soared to and fro, indifferent to the ships that ploughed
    (D) Bright colored birds soared to and fro, indifferently with the ships, they ploughed
    (E) Brightly colored birds soaring to and fro, indifferent with the ships that ploughed

15. The Metropolitan Museum of Art's collection of medieval sculptures, like so many other aspects of the museum, have benefited significantly from the generosity of J. Pierpont Morgan, the financier.

- (A) sculptures, like so many other aspects of the museum, have benefited significantly from
- (B) sculptures, like so many other aspects of the museum, have significant benefits from
- (C) sculptures, like so many other aspects of the museum, has benefited significantly from
- (D) sculptures, similar to many other aspects of the museum, have benefited significantly from
- (E) sculptures, like so many other aspects of the museum, have benefited significantly through

16. Native Americans did not fare well in the mission system, perishing in vast numbers from measles and other diseases introduced by the Spanish.

- (A) fare well in the mission system, perishing
- (B) fare good in the mission system, perishing
- (C) fare well in the mission system, they perished
- (D) fare well from the mission system, perishing
- (E) fare well in the mission system, despite perishing

17. Standoffish and reserved, Charles Lindbergh was uncomfortable with the applause he received from the crowds which have cheered his historic flight.

- (A) received from the crowds which have cheered his historic flight
- (B) receives from the crowds which cheer his historic flight
- (C) received from the cheering crowds about his historic flight
- (D) received from the crowds when they cheer his historic flight
- (E) received from the crowds that cheered his historic flight

18. Study-abroad programs can enhance students' acquisition of a foreign language, improve their knowledge of the host culture, and even their world views can be transformed.

- (A) culture, and even their world views can be transformed
- (B) culture, and even can transform their world views
- (C) culture, and their world views can even be transformed
- (D) culture, and even transform their world views
- (E) culture, and even transforming their world views

19. <u>Once dried and pinned as specimens, dragonflies lose most of their color and become increasing fragile.</u>

    (A) Once dried and pinned as specimens, dragonflies lose most of their color and become increasing fragile.

    (B) Once dried and pinned as a specimen, dragonflies lose most of their color and become increasing fragile.

    (C) Once they have been dried and pinned as specimens, dragonflies lose most of their color, becoming increasing fragile.

    (D) They were once dried and pinned as specimens, and then dragonflies lose most of their color and become increasingly fragile.

    (E) Once dried and pinned as specimens, dragonflies lose most of their color and become increasingly fragile.

20. By the time Jews began to arrive in the United States in significant numbers in the early twentieth century, <u>they already have established an affinity with</u> political liberalism in Europe.

    (A) they already have established an affinity with

    (B) they all ready have established an affinity with

    (C) they already have established an affinity for

    (D) an affinity had already been established by them toward

    (E) they already had established an affinity with

The sentences in this section may contain errors in grammar, usage, choice of words, or idioms. There is either just one error per sentence or the sentence is correct. Some words or phrases are underlined and lettered; everything else in the sentence is correct.

If an underlined word or phrase is incorrect, choose that letter; if the sentence is correct, select <u>No error</u>. Then blacken the appropriate space on your Answer Sheet.

EXAMPLE:

The region has a climate <u>so severe that</u> plants
                        A
<u>growing there</u> <u>rarely had been</u> more than
      B   C
twelve inches <u>high</u>. <u>No error</u>   Ⓐ Ⓑ ● Ⓓ Ⓔ
              D   E

21. <u>After</u> his heart attack, he <u>was ordered</u> <u>to lay</u> in bed and rest <u>for</u> two weeks.
    A   B   C   D

    <u>No error</u>
    E

22. While <u>my</u> aunt and I <u>were traveling</u> <u>through</u> our National Parks, my aunt was
          A   B   C

    <u>frightened</u> by a bear. <u>No error</u>
    D   E

23. <u>Only</u> recently, the <u>newly</u> organized football association <u>added</u> two new teams
    A   B   C

    to <u>their</u> league. <u>No error</u>
       D   E

24. <u>In view of</u> the controversy with the school board, neither the teachers <u>nor</u> the
    A   B

    principal <u>are being</u> considered for promotion <u>at this time</u>. <u>No error</u>
              C   D   E

25. While we <u>have rummaged</u> <u>through</u> the attic, we found <u>not only</u> an album of
             A   B   C

    our trip to Europe, but also a <u>multitude of</u> old news clippings. <u>No error</u>
                                   D   E

26. Of <u>all</u> the <u>members of</u> the United States team, Greg Lemond <u>became</u> the first
      A   B   C

  <u>to win</u> the prestigious Tour de France bike race. <u>No error</u>
   D   E

27. Before we <u>adopt</u> this legislation, we <u>ought to</u> consider the <u>affect</u> the new law
              A   B   C

  will have on <u>our</u> retired and disabled citizens. <u>No error</u>
              D   E

28. The legendary Mark McGwire <u>has established</u> an <u>enviable</u> <u>record, and it</u> prob-
                                   A   B   C

  ably will not <u>be broken</u> during the next fifty years. <u>No error</u>
              D   E

29. Toni Cade Bambara, <u>who</u> is a black American writer, <u>has been active</u> in civil
                         A   B

  rights and women's issues, <u>nor is she</u> <u>attuned to</u> Afro-American relationships.
                             C   D

  <u>No error</u>
   E

30. The boom of video cassette recorder sales <u>can be</u> <u>attributed to</u> <u>numerous</u>
                                                A   B   C

  things, <u>including being</u> price reduction and the growth of rental stores.
          D

  <u>No error</u>
   E

31. <u>After</u> a six-month study semester abroad, she <u>was</u> <u>happy</u> to get home to
   A   B   C

  <u>comfortable familiar</u> surroundings and appetizing food. <u>No error</u>
          D   E

32. <u>Much more</u> experimental data <u>are</u> required <u>before</u> we can accept <u>this theory</u>.
        A   B   C   D

  <u>No error</u>
   E

33. Because he <u>has been warned</u> <u>only</u> about the danger of <u>walking</u> on the railroad
$\qquad\qquad$ A $\qquad\qquad$ B $\qquad\qquad\qquad\qquad$ C

trestle, he dared <u>several of</u> his friends to walk on the tracks. <u>No error</u>
$\qquad\qquad\qquad$ D $\qquad\qquad\qquad\qquad\qquad\qquad\qquad$ E

34. Where is it possible to find <u>if</u> <u>it was</u> Lowell <u>or</u> Longfellow <u>who</u> wrote
$\qquad\qquad\qquad\qquad\qquad\qquad$ A $\quad$ B $\qquad\qquad$ C $\qquad\qquad\qquad$ D

"Hiawatha"? <u>No error</u>
$\qquad\qquad$ E

The passage below is the unedited draft of a student's essay. Some of the essay needs to be rewritten to make the meaning clearer and more precise. Read the essay carefully.

The essay is followed by five questions about changes that might improve all or part of its organization, development, sentence structure, use of language, appropriateness to the audience, or its use of standard written English. Choose the answer that most clearly and effectively expresses the student's intended meaning. Indicate your choice by filling in the corresponding space on the answer sheet.

---

[1] *Although some people believe that certain celebrations have no point, celebrations are one of the few things that all people have in common. [2] They take place everywhere. [3] Listing all of them would be an impossible task. [4] People of all kinds look forward to celebrations for keeping traditions alive for generation after generation. [5] Those who criticize celebrations do not understand the human need to preserve tradition and culture.*

[6] *In the Muslim religion, the Ead is a celebration. [7] It begins as soon as Ramadan (the fasting month) is over. [8] During the Ead, families gather together. [9] New clothes are bought for children, and they receive money from both family and friends. [10] Also, each family, if they can afford it, slaughters a sheep or a cow. [11] They keep a small fraction of the meat, and the rest must give to the poor. [12] They also donate money to a mosque.*

[13] *Many celebrations involve eating meals. [14] In the United States, people gather together on Thanksgiving to say thank you for their blessings by having a huge feast with turkey, sweet potatoes, and cranberry sauce. [15] Christmas and Easter holiday dinners are a custom in the Christian religion. [16] They have a roast at Christmas. [17] At Easter they serve ham. [18] The Jewish people celebrate Passover with a big meal called a seder. [19] They say prayers, drink wine, and sing*

songs to remember how Jews suffered centuries ago when they escaped from slavery in Egypt.

[20] A celebration is held each year to honor great people like Dr. Martin Luther King. [21] His birthday is celebrated because of this man's noble belief in equality of all races. [22] People wish to remember not only his famous speeches, including "I Have A Dream," but also about him being assassinated in Memphis in 1968. [23] He died while fighting for the equality of minorities. [24] Unlike religious celebrations, celebrations for great heroes like Martin Luther King are for all people everywhere in the world. [25] He is a world-class hero and he deserved the Nobel Prize for Peace that he won.

35. To improve the unity of the first paragraph, which of the following is the best sentence to delete?

(A) Sentence 1   (B) Sentence 2   (C)   Sentence 3

(D) Sentence 4   (E)   Sentence 5

36. In the context of the third paragraph, which is the best way to combine sentences 15, 16, and 17?

(A) A roast at Christmas, ham at Easter—that's what Christians eat.

(B) Christians customarily serve a roast for Christmas dinner, at Easter ham is eaten.

(C) At customary holiday dinners, Christians eat a roast at Christmas and ham is for Easter dinner.

(D) Christians often celebrate the Christmas holiday with a roast for dinner and Easter with a traditional ham.

(E) Christmas and Easter dinners are the custom in the Christian religion, where they have a roast at Christmas and ham at Easter.

37. In an effort to provide a more effective transition between paragraphs 3 and 4, which of the following would be the best revision of sentence 20 below?

A celebration is held each year to honor great people like Dr. Martin Luther King.

(A) There are also some celebrations to honor great people like Dr. Martin Luther King.

(B) Martin Luther King is also celebrated in the United States.

(C) In the United States, celebrating to honor great people like Dr. Martin Luther King has become a tradition.

(D) In addition to observing religious holidays, people hold celebrations to honor great leaders like Dr. Martin Luther King.

(E) Besides holding religion-type celebrations, celebrations to honor great people like Dr. Martin Luther King are also held.

38. Which is the best revision of the underlined segment of sentence 22 below?

People wish to remember not only his famous speeches, including "I Have A Dream," but also about him being assassinated *in Memphis in 1968.*

(A) that his assassination occurred

(B) about his being assassination

(C) the fact that he was assassinated

(D) about the assassination, too,

(E) his assassination

39. Considering the essay as a whole, which one of the following best explains the main function of the last paragraph?

(A) To summarize the main idea of the essay

(B) To refute a previous argument stated in the essay

(C) To give an example

(D) To provide a solution to a problem

(E) To evaluate the validity of the essay's main idea

IF YOU FINISH IN LESS THAN 30 MINUTES, YOU MAY CHECK YOUR WORK ON THIS SECTION ONLY. DO NOT TURN TO ANY OTHER SECTION IN THE TEST.

S T O P

Answer Key

Section 1 Critical Reading

1. D	9. E	17. C
2. C	10. C	18. D
3. A	11. D	19. C
4. B	12. E	20. C
5. E	13. D	21. E
6. C	14. C	22. E
7. C	15. B	23. B
8. B	16. C	24. C

Section 2 Mathematical Reasoning

1. E	8. A	15. D
2. C	9. C	16. E
3. C	10. C	17. C
4. B	11. D	18. E
5. C	12. D	19. E
6. A	13. D	20. A
7. B	14. D	

Section 3 Critical Reading

25. E	33. C	41. C
26. B	34. E	42. A
27. E	35. A	43. C
28. A	36. B	44. B
29. D	37. E	45. E
30. E	38. B	46. C
31. C	39. B	47. C
32. E	40. D	48. C

Section 4 Mathematical Reasoning

21. C	24. A	27. C
22. B	25. D	28. B
23. C	26. C	

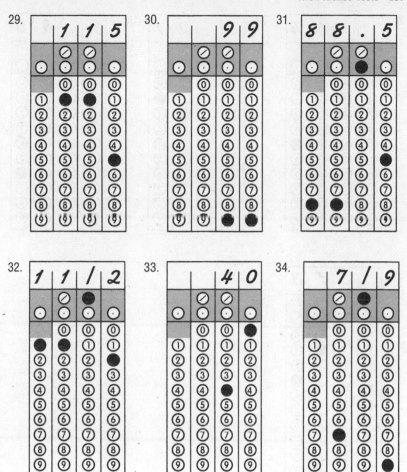

29. 1 1 5
30. 9 9
31. 8 8 . 5
32. 1 1 / 2   or 5 . 5
33. 4 0
34. 7 / 9   or .777 or .778

35. 4 4

36. 2 1

37. 9 . 3 6

38. 1 3

Section 5 Writing Skills

1. **C**	9. **C**	17. **B**	25. **A**	33. **A**
2. **C**	10. **A**	18. **D**	26. **E**	34. **A**
3. **D**	11. **A**	19. **E**	27. **C**	35. **C**
4. **C**	12. **A**	20. **E**	28. **C**	36. **D**
5. **B**	13. **E**	21. **C**	29. **C**	37. **D**
6. **D**	14. **C**	22. **E**	30. **D**	38. **E**
7. **D**	15. **C**	23. **D**	31. **D**	39. **C**
8. **A**	16. **A**	24. **C**	32. **E**	

Answer Explanations

Section 1 Critical Reading

1. **(D)** Such an extraordinarily useful material would *revolutionize* or make radical changes in an industry.

2. **(C)** A contrast is set up here by the expression "no matter how." It tells us that, although future "revelations" (surprising news) may be *striking*, they will not equal past ones. These past revelations *radically* transformed or thoroughly changed our view.

3. **(A)** Since "few other plants can grow beneath the canopy of the sycamore," it must be *inhibiting* or restraining the other plants.

4. **(B)** Certain authors have been *relegated* or sent off to "obscurity," a state of being hidden or forgotten. There they must be "rediscovered."

5. **(E)** Critics sometimes praise but more often *decry* or condemn things. Here the critics see the "saccharine" (too sweet) mood of the movie as inconsistent with the *acerbic* (sour, bitter) tone of the book.

6. **(C)** If poetry fans can fill an entire football stadium, there must be a lot of them. Thus, the reference to the football stadium suggests the size of the audience for poetry and thus *emphasizes the popularity of poetry in the period*.

7. **(C)** To say that literature enjoyed a central place in the culture is to say that literature *possessed* or occupied such a place.

8. **(B)** The statement "we're dying anyway" is an example of a *metaphor* or implicit comparison. The author does not mean that he and his fellow poets are literally dying; they are dying metaphorically (figuratively), for their poetry does not matter to anyone, and to be ignored feels like death.

9. **(E)** The time when poetry mattered "is long gone." In America "no one cares." Clearly the authors of Passage 1 and Passage 2 agree that *the climate for poetry in America is inauspicious* (unfavorable).

10. **(C)** Among other clues, Mr. Collins states that he hopes to lead Elizabeth "to the altar ere long."

11. **(D)** Elizabeth is "sensible of the honour" Mr. Collins is paying her by proposing. She is all too *keenly aware* of his intentions and wants nothing to do with them.

12. **(E)** Elizabeth expects that by refusing Mr. Collins' proposal she will *put an end to his suit*; that is the result she desires. However, her rejection *fails* to have this intended effect. Instead, Mr. Collins in his stubbornness and conceit continues to pursue her and even takes her refusal as an encouraging sign.

13. **(D)** Mr. Collins breaks off in the middle of a sentence that begins: "Were it certain that Lady Catherine would think so—." He then finishes it awkwardly

by saying, "but I cannot imagine that her ladyship would at all disapprove of you." By implication, his unspoken thought was that, if Lady Catherine *didn't* approve of Elizabeth, then Mr. Collins wouldn't want to marry her after all.

14. **(C)** Mr. Collins plans to praise Elizabeth to Lady Catherine in order to ensure Lady Catherine's approval of his bride. Elizabeth insists all such praise will be unnecessary because she *has no intention of marrying Mr. Collins* and thus has no need of Lady Catherine's approval.

15. **(B)** *Obtuse* means thick-headed and *obstinate* means stubborn. Both apply to Mr. Collins, who can't seem to understand that Elizabeth is telling him "no."

16. **(C)** The author's emphasis is on the elephant as an important "creator of habitat" for other creatures.

17. **(C)** To mount an effort to rescue an endangered species is to *launch* or initiate a campaign.

18. **(D)** The elephant is the architect of its environment in that it *physically alters its environment*, transforming the landscape around it.

19. **(C)** The author states that it is the elephant's metabolism and appetite—in other words, its voracity or *ravenous hunger*—that leads to its creating open spaces in the woodland and transforming the landscape.

20. **(C)** Since the foraging of elephants creates a varied landscape that attracts a diverse group of plant-eating animals and since the presence of these plant eaters in turn attracts carnivores, it follows that elephants *have an indirect effect on the hunting patterns of carnivores*.

21. **(E)** Here the phrase "keystone species" *is being used in a special or technical sense* to mean a species whose very presence contributes to a diversity of life and whose extinction would consequently lead to the extinction of other forms of life.

22. **(E)** You can arrive at the correct answer choice through the process of elimination.

    Question I is answerable on the basis of the passage. The elephant's foraging opens up its surroundings by knocking down trees and stripping off branches. Therefore, you can eliminate Choices B and D.

    Question II is answerable on the basis of the passage. Gazelles are grazers; giraffes are browsers. Therefore, you can eliminate Choice A.

    Question III is answerable on the basis of the passage. The concluding sentence states that when elephants disappear the forest reverts. Therefore, you can eliminate Choice C.

    Only Choice E is left. It is the correct answer.

23. **(B)** The author is listing the many species that depend on the elephant as a creator of habitat. Thus, the host of smaller animals is the *very large number* of these creatures that thrive in the elephant's wake.

24. **(C)** The author is in favor of the effect of elephants on the environment; he feels an accidental or *fortuitous result* of their foraging is that it allows a greater variety of creatures to exist in mixed-growth environments.

Section 2 Mathematical Reasoning

In each mathematics section, for some of the problems, an alternative solution, indicated by two asterisks (**), follows the first solution. When this occurs, one of the solutions is the direct mathematical one and the other is based on one of the tactics discussed in Chapter 6.

1. **(E)** $b - 8 = 0 \Rightarrow b = 8 \Rightarrow b + 8 = 16.$

2. **(C)** If Isaac has twice as many toys as Sydney, then Sydney has half as many as Isaac: $\frac{t}{2}$. This is so easy that you shouldn't have to plug in a number, but you could: If Sydney has 10 toys, then Isaac has 5, and only Choice C equals 5 when b is 10.

3. **(C)** By **FACT 42**, the measure of an exterior angle of a triangle is equal to the sum of the measures of the two opposite interior angles, so
   $140 = x + x = 2x \Rightarrow x = 70.$
   **Let the third angle in the triangle be y. Then $140 + y = 180 \Rightarrow y = 40$; and $40 + x + x = 180 \Rightarrow x = 70.$

4. **(B)** Since $1{,}000{,}000 = 10^6$, then
$$2n + 1 = 6 \Rightarrow 2n = 5 \Rightarrow n = 2.5.$$

5. **(C)** Use your calculator: $1.5 \times 1.7 = 2.55$, which, to the nearest tenth, is 2.6.

6. **(A)** Since the circle's diameter is 4, its radius is 2, and its area is $\pi(2)^2 = 4\pi$. Since the area of the square is also 4π, the length of each side is $\sqrt{\pi 4} = 2\sqrt{\pi}$.

7. **(B)** Set up a proportion and cross-multiply:
$$\frac{\text{inches}}{\text{miles}} = \frac{\frac{1}{3}}{14} = \frac{x}{30}.$$

Then, $14x = 30\left(\frac{1}{3}\right) = 10$, and $x = \frac{10}{14} = \frac{5}{7}.$

8. **(A)** Since the area of the square is 36, its sides are 6, and its perimeter is 24. Since the perimeter of the hexagon is also 24, each of its six sides is 4.

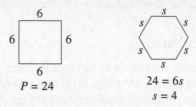

$$P = 24$$
$$24 = 6s$$
$$s = 4$$

9. **(C)** The first step is to calculate $(3◇)(♦5)$:
$$(3◇)(♦5) = (3 + 1)(5 − 1) = 4 × 4 = 16.$$
Now check each answer until you find one that is NOT equal to 16.
A: $(1◇)(♦9) = (1 + 1)(9 − 1) = (2)(8) = 16.$
B: $(7◇)(♦9) = (7 + 1) + (9 − 1) = 8 + 8 = 16.$
C: $(4◇)(♦4) = (4 + 1)(4 − 1) = 5 × 3 ≠ 16.$

10. **(C)** Pick an integer for $\frac{n + 2}{5}$, say 2. Then
$$\frac{n + 2}{5} = 2 ⇒ n + 2 = 10 ⇒ n = 8,$$
and 5 goes into 8 once with a remainder of 3.

11. **(D)** Let n represent the number of students in the class other than Michelle. These n students earned a total of $85n$ points (**FACT 31**). When Michelle was included, there were $n + 1$ students who earned a total of $85n + 30$ points. Since the class average was then 80:
$$80 = \frac{85n + 30}{n + 1} ⇒$$
$$85n + 30 = 80(n + 1) = 80n + 80 ⇒$$
$$5n = 50 ⇒ n = 10, \text{ and so } n + 1 = 11.$$

 Use **TACTIC 1: backsolve, starting with Choice C. If there were 10 children in the class, the 9 students other than Michelle would have earned $9 × 85 = 765$ points, and so including Michelle, the total number of points earned would have been $765 + 30 = 795$ points. The class average, then, would have been $\frac{795}{10} = 79.5$, which is just a little too low. Eliminate Choices A, B, and C, and try Choice D, which works.

12. **(D)** At the regular price, a CD costs d dollars; at 20% off, each one costs 80% of d dollars: $\frac{80}{100}(d) = \frac{80d}{100} = \frac{4d}{5}$ dollars. To find out how many you can buy, divide the amount of money, m, by the price per CD, $\frac{4d}{5}$: $m ÷ \frac{4d}{5} = m\left(\frac{5}{4d}\right) = \frac{5m}{4d}.$

Use **TACTIC 3 and plug in easy-to-use numbers. If CDs regularly cost $10, then on sale at 20% off, they cost $8 each. How many can be purchased on sale for $40? The answer is 5. Which of the choices equals 5 when $d = 10$ and $m = 40$? Only $\frac{5m}{4d}$.

13. **(D)** Since 16 of the 40 people have neither a dog nor a cat, 24 people have at least one, possibly both. Since 18 of those 24 have cats, 6 of them have dogs, but no cat. But since 13 have dogs, it must be that 7 dog owners also have cats.

    **A Venn diagram may make this easier.

    Let $x =$ the number of people who have both a cat and a dog.

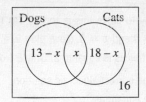

$$(13 - x) + x + (18 - x) = 24 \Rightarrow$$
$$31 - x = 24 \Rightarrow x = 7.$$

14. **(D)** $3|x| + 1 < 16 \Rightarrow 3|x| < 15 \Rightarrow |x| < 5$. There are 9 integers whose absolute value is less than 5: $-4, -3, -2, -1, 0, 1, 2, 3, 4$.

15. **(D)** The mode is 8, since more people have 8 teddy bears than any other number. Since there are 15 members, the median is the eighth piece of data when arranged in increasing order; so the median is 10. Finally, the average of 8 and 10 is 9.

16. **(E)** By **FACT 14**, $3^{\frac{1}{2}} \times 3^{\frac{1}{3}} \times 3^{\frac{1}{6}} = 3^{\left(\frac{1}{2} + \frac{1}{3} + \frac{1}{6}\right)} = 3^1 = 3$

    **Just enter the given expression into your calculator.

17. **(C)** Let s and S be the sides of the small and large squares, respectively.

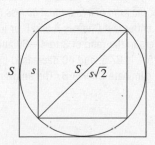

Then S and $s\sqrt{2}$ are each equal to the diameter of the circle; so

$$S = s\sqrt{2} \Rightarrow \frac{S}{s} = \sqrt{2} \Rightarrow \frac{S^2}{s^2} = 2.$$

Since s^2 and S^2 are the areas of the squares, the desired ratio is $2:1$.

18. **(E)** Since the diameter of the circle is 10, the radius is 5 and the area is 25π. Also, since the area of the shaded region is 20π, it is $\frac{20}{25} = \frac{4}{5}$ of the circle, and the white area is $\frac{1}{5}$ of the circle. Then the sum of the measures of the two white central angles is $\frac{1}{5}$ of $360°$, or $72°$. The sum of the measures of all six angles in the two triangles is $360°$, so $a + b + c + d = 360 - 72 = 288.$

19. **(E)** An easy way to solve this is to use **TACTIC 3**. Let $r = 2$ and $s = 1$. So $rs = 2$, $a = 4$ and $b = 0$. Now, plug in 4 for a and 0 for b and see which of the five choices is equal to 2. Only E works: $\frac{a^2 - b^2}{8} = \frac{4^2 - 0^2}{8} = \frac{16}{8} = 2$.

**Here is the correct algebraic solution.

Add the two equations:

$$r + 2s = a$$
$$\underline{+\ r - 2s = b}$$
$$2r = a + b$$

Divide by 2:

$$r = \frac{a+b}{2}$$

Now, multiply the second equation by -1 and add it to the first:

$$r + 2s = a$$
$$\underline{+\ -r + 2s = -b}$$
$$4s = a - b$$

Divide by 4:

$$s = \frac{a-b}{4}$$

So, $rs = \frac{a+b}{2} \cdot \frac{a-b}{4} = \frac{a^2 - b^2}{8}$.

This is the type of algebra you want to avoid.

20. **(A)** $a + 25\%(a) = 1.25a$, and $b - 25\%(b) = 0.75b$.

So, $1.25a = .75b$, and $\frac{a}{b} = \frac{.75}{1.25} = \frac{3}{5}$

**If after increasing a and decreasing b the results are equal, a must be smaller than b. So, *the ratio of a to b must be less than 1.* Eliminate Choices C, D, and E. Now, either test Choices A and B or just guess. To test Choice B, pick two numbers in the ratio of 3 to 4—30 and 40, for example. Then, 30 increased by 25% is 37.5, and 40 decreased by 25% is 30. The results are not equal, so eliminate Choice B. The answer is $\frac{3}{5}$. (50 decreased by 25% *is* 37.5.)

Section 3 Critical Reading

25. **(E)** To make the correct decisions, the lawmakers must be able to *discern* or recognize the truth.

26. **(B)** There is a chance that *serious* women may not be attracted by an inappropriate *frivolity* or lightheartedness in style—hence the gamble.

27. **(E)** A customer service agent would try to *mollify* or soothe an *angry* passenger by giving her an upgrade to a better class of service.

28. **(A)** If you started falling asleep at times you wouldn't normally wish to do so, you clearly would strike yourself as unusually *lethargic* (drowsily slow to respond; sluggish; listless).

29. **(D)** A *euphemism* is by definition a mild expression used in place of a more unpleasant or distressing one. The blunt expression "he died" is unpleasantly direct for some people, who substitute the vague euphemism "he passed away."

30. **(E)** *Despite* signals a contrast. If someone writes an enormously popular book, you would expect his career to prosper. Instead, White's career *foundered* or came to grief.

31. **(C)** Because it was written immediately after the assassination, the book has *immediacy*, but it lacks *perspective*; the author had not had enough time to distance himself from his immediate reactions to the event and think about it.

32. **(E)** The key word here is "chagrin." Because Costner has triumphed, the critics who predicted his *failure* feel chagrin (great annoyance mixed with disappointment or humiliation). Costner, for his part, greatly enjoys his success and especially enjoys or *savors* their embarrassment and vexation.

33. **(C)** The next sentence says that these stones in actuality are plants. Thus, the quotation marks around the word "stones" serve to underscore that these stonelike objects *are not literally stones*.

34. **(E)** Examine the context: "These stones are in actuality *plants*, members of the genus Lithops, some of the strangest succulents in the world." A succulent is clearly a *kind of plant*.

35. **(A)** Chomsky and others contend that the capacity for language is a uniquely human property or *trait*.

36. **(B)** Where Chomsky and Savage-Rambaugh differ has to do with the primates' capacity to use language, in other words, their *abilities in language acquisition*.

37. **(E)** The italicized introduction states that the author has had his manuscript rejected by his publisher. He is consigning or committing it to a desk drawer *to set it aside as unmarketable*.

38. (B) The rejected author identifies with these baseball players, who constantly must face "failure." *He sees he is not alone in having to confront failure and move on.*

39. (B) The author uses the jogger's comment to make a point about the *mental impact Henderson's home run must have had on Moore*. He reasons that, if each step a runner takes sends so many complex messages to the brain, then Henderson's ninth-inning home run must have flooded Moore's brain with messages, impressing its image indelibly in Moore's mind.

40. (D) The author is talking of the impact of Henderson's home run on Moore's mind. Registering in Moore's mind, the home run *made an impression* on him.

41. (C) The author looks on himself as someone who "to succeed at all ... must perform at an extraordinary level of excellence." This level of excellence, he maintains, is not demanded of accountants, plumbers, and insurance salesmen, and he seems to pride himself on belonging to such a demanding profession. Thus, his attitude to members of less demanding professions can best be described as *superior*.

42. (A) The description of the writer defying his pain and extending himself irrationally to create a "masterpiece" despite the rejections of critics and publishers is a highly romantic one that elevates *the writer as someone heroic in his or her accomplishments*.

43. (C) The author of Passage 2 discusses the advantages of his ability to concentrate. Clearly, he prizes *his ability to focus* on the task at hand.

44. (B) When one football team is ahead of another by several touchdowns and there seems to be no way for the second team to catch up, the outcome of the game appears *decided* or settled.

45. (E) The "larger point of view" focuses on what to most people is the big question: the outcome of the game. The author is indifferent to this larger point of view. Concentrating on his own performance, he is *more concerned with the task at hand than with* winning or losing the game.

46. (C) Parade ground drill clearly does not entirely prepare a soldier for the reality of war. It only does so "to an extent." By using this phrase, the author is *qualifying his statement*, making it less absolute.

47. (C) One would expect someone who dismisses or rejects most comparisons of athletics to art to avoid making such comparisons. The author, however, *is making such a comparison*. This reversal of what would have been expected is an instance of irony.

48. (C) To learn to overcome failure, to learn to give one's all in performance, to learn to focus on the work of the moment, to learn "the selfish intensity needed to create and to finish a poem, a story, or a novel"—these are hard lessons that *both athletes and artists learn*.

Section 4 Mathematical Reasoning

21. **(C)** The weight of the fruit is $5 + 3 + 1 = 9$ pounds, of which 3 pounds are oranges. Hence, the desired fraction is $\frac{3}{9} = \frac{1}{3}$

22. **(B)** Since the sum of the five angles is 180°:
$$4a + 40 = 180 \Rightarrow 4a = 140 \Rightarrow a = 35.$$

23. **(C)** Use **TACTIC 3** and choose an easy-to-use number. Since $\frac{5}{8}$ of the members are boys, assume there are 8 members, 5 of whom are boys. Then the other 3 are girls, and the ratio of girls to boys is 3 to 5, or $\frac{3}{5}$.

24. **(A)** Refer to the figures below.

The circumference of a circle of radius 3 is 6π (**FACT 54**). By **FACT 56**, the perimeter of a rectangle is $2(\ell + w)$, so $6\pi = 2(\ell + 3) \Rightarrow$
$$\ell + 3 = 3\pi \Rightarrow \ell = 3\pi - 3.$$

25. **(D)** $13 - 11 = 2$, so I could be true. Since $5 + 7 + 11 = 23$, III could be true. Since all primes greater than 5 are odd, $p + q$ must be even, and so cannot be a prime. (Statement II is false.) Statements I and III only are true.

26. **(C)** Use the distance formula, **FACT 61**, to calculate the length of diameter $\overline{AB}$:
$$AB = \sqrt{(7-3)^2 + (2-(-2))^2} = \sqrt{4^2 + 4^2} = \sqrt{32}.$$
So the diameter is $\sqrt{32}$ and the radius is $\frac{\sqrt{32}}{2}$. Then the area is:
$$A = \pi r^2 = \pi \left(\frac{\sqrt{32}}{2}\right)^2 = \pi \left(\frac{32}{4}\right) = 8\pi.$$

Note: You do not need to simplify $\sqrt{32}$. You also don't need to use your calculator to evaluate $\sqrt{32}$, but if you do, don't round off. Take whatever appears in your calculator's window, divide it by 2 and then square it—you will get exactly 8. Of course, *do not* multiply by 3.14.

27. **(C)** $13 - 2\sqrt{x} = 7 \Rightarrow -2\sqrt{x} = -6 \Rightarrow \sqrt{x} = 3 \Rightarrow x = 9.$

   You can use **TACTIC 1 and backsolve. Choice C, 9, works.

28. (B) The trust received 80% of the estate (10% went to the man's wife, 5% to his children, and 5% to his grandchildren). If *E* represents the value of the estate, then

$$0.80E = 1,000,000 \Rightarrow$$
$$E = 1,000,000 \div .80 = 1,250,000.$$

Each grandchild received 1% (one fifth of 5%) of the estate, or $12,500.

29. (115) We can find any or all of the angles in the figure. The easiest way to get *w* is to note that the measure of $\angle PST = 25$ and so by **FACT 42**, $w = 25 + 90 = 115$.

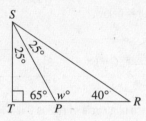

30. (99) From the 109 people in front of Wendy, remove Peter plus the 9 people in front of Peter: $109 - 10 = 99$.

31. (88.5) $(x + 1) + (x + 2) = 180 \Rightarrow$
$2x + 3 = 180 \Rightarrow 2x = 177 \Rightarrow x = 88.5.$

32. ($\frac{11}{2}$ **or 5.5**) To make the fraction $\frac{r-s}{t}$ as large as possible, make the numerator, $r - s$, as large as you can, and the denominator *t*, as small as you can. So let *t* be 2, the smallest prime. In order for the difference $r - s$ to be as large as possible, let *r* be large, and subtract as little as possible. Therefore, let *r* be 13, the largest prime less than 15, and let *s* be 2, the smallest prime. (Note that the question did not say that *s* and *t* had to be different, only that they had to be primes.) Finally, $\frac{r-s}{t} = \frac{13-2}{2} = \frac{11}{2}$ or 5.5.

33. (40) To solve the equation $\frac{2}{x} + \frac{3}{4} = \frac{4}{5}$, subtract $\frac{3}{4}$ from each side:

$$\frac{2}{x} + \frac{3}{4} = \frac{4}{5} \Rightarrow \frac{2}{x} = \frac{1}{20} \Rightarrow x = 40$$

Note: Do not waste time getting a common denominator; just use your calculator.

34. ($\frac{7}{9}$ **or .777 or .778**) Since the radius of the large circle is 3, its area is 9π. Each of the small circles has a radius of 1 and an area of π. So the total area of the white region is 2π, leaving 7π for the area of the shaded region. Therefore, the probability that *P* lies in the shaded region is $\frac{7\pi}{9\pi} = \frac{7}{9}$.

35. (44) Since the diameters of the circles are in the ratio of 12:10 or 6:5, the ratio of their areas is $6^2:5^2 = 36:25$. Convert the ratio to a percent: $36:25 = \frac{36}{25} = \frac{144}{100} = 144\%$. So, the area of the large circle is 144% of the area of the small one, or is 44% *more* than the area of the small one.

**With your calculator, actually calculate the areas. The radius of the large circle is 6, so its area is $\pi(6)^2 = 36\pi$. Similarly, the radius of the small circle is 5 and its area is $\pi(5)^2 = 25\pi$. The difference in the areas is $36\pi - 25\pi = 11\pi$, and 11π is 44% of 25π $\left(\frac{11\pi}{25\pi} = \frac{11}{25} = \frac{44}{100}\right)$.

36. (21) For the third place share to be as large as possible, the fourth place share must be as small as possible. However, it must be more than 10, so let it be 11. Then the amount, in dollars, left for second and third place is $100 - (35 + 11 + 10) = 100 - 56 = 44$. So, the second place share could be $23 and the third place share $21.

37. (9.36) For the average to be as high as possible, each student needs to have scored the maximum number of points. Therefore, assume that each of the 22 students who passed earned a grade of 10, that only one student earned a 2, and that the other two students who failed each earned a 6, the highest possible failing grade. Then the average is $\frac{10(22) + 2 + 2(6)}{25} = \frac{234}{25} = 9.36$.

38. (13) Since π is approximately 3.14, 2π is approximately 6.28, and $[2\pi] = 6$. Now, be careful: -2π is approximately -6.28, and the largest integer less than -6.28 is -7. Finally,

$$[2\pi] - [-2\pi] = 6 - (-7) = 6 + 7 = 13.$$

Section 5 Writing Skills

1. **(C)** Comma splice. Choices A, D, and E are run-on sentences. Choice B is constructed awkwardly.

2. **(C)** Comparison of modifiers. When comparing two things, you should use the comparative degree (*better*) rather than the superlative degree (*best*).

3. **(D)** This choice corrects the sentence fragment.

4. **(C)** Error in coordination and subordination. The subordinating conjunction *Although* best connects the sentence's two clauses.

5. **(B)** Comma splice. Choices A, C, and E are run-on sentences; Choice D is unidiomatic.

6. **(D)** Error in parallelism. Parallel structure is maintained in Choice D.

7. **(D)** Choices A, B, and E contain sentence fragments; Choice C creates a comma splice.

8. **(A)** Error in coordination and subordination. The past tense and the subordinating conjunction *When* are correctly used in Choice A.

9. **(C)** Choice C expresses the author's meaning directly and concisely. All other choices are either indirect or ungrammatical.

10. **(A)** Choices B, C, D, and E are sentence fragments.

11. **(A)** Sentence is correct.

12. **(A)** Sentence is correct.

13. **(E)** The errors in pronoun case and subject-verb agreement are corrected in Choice E. *I* should be used instead of *me* because it is the predicate nominative of the verb *is*. *Who*, having as its antecedent the pronoun *I*, is a first person singular pronoun. The first person singular verb *am* should be used.

14. **(C)** Error in idiomatic usage. The birds are indifferent *to* the ships.

15. **(C)** Error in subject-verb agreement. The subject of the sentence, *collection*, is singular; the verb should be singular as well.

16. **(A)** Sentence is correct.

17. **(B)** Error in sequence of tenses. *Was* and *received* are in the simple past tense. Both indicate a definite time in the past. *Have cheered* is in the present perfect tense. It indicates sometime before now but not a definite time. The sequence is illogical.

18. **(D)** Error in parallelism. Choice D corrects the lack of parallel structure.

19. **(E)** Adjective-adverb confusion. The dragonflies become *increasingly fragile*.

20. **(E)** Error in sequence of tenses. The *had* before *established* indicates a time prior to *began to arrive*.

21. **(C)** Error in diction. Use *lie* instead of *lay*.

22. **(E)** Sentence is correct.

23. **(D)** Error in pronoun number agreement. Since antecedent is *association*, change *their* to *its*.

24. **(C)** Error in subject-verb agreement. In a neither-nor construction the verb agrees with the noun or pronoun which comes immediately before the verb. *Principal is being considered* is correct.

25. **(A)** Error in tense. Change *have rummaged* to *were rummaging*.

26. **(E)** Sentence is correct.

27. **(C)** Error in diction. Use *effect* instead of *affect*.

28. **(C)** Error in coordination and subordination. Delete the comma and substitute *that* for *and it*. The second clause describes McGwire's record.

29. (C) Error in coordination and subordination. Change conjunction and word for *nor is she* to *and she is* to clarify the relationship between the clauses.

30. (D) Error in diction. The word *being* is unnecessary. Change *including being* to *including*.

31. (D) Adjective and adverb confusion. Change *comfortable* to *comfortably*.

32. (E) Sentence is correct.

33. (A) Error in tense. Change *has been warned* to *had been warned*.

34. (A) Error in diction. Use *if* to indicate a condition. Substitute *whether*.

35. (C) All sentences except sentence 3 contribute to the paragraph's main point, that celebrations help to unite people and keep traditions alive. Therefore, Choice C is the best answer.

36. (D) Choice A is fresh, but its tone is not consistent with the rest of the essay.
Choice B contains a comma splice between *dinner* and *at*.
Choice C emphasizes the idea properly, but contains an error in parallel construction.
Choice D places the emphasis where it belongs and expresses the idea effectively. It is the best answer.
Choice E is repetitious, and it contains an error in pronoun reference. The pronoun *they* has no specific referent.

37. (D) Choice A does not provide a significantly better transition.
Choice B does nothing to improve the relationship between paragraphs 3 and 4.
Choice C is awkwardly worded and does not include transitional material.
Choice D provides an effective transition between paragraphs. It is the best answer.
Choice E tries to provide a transition, but it is wordy and it contains a dangling participle.

38. (E) Choice A places emphasis on the location of the assassination instead of on the event itself, an emphasis that the writer did not intend.
Choice B contains a nonstandard usage. The phrase *to remember about* is not standard.
Choice C is grammatically correct but wordy.
Choice D is the same as B.
Choice E is a succinct and proper revision. It is the best answer.

39. (C) The main purpose of the last paragraph is to provide an example of a celebration that unites people and preserves tradition. Therefore, Choice C is the best answer.

After the PSAT/NMSQT

After the scores of the PSAT/NMSQT are received, you, your parents, and your guidance counselor can begin to make plans for college. Here are some Barron's reference books that will be very helpful to you.

Barron's SAT by Sharon Weiner Green and Ira K. Wolf (2008, 24th Edition). This classic includes a diagnostic test and five additional practice tests that enable you to practice under exact SAT format and test conditions; all tests have answer keys and answer explanations. Extensive review and practice is provided for each type of test question. The Critical Reading review also includes the 3500 word list, with definitions and parts of speech. The Writing review includes common grammar and usage errors. The Mathematical Reasoning review covers basic arithmetic through high school algebra and geometry. Testing tactics and strategies are featured. Two additional practice tests are provided on an optional CD-ROM.

Critical Reading Workbook for the SAT by Sharon Weiner Green (2006, 12th Edition), *Math Workbook for the SAT* by Lawrence Leff (2004, 3rd Edition), *Writing Workbook for the SAT* by George Ehrenhaft (2005). These workbooks provide the detailed review you may need for specific sections of the test. Each book contains hundreds of practice questions with answers and extensive review specific to the topic.

Grammar Workbook for the SAT, ACT...and More by George Ehrenhaft (2006). This workbook provides a review of the grammatical issues you are most likely to be asked about on the SAT, ACT, and other standardized tests. You'll learn terms you need to know and how to avoid the grammar pitfalls that give almost everyone a headache. And you will learn how to write a proper exam essay. The book includes plenty of practice questions with complete answer explanations.

Hot Words for the SAT by Linda Carnevale (2007, 3rd Edition). This book includes hundreds of words, grouped by concept, with definitions, sample sentences, and quizzes.

SAT 2400 by Linda Carnevale and Roselyn Teukolsky (2008, 2nd Edition). Written for the student who is aiming for that perfect score, this book breaks down the toughest questions and analyzes why they are tough. Practice tests are provided for each of the three SAT sections: critical reading, writing, and math. An optional CD-ROM contains a complete practice SAT test and fifty additional practice questions.

SAT Flash Cards by Sharon Weiner Green and Ira K. Wolf (2008). This handy boxed set includes 200 math cards with 75 important math facts, strategies, and sample multiple-choice and grid-in questions; 200 grammar cards covering parts of speech, sentence construction, and more; and 100 vocabulary cards with definitions and sample sentences.

Essays that Will Get You into College by Daniel Kaufman, Chris Dowhan, and Adrienne Dowhan (2003, 2nd Edition). More than fifty model essays that have worked for applicants, with advice, discussion, and commentary, reveal the secrets of successful essay writing.

Barron's Profiles of American Colleges (2008, 28th Edition). Profiles of more than 1,600 regionally accredited four-year American colleges and universities give the prospective student a preview of his or her relationship to a particular college—based on its facilities, outstanding features and programs, admission requirements, costs, available financial aid, extracurricular activities, programs and major offerings, degrees awarded, enrollment, religious affiliation, housing facilities, and social and honorary societies. CD-ROM included.